# Contemporary Perspectives on Ecofeminism

Why is ecofeminism still needed to address the environmental emergencies and challenges of our times? Ecofeminism has a chequered history in terms of its popularity and its perceived value in conceptualizing the relationship between gender and nature as well as feeding forms of activism that aim to confront the environmental challenges of the moment.

This book provides a much needed comprehensive overview of the relevance and value of using ecofeminist theories. It provides a broad coverage of traditional and emerging ecofeminist theories, exploring their various contributions and spanning various strands of ecofeminist thinking. The origins of influential ecofeminist theories are discussed, including key themes, and some of its leading figures (contributors include Erika Cudworth, Greta Gaard, Trish Glazebrook and Niamh Moore) outline its influence on how scholars might come to a more generative understanding of the natural environment. The book examines ecofeminism's potential contribution to advancing current discussions and research on the relationships between the humans, and more-than-humans, that share our world.

This timely volume makes a distinctive scholarly contribution and is a valuable resource for students and academics in the fields of environmentalism, political ecology, sustainability and natural resource management.

**Mary Phillips** is Reader in Organization Studies at The School of Economics, Finance and Management, University of Bristol, UK.

**Nick Rumens** is Professor of Organization Behaviour and Head of Department (Leadership, Work & Organization) at Middlesex University, UK.

# Routledge Explorations in Environmental Studies

# Contemporary Perspectives on Ecofeminism

Edited by
Mary Phillips and Nick Rumens

Routledge
Taylor & Francis Group
LONDON AND NEW YORK

earthscan
from Routledge

First published 2016
by Routledge

2 Park Square, Milton Park, Abingdon, Oxfordshire OX14 4RN
711 Third Avenue, New York, NY 10017

*Routledge is an imprint of the Taylor & Francis Group, an informa business*

First issued in paperback 2017

*British Library Cataloguing in Publication Data*
A catalogue record for this book is available from the British Library

*Library of Congress Cataloging in Publication Data*
Names: Phillips, Mary, 1955- editor. | Rumens, Nick, editor.
Title: Contemporary perspectives on ecofeminism / edited by Mary Phillips and Nick Rumens.
Description: Abingdon, Oxon ; New York, NY : Routledge is an imprint of the Taylor & Francis Group, an Informa Business, [2016] | Series: Routledge explorations in environmental studies
Identifiers: LCCN 2015021326| ISBN 9781138019744 (hb) |
ISBN 9781315778686 (e-book)
Subjects: LCSH: Ecofeminism. | Women and the environment. |
Human ecology.
Classification: LCC HQ1194 .C66 2016 | DDC 304.2082--dc23
LC record available at http://lccn.loc.gov/2015021326

ISBN: 978-1-138-01974-4 (hbk)
ISBN: 978-0-8153-5555-7 (pbk)

Typeset in Goudy
by Taylor & Francis Books

Mary: For Martin and Matthew for always being there and keeping things real.

Nick: For Jamie, Fergus and Meisha, with love, for their unconditional love and affection.

# Contents

# Illustrations

**Figure**

**Box**

# Acknowledgements

We would both like to thank Martin and Peter, Mary's and Nick's respective partners, and their families, friends and pets, for providing us with unending fortitude, love and encouragement throughout the process of developing this book.

The book would not have happened without the insight, energy and commitment of our contributors. We would like to thank them for providing us with engaging and pertinent chapters that breathe fresh air into contemporary ecofeminist issues and perspectives. We also pay heartfelt tribute to those activists and scholars who first nurtured and developed the principles of ecofeminism. We hope that this volume will add to the growing chorus of voices calling for more equal, hopeful and healthy ways to engage with the planet of which we are a part and for which ecofeminists have tirelessly striven.

Equally, this book benefited from the generous support and patience of the Editorial and Commissioning team at Routledge. It has been a pleasure to work with Routledge and we extend our appreciation to Khanam Virjee and Margaret Farrelly, and production and marketing staff at Routledge, all of whom have supported this project from the beginning.

# Contributors

## Editors

**Mary Phillips** is Reader in Organization Studies at the University of Bristol, UK, and Director of the Action Research and Critical Inquiry in Organizations research centre. Her current work critically analyses the gendered and embodied ethico-politics of corporate environmentalism and asks how they might be re-imagined. She has published over 40 scholarly articles, chapters and books and is Associate Editor of *Gender, Work & Organization*.

**Nick Rumens** is Professor in Organization Behaviour at Middlesex University, London, UK. He has a recently discovered passion for ecofeminism and how it intersects with critical studies on men and masculinities and queer theory. He is Associate Editor of the journal *Gender, Work & Organization* and has published journal articles on queer theory in *Gender, Work & Organization*, *Critical Perspectives on Accounting* and *British Journal of Management*. His forthcoming book, *Queer Business: Queering Sexualities of Organisation*, will be published by Routledge.

## Contributors

**Adelheid Biesecker** is Emeritus Professor at the Institute for Institutional and Social Economics at the University of Bremen, Germany. Her main research interests include microeconomics from a social-ecological perspective, history of economic thought, ecological economics, feminist economics and the future of work.

**Mary Brydon-Miller**, PhD, directs the Action Research Center at the University of Cincinnati, USA, and is Professor of Educational and Community-based Action Research in the Educational Studies Program in the College of Education, Criminal Justice, and Human Services. She is a participatory action researcher who conducts work in both school and community settings. She recently completed work on the *Sage Encyclopedia of Action Research* with co-editor David Coghlan. Other recent publications focus on the development of new frameworks for understanding research ethics in educational and community settings.

**Erika Cudworth** is Reader in Political Sociology and Critical Animal Studies at the University of East London, UK. Her research interests include complexity theory, gender, and human relations with non-human animals, particularly theoretical and political challenges to exclusive humanism. Her books include *Environment and Society* (2003), *Developing Ecofeminist Theory* (2005), *Social Lives with Other Animals* (2011), and *Posthuman International Relations* (2011). Erika's current projects are on companion animals, animals and war and posthuman emancipation.

**Greta Gaard** is Professor of English and Coordinator of the Sustainability Faculty Fellows at University of Wisconsin-River Falls, USA. Her work emerges from the intersections of feminism, environmental justice, queer studies and critical animal studies, exploring a wide range of issues, from interspecies justice, material perspectives on fireworks and space exploration, postcolonial ecofeminism, and the eco-politics of climate change. Author or editor of five books, Gaard's most recent volume is *International Perspectives in Feminist Ecocriticism* (2013), co-edited with Simon Estok and Serpil Oppermann. Her creative non-fiction eco-memoir, *The Nature of Home* (2007), is being translated into Chinese and Portuguese.

**Trish Glazebrook** is Professor and Chair of Philosophy at the University of North Texas, USA. Her main research interests include ancient philosophy, ecophenomenology, environmental philosophy, feminism, gender and environmental policy, Heidegger, international development, and the philosophy of science and technology. She has published widely on these topics in chapters in edited books, journals such as *Hypatia* and *Ethics and the Environment*, and books including *Heidegger on Science* (2012).

**Anne Inga Hilsen**, PhD is a senior researcher at Fafo, Institute for Labour and Social Research in Oslo, Norway. She is an action researcher who works mainly on work life issues, from enterprise development and industrial relations to active ageing and occupational safety and health (OSH).

**Christine Katz** (Dipl. Biol. Dr. rer. nat.) is a biologist and ecosystem researcher. She has worked for six years as a scientific consultant at the German Parliament (Technology Assessment), before returning to Leuphana University, Lüneburg, Germany, to carry out socio-ecological research and teaching. Since 2014, she has been the general secretary at diversu e.V. (institute for diversity, nature, gender and sustainability). Her main research interests are gender, diversity and nature, gender relations and nature management practices, intercultural participation, gender and sustainability and the effect of spirituality on human–nature relations.

**Niamh Moore** is a Chancellor's Fellow in Sociology at the University of Edinburgh, UK. She is the author of *The Changing Nature of Eco/feminism: Telling Stories of Clayoquot Sound* (2015). She is currently working on a number of research projects on community food growing, sustainable transport, feminist community archiving and participatory story-telling methodology.

**Ida Sabelis** is Associate Professor and Program Leader for MSc Culture, Organization and Management (organizational anthropology) at VU University Amsterdam, the Netherlands. Her research entails gender studies, time/s and sustainability in organizations, and a focus on critical-creative methods. Her publications include 'Frayed careers: exploring rhythms of working lives' in *Gender, Work & Organization* (2013) with Elisabeth Schilling; and 'Juggling difference and sameness: rethinking strategies for diversity in organizations' in *Scandinavian Journal of Management* (2013) with Halleh Ghorashi. She is joint Editor-in-Chief for the journal *Gender, Work & Organization*.

**Scott Taylor** is Reader in Leadership and Organization Studies at Birmingham Business School, University of Birmingham, UK. He has a long-standing research interest in the intersection of New Age spiritualities and the workplace.

**Tamarisk van Vliet** is an alumna at the Department of Organization Studies of VU University Amsterdam, the Netherlands, finishing her MSc Culture, Organization and Management in 2011 with the first study on game rangers' wives, titled '"A woman's wilderness": when ignored contributions, nature conservation, and romantic landscape notions collide in the context of game reserves in KwaZulu-Natal, South Africa'. Currently she works as HR Expert at Swarovski Benelux, Amsterdam.

**Harry Wels** is Associate Professor at VU University Amsterdam, The Netherlands, Extraordinary Professor at the University of the Western Cape, South Africa, and Publication Manager at the African Studies Centre, Leiden, The Netherlands. His publications include *Securing Wilderness Landscapes in South Africa: Nick Steele, Private Wildlife Conservancies and Saving Rhinos* (2015) and a co-authored article (with Malcolm Draper and Marja Spierenburg) titled, 'African dreams of cohesion: elite pacting and community development in Transfrontier Conservation Areas in southern Africa', published in the journal *Culture and Organization* (2004).

**Uta von Winterfeld** is a private lecturer at the Department of Political and Social Sciences at the Freie Universität, Berlin, Germany. She is also a Project Co-ordinator at the Wuppertal Institute for Climate, Environment and Energy. Her main research interests include societal relations and nature, sustainability and gender, participation, governance and democracy, and adaptation on climate change.

**Laura Wright** is Associate Professor and Department Head of English at Western Carolina University, USA, where she specializes in postcolonial literature and theory, ecocriticism and animal studies. Her monographs include *Writing Out of All the Camps: J. M. Coetzee's Narratives of Displacement* (2006 and 2009) and *Wilderness into Civilized Shapes: Reading the Postcolonial Environment* (2010). She is lead editor (with Jane Poyner and Elleke Boehmer) of *Approaches to Teaching Coetzee's Disgrace and Other Works* (2014). Her monograph *The Vegan Studies Project: Food, Animals, and Gender in the Age of Terror* is forthcoming from the University of Georgia Press in 2015.

**Ali Young** was awarded her doctorate in leadership and spirituality by The Centre for Leadership Studies at Exeter University, UK, in 2015. Coming to this with a background in the National Health Service, her interests include wellbeing, sustainable organizational practices and critical perspectives on contemporary leadership discourses.

# Introducing contemporary ecofeminism

*Mary Phillips and Nick Rumens*

This book is about contemporary forms of ecofeminism and why we need them now more than ever. *Contemporary Perspectives on Ecofeminism* brings together 11 original chapters in which scholars and activists were asked to rethink ecofeminism, providing fresh theoretical and empirical insights into the contemporary salience of the subject. Despite the different approaches and disciplinary spaces adopted by the authors, the chapters are united by an underpinning question: why is ecofeminism still needed to address the environmental emergencies and challenges of our times? The resulting collection traverses disciplines and geopolitical locations, bringing together (pro) ecofeminist scholars and activists who address contemporary concerns such as: corporeality and the animal; materially based analysis of economic, social and political systems of domination; community-based, participative research; colonializing, majority world development; spirituality; the management of nature and the ways in which the natural world and its degradation are represented in popular culture. The divergent foci of interest amongst contributors illustrate the importance and the role of this book in advancing cutting-edge theoretical and empirical contributions in the field of ecofeminism. Although there is a sustained concern in this book with demonstrating the contemporary relevance and importance of ecofeminism, this has not always been the case. Ecofeminism has a chequered history in terms of its popularity and its perceived value in conceptualizing the relationship between gender and nature, as well as feeding forms of activism that aim to confront the environmental challenges of the moment. Indeed, the inspiration for this book partly derives from this understanding of the history of ecofeminism and a current concern to engage critically with the contours of contemporary ecofeminism. In the remainder of this chapter, we unpack the history of ecofeminism, elaborate the genesis and rationale of this edited collection, and conclude by discussing the structure and organization of the book. To begin, we can think of no better person to turn toward than ecofeminist philosopher Karen Warren.

Recognizing the rich diversity of ecofeminist thinking, Karen Warren referred to it as a quilt: 'An ecofeminist philosophical quilt will be made up of different "patches", constructed by quilters in particular social, historical and materialist contexts' (2000: 66). This is an appropriate metaphor that draws on the history of quilting as women's work, as often a collective endeavour and as a means of both celebrating and subverting the culturally produced norms of femininity (Parker 1984). It also captures the idea that, as with a quilt, different colours, patterns and textures contribute to an over-arching ecofeminist whole that is bounded by a commitment to ideals such as care and justice (Cuomo 2002). This book therefore offers a selection of 'patches' that represent contemporary thinking in ecofeminism. Some of them are new so that they add to the diversity and richness of the quilt. Others revisit areas that have long been included, but which have perhaps become a little faded and threadbare, to incorporate new stitching and materials. These patches remind us that ecofeminism is and should be a social, political and theoretical movement and one that is continually developing. But before describing them in more detail, we need to examine the foundational concepts of ecofeminism and the history of this quilt, and then to argue why we need it now more than ever.

In 1997, Karen Warren asked: 'Trees, forests and deforestation. Water, drought and desertification. Food production, poverty and toxic wastes. Environmental destruction and women. And women? What do these environmental issues have to do with women?' (Warren 1997: 3). Warren went on to answer her own question; namely that the subordination, appropriation and exploitation of women and the natural world are interconnected and that such connections extend to the treatment of ethnic and racial minorities in the Global North, most of the Global South, the poor, the aged, the differently abled, and lesbian, gay, bisexual and trans (LGBT) communities. Such relationships exist because of a logic of identity that has become reified as 'objectively real' through discourses, institutions and material practices. This logic rests on hierarchical and interrelated dualisms, such as mind/body, reason/nature, reason/emotion, masculine/feminine and human/nature, to define what is authentically human in opposition to the spheres of the natural, physical or biological. The feminine, women, nature and other subordinated groups are deemed not to possess attributes such as rationality and autonomy, which are associated with the dominant terms in these dualisms, and they are therefore 'othered' to confirm and justify their exclusion. They are considered as less than human or non-human or, at best, an inferior copy. For ecofeminism, striving for new connectivities of care, responsibility and justice therefore has to be extended to social *and* natural realms as they are bound in the same systems of oppression. An atomized approach to injustice will not be effective, and re-fashioning the world as fair and respectful means fairness and respect for all. In such a world, hierarchical distinctions between human and more-than-human are dissolved. Humanity no longer positions itself and its needs as transcending 'nature' but regards itself as being immanent within an ecological system on which it depends. Humans recognize themselves as inextricably immersed in relationships with nature and others but in ways that acknowledge difference, rather than submerge it in an imposition of the self. Such relations value 'the other's boundary and opacity of being' (Plumwood 1993: 178) which is part of respect for the other. Our evaluation of living beings, including nature and those people and groups once categorized as 'non-human', is based neither on their instrumental use value, nor on giving moral considerability to those parts of nature that share certain characteristics deemed to separate humanity from nature. These might include consciousness of a self, ability to feel pain or distress, ability to communicate or to strategize. Such an evaluation is rejected as one based in anthropocentrism and a logic of the same which privileges such characteristics as morally more deserving than others. However, this ecofeminist way of thinking does not marginalize the human and human concerns in relation to nature, and holds that a focus on the larger social, political and historical contexts in which nature *and* humanity are situated is essential to address the full range of issues at stake in meeting real environmental challenges (Plumwood 2006). These ideas provide the foundations for the plethora of approaches broadly identified as 'ecofeminism'. That is ecofeminism's vision for the future. We now turn to consider, albeit briefly, ecofeminism's past.

## On the history of ecofeminism

A history and genealogy of ecofeminism has been addressed elsewhere (e.g. Gaard 2011; Moore 2008; Sturgeon 1997; Thompson 2006). It is generally agreed that ecofeminism arose in the late 1970s to early 1980s from roots in activist social movements, the anti-nuclear and peace movements in particular, and from a growing sense of discontent with what was perceived as gender blindness and sexism in other environmental groups. Ecofeminism has always been an activist and an academic movement; activist groups and scholars pondering ecofeminist philosophical questions developed in the USA, Europe and Australia. Ecofeminists have been involved in a wide range of issues such as toxic waste, animal rights, deforestation and agricultural development in minority and majority worlds. Ecofeminists taking direct action could be found in campaigns such as Greenham Common in the UK or Earth First! (the latter, as Sturgeon 1997 notes, somewhat controversially) and, more recently, ecofeminists have participated in the Occupy movement in the USA, using their skills and experience in non-violent protest. The Women and Life on Earth conference at Amherst in 1980 was attended by over 650 women and inspired other conferences and groups in the USA and beyond, including Australia, Canada, France, Japan, Germany and the UK. Ecofeminist scholars, and those interested in ecofeminism, have created and critiqued theory and have published books, journal articles and special issues across a wide range of subject disciplines (Sturgeon 1997).

However, in the years immediately following 2000, when Warren published the words which opened this Introduction, ecofeminist voices became relatively muted and some would argue were actively silenced (e.g. Moore

2008; Sturgeon 1997; Thompson 2006; Twine 1997) by a backlash centred mainly around charges of essentialism, often originating from other feminists. Niamh Moore engages fully with this debate in chapter 1 of this collection. In brief, critics claimed ecofeminism argued for women's special affinity with and closeness to nature based in biologically determined and embodied experiences of, for example, childbirth and menstruation. As Thompson puts it: 'Women's ways of being and thinking, the ecofeminist movement maintained, made them natural (in many senses of the word) inhabitants and guardians of Mother Nature's garden in an anti-patriarchal and oft-times pre-lapsarian imaginary' (Thompson 2006: 506; see also Sandilands 1999). It was said that this, and a perceived celebration of 'womanly' values such as nurturing, were supportive of and colluded with patriarchal ideas where the disordered and anarchic female body provides the explanation for the inherent inferiority of women. Similarly dismissive claims were made against ecofeminist explorations of human–animal relations while ecofeminist versions of Earth-based spirituality were dismissed as goddess-worship (see Gaard 2011 for a full discussion). Moreover, critics claimed that such positions ignored the complexity of women's experiences which are mediated by intersections of class, ethnicity, sexuality and able-bodiedness. In particular, it was argued that ecofeminism was a white women's movement that ignored women of colour. Gaard (2011) has comprehensively rebutted such claims, as have Sturgeon (1997) and Moore (2008 and chapter 1 in this volume), who argue that ecofeminisms are situated in multiple forms of action and theory that contest relations of power and that much of this criticism was unfair, decontextualized and inaccurate.

As well as the attack on ecofeminism for its supposed essentialism, post-structuralist feminism tended to ignore or criticize ecofeminism because of its central tenet that linked structurally the oppression of women and of nature. Poststructuralist feminism, exemplified in the work of Luce Irigaray, Hélène Cixous, Lois McNay and Rosi Braidotti (to name but a few), draws on the work of French theorists such as Derrida, Lacan and Foucault to contest ahistorical and deterministic appeals to structure as an external given that we can apprehend independently of the institutional, cultural and other practices by which it is named, reinforced and measured. However, Thompson argues that such critiques when applied to ecofeminism are misdirected if they view accounts with a structural argument as 'static and hopelessly beguiled by the singularity of truth and reason' (Thompson 2006: 511). Most ecofeminist theorists eschew structuralist thinking that would posit a fixed and ahistorical relation between women, nature and their interrelated causes of oppression. On the contrary, they argue that such causes are historically and culturally determined, and embrace post-structuralist repudiation of determinism and its focus on multiplicity and difference (e.g. Sandilands 1999). At the same time, and from a different direction, academic ecofeminists were accused of threatening the pluralism of ecofeminism and of privileging philosophical approaches. This was described as a colonizing strategy, employed to gain academic standing that excluded activist, spiritual and majority world ecofeminists (Cook 1998).

Others argued that ecofeminism romanticized the experiences of indigenous cultures and practices, which amounted to a form of colonialist appropriation (see Moore, chapter 1 in this volume and Sturgeon 1997, especially ch. 4, for a detailed review). Several ecofeminists have themselves pointed out that this amounts to an unethical exploitation of such women in order to develop academic theory. For example, Gaard writes:

> Naming the activism of others in a way that they have not, effectively puts words in their mouths; contradicts, silences or erases their activist speech and colonizes or appropriates their labors for the use of others. The problem becomes obvious, finally, when one realizes that the naming and appropriation is taking place across the lines of races, class or nationality ... and those most likely to engage in such naming tend to be white, middle-class academic women in industrialized nations.
>
> (Gaard 1998: 13)

The accusations and pressures with which ecofeminism was assailed were such that many erstwhile ecofeminists no longer called themselves such (Gaard 2011; Sturgeon 1997). The rate of publication of books and journal articles admitting an ecofeminist perspective slowed considerably. This is a serious concern, to which this edited volume responds.

## Why this book, why now?

As we and the contributors in this edited collection argue, it is now even more urgent that we develop the means to move from 'unhealthy, life-denying systems and relationships to healthy, life-affirming ones' (Warren 2000: 200) so that we can live in this world in a way that 'recognizes and accommodates the denied relationships of dependency and enables us to acknowledge our debt to the sustaining others of the earth' (Plumwood 1993: 196). In the 30 or more years since ecofeminists first argued that nature must be included in theorizing and acting against constellations of injustice and exploitation, the environmental, economic, social and political crises caused by those constellations have grown deeper. Below, for example, we argue that the carrying capacity of the planet is collapsing and yet our dominant economic and political ideologies exacerbate catastrophe. A deployment of radical ideas, strategies and politics which re-connect the human and more-than-human world is needed now more than ever. As Gaard points out:

> An intersectional ecological-feminist approach frames these issues [of eco-justice] in such a way that people can recognize common cause across the boundaries of race, class, gender, sexuality, species, age,

ability, nation – and affords a basis for engaged theory, education and activism.

(Gaard 2011: 44).

The degradation of the environment continues apace. The World Wildlife Fund's (2014a,b) *Living Planet Report* shows that between 1970 and 2010, populations of mammals, birds, reptiles, amphibians and fish around the globe dropped 52 per cent (World Wildlife Fund 2014a). That we have lost half of the world's living creatures in fewer than two generations is both appalling and heartbreaking. The reasons given for what can only be described as a form of genocide are habitat loss and fragmentation, pollution, unsustainable use of land and overfishing of the seas, and the poaching and killing of higher mammals for their body parts in traditional medicines or for food. We are ripping up the natural fabric of our planet that supports all life. A summary of *The Living Planet Report* goes on to say:

> In addition to the precipitous decline in wildlife populations the report's data point to other warning signs about the overall health of the planet. The amount of carbon in our atmosphere has risen to levels not seen in more than a million years, triggering climate change that is already destabilizing ecosystems. High concentrations of reactive nitrogen are degrading lands, rivers and oceans. Stress on already scarce water supplies is increasing. And more than 60 percent of the essential 'services' provided by nature, from our forests to our seas, are in decline.
>
> (World Wildlife Fund 2014b: n.p.)

So, alongside the insidious degradation of nature to which it is contributing, climate change is now recognized as having the potential to destroy much of the life on the planet – including human life. There is an overwhelming scientific consensus that human activity is causing climate change that will have, indeed is already having, serious negative impacts (Cook et al. 2013; Maibach et al. 2014). The Intergovernmental Panel on Climate Change (IPCC) Fifth Assessment Report (IPCC 2014) points to the effects of warming in the melting of polar ice and glaciers, leading to rising sea levels, to increasing salination and scarcity of water supplies, and to desertification even in what are now temperate zones of the planet. It warns that extreme weather events such as rainfall and storms in some places, and prolonged drought in others, will become even more severe and more frequent. In the anodyne language of its *Synthesis Report*, the report is abundantly clear on the potential consequences:

> Without additional mitigation efforts beyond those in place today, and even with adaptation, warming by the end of the 21st century will lead to high to very high risk of severe, widespread, and irreversible impacts globally (high confidence). Mitigation involves some level of co-benefits

and of risks due to adverse side-effects, but these risks do not involve the same possibility of severe, widespread, and irreversible impacts as risks from climate change, increasing the benefits from near-term mitigation efforts.

(IPCC 2014: 17)

The Overseas Development Institute found that climate change would impact directly on development goals such as food security, availability of water and health outcomes, and that these would then negatively affect gender equality, employment and income poverty (ODI 2014). Those who currently have the smallest share of resources will be most affected such that current global inequalities will be amplified.

At the same time, global institutions, many national governments and business continue to drag their feet in terms of making the transformative changes that are required to mitigate against disaster. When the United Nations Climate Change Conference is held in Paris in December 2015, it will be over 20 years since the 1992 Rio Earth Summit, at which a small number of countries agreed to limit greenhouse gas emissions. There has been some response in terms of developing climate legislation, and groups such as the We Mean Business coalition (formed in June 2014 and made up of over 500 global companies – see www.wemeanbusinesscoalition.org) are calling for stronger agreement and action, although this is based on a business case approach that sees growth opportunities in mitigation (Phillips 2014, 2015). Little if any real progress has been achieved. Indeed, the 2009 climate summit in Copenhagen was an opportunity for 115 world leaders to make a binding agreement regarding carbon reduction, but it was an opportunity squandered as it descended into bickering and fiasco. The Copenhagen Accord that was cobbled together did not last and had little impact. Most Western national governments have sidelined a focus on carbon emissions in favour of economic growth following the global 2008 crash (Ellis and Bastin 2011). Public opinion too is weaker in terms of recognition of how dangerous climate change is and in terms of the actions that should be taken to mitigate it (Doan 2014). This is, in part, a result of disinformation produced by powerful vested interests, the remoteness of the discourses through which climate science is disseminated and feelings of powerlessness when confronted with the scale of the problem. However, to quote Naomi Klein:

> We know that if we continue on our current path of allowing emissions to rise year after year, climate change will change everything about our world. ... And we don't have to do anything to bring about this future. All we have to do is nothing.

(Klein 2014: 4)

This brings us to the next reason why contemporary perspectives on eco-feminism are needed. Over a period when it was argued that governments needed to act together to produce robust regulatory frameworks and other means to reduce carbon emissions and prevent natural degradation, they have instead done the opposite. Most Western governments and businesses support economic and political positions that broadly subscribe to the ideology of neoliberalism. While neoliberalism is a polysemic and contested term, it is broadly deployed in this text as a mode of political and economic rationality that has been characterized by deregulation of labour markets and privatization. As Harvey argues, it is a 'theory of political and economic practices that proposes that human wellbeing can be best advanced by liberating individual entrepreneurial freedoms and skills within an institutional framework characterized by strong private property rights, free markets and free trade' (Harvey 2005: 2). While neoliberalism is not an end-state, such that it is more accurate to say that processes of neoliberalization are taking place, the current political consensus is that the interests of a society, conceptualized as a set of atomized individuals, are best served through the operation of market forces. From a neoliberal perspective, the supposed economic rationality of the market will provide solutions to challenges such as climate change. Governments are positioned as having a minimal role in imposing regulation, striving instead to provide the conditions in which markets can operate (Dowling and Harvie 2014). Voluntary initiatives and complex market mechanisms created by corporations, industry associations, and even some environmental campaigners working in concert are seen as more attractive and more effective than direct regulation. This has resulted in the increasing commoditization of nature such that its value is calculated in economic terms and it is acquired and regulated by means of the market (Böhm et al. 2012). Concurrently, neoliberal economic policy and the politics of austerity have resulted in flows of assets, wealth and income to an increasingly small elite and to richer countries (Böhm et al. 2012; Cingano 2014), increasing inequality and making it even more difficult for individuals and majority world states to undertake the mitigation and adaptation measures necessary to combat climate change impacts. Current government, business and even many NGOs' approaches to environmental issues such as climate change are thus based in the imperatives of the market. This has resulted in a regime which Newell and Paterson (2010) call 'climate capitalism', where strategies of 'decarbonization' and 'greening' offer only minimal disruption to patterns of economic growth and expansion of the global economy, and are presented as opportunities for further capital accumulation.

Through its focus on the ways in which rationality is thus privileged, ecofeminism provides resources from which to illuminate and challenge the current orthodoxies which are further cementing ecological, social and economic crises. Ecofeminist philosopher Val Plumwood (1993, 2006) has charted how the foregrounding of reason accompanied the rise of capitalism. Systems which privilege and facilitate the self-interest of the rational, and therefore fully human, individual deny both human and Earth others. Those associated with the more-than-human, reproduction, the body and the unpaid labour of those demarcated into nature's sphere become invisible and unvalued inputs to an increasingly rationalized economy. The characteristics of *Homo œconomicus*, natural because economic rationality is deemed to be inherent in all persons, underpin and legitimate neoliberal concepts in which supposedly rational motives take primacy over and above other conflicting and transient motivations such as emotions, desires and attachments (Langley and Mellor 2002; Held 2006). This has justified regarding nature instrumentally: as a resource to be consumed rather than given status and value in its own right, which has had devastating consequences for nature, but which also increasingly threatens humanity as we have outlined above. For Plumwood, the forms of logic and rationality associated with current dominant political and economic models are thus inherently illogical and irrational, and carry within them the seeds of their own destruction. Such forms are unable to account for and recognize:

> in biospheric nature a unique, non-tradeable, irreplaceable other on which all life on the planet depends. Because it has not fully come to terms with its earthian existence, but clings to illusions of identity outside nature, the master rationality is unable to grasp its peril …
>
> (Plumwood 1993: 194)

This results in 'the kind of use of an earth other which treats it entirely as a means to another's ends, as one whose being creates no limits on use and which can be entirely shaped to ends not its own' (Plumwood 1993: 142). In contrast, the ecofeminist imperative is to consider how to create the 'possibility of meaningful, equitable and pleasant lives for all people in the present, [that] does not destroy either its ecological foundations or its capacity for social and physical reproduction in the future' (Perkins 2007: 227). It seeks to contribute to humanity's collective understanding of how to build more sustainable socio-economies-ecologies through a concern for nature and for equity within and between species and between generations. As Val Plumwood argues, ecofeminism should be seen as 'an attempt to obtain a new human and new social identity in relation to nature' (1993: 186) in an act of opposition and resistance to the instrumentalization and commodification characteristic of current social and economic life.

It is also the case that debates within feminist and environmental philosophies have moved forward in the past 15 years or so, often building on ideas first developed in ecofeminist thinking (Gaard 2011). The accusations levelled against ecofeminism now seem outdated and irrelevant. Feminist critiques of essentialism have, in turn, been critiqued (see Moore, chapter 1 in this volume). A 'material turn' and a 'corporeal turn' have made addressing the body, embodiment and materialism important elements of feminist thinking (e.g. Alaimo and Heckman 2007; Barad 2003) resonating with Glazebrook's (2005) call for approaches that recognize that 'the category of "woman" is neither universal, nor shattered irreparably into fragmented individualism'

(76–77). As she points out, 'We [women] have no access to our biology free of social construction, and our social construction has its reproductive under-pinning' (88). Concepts around 'nature' are also recognized as made from assemblages of cultural norms, social ideologies and scientific discourses so that they are irreducible to the 'natural' but, at the same time, nature is also embodied and has a material basis that cannot be subsumed within human construction (Thompson 2006). Postcolonialism and ideas around the post-human are widely debated within and without feminism, and exploring and interrogating forms of spirituality are no longer dismissed. Within the UK, the value of academics, activists and community groups working together is becoming more widely recognized. This is at least partly driven by the policies of government-sponsored funding councils and the requirements of the Research Excellence Framework which has introduced the measurement of non-academic impact.[1] However, the result is that such 'real world' effects are increasingly regarded as of equal importance to academic theoretical development – something long recognized in action research. While eco-feminism was not immune to at times damaging typologizing that sought to distinguish academic from activist (see Sturgeon 1997 for a full discussion), there has always been a strong current within the field that emphasizes the need for solidarity and coalition-building between all those striving for social and environmental justice (e.g. Plumwood 2006; Warren 1987) and that sees activism as central to, not separate from, feminist theorization.

It was in recognition both of the urgency of environmental challenges and of the changing nature of debates within feminism that this collection had its genesis. The first editor and one of our chapter authors, Mary Phillips, stumbled across ecofeminism almost by accident. She was becoming increasingly disenchanted with the ways in which her discipline of critical management and organization studies ignored the gendered dimensions of debates around sustainability and corporate environmentalism. She was also frustrated by the anthropocentrism of much feminist thinking. The philosophical debates, coupled with the focus on action, offered by ecofeminism provided a highly salient lens through which to critique the functionalist approaches to the environment that are dominant in the field of academic management. More-over, she was struck how these debates pre-figured much of what would become 'mainstream' in feminist thinking. Two conference streams followed in 2012 and 2014 at the 'Gender, work and organization' meetings held at Keele University, UK. There were two aims: first, to introduce ecofeminist philoso-phies into studies of management; second, to contribute to a wider recognition of and recuperation of ecofeminism. Both attracted a healthy number of papers offered by academics working in Australia, continental Europe, South Africa, the UK and the USA, some of which have been further developed for inclusion in this volume. It is the case that a growing number of scholars are recognizing that ecofeminism is needed now more than ever.

Indeed the second editor, Nick Rumens, is another example. Working with Mary Phillips, Nick has come to recognize the absolute necessity of ecofeminism in a context of wasted opportunities to intervene in ecological care of the world which we inhabit, and at a time when multifarious neoliberalisms and forms of transnational power are in play. Specifically, the pressing importance and salience of contemporary forms of ecofeminism is the chorus of criticism it directs towards the role of men and masculinities in perpetuating these missed opportunities and systems of domination and inequality. As many of the chapter contributors rightly point out, men have historically dominated women and nature to the detriment of both. For Nick, ecofeminism has a crucial role to play in nourishing the minds of men who are implicated in and responsible for reproducing male hegemonic power and ideologies, as some of the chapters in this volume illustrate vividly. However, as this edited collection also reveals, the limited number of contributions from pro-ecofeminist male writers underscores the need for more research on the complex relationship between men and masculinities in order to understand more fully the connections among racism, sexism, colonialism, speciesism and the environment. For men wishing to participate in this endeavour, they must start from the recognition of a transnational field that is riven with radically uneven power relations, gender differences and inequalities, challenging both men and women to generate modes of engagement that take seriously the environmental emergencies of the current moment.

And so, we now turn to the 'patches' offered here to the expanding ecofeminist quilt, which address contemporary concerns such as corporeality and the animal; materially based analysis of economic, social and political systems of domination; community-based, participative research; colonializing, majority world development; spirituality; the management of nature; and the ways in which the natural world and its degradation are represented in popular culture.

## Structure and organization of the book

### Part I: Theory

*Contemporary Perspectives on Ecofeminism* is divided into two thematically organized sections. The first section examines the theoretical richness of ecofeminism, its genealogy and how it might be reinvigorated by new conceptual approaches. However, as stated above, ecofeminism has never been solely concerned with theory. Ecofeminist theories are an extension of ecofeminism into the realm of theoretical and philosophical discourse but they are also linked to action and forms of activism, insisting we should push for progressive environmental change and gender equality. In this section, then, bridging ecofeminist theories with practice forms an important theme that unites not only these chapters, but also those that follow in the second section of the book on Practice.

Niamh Moore (chapter 1) begins with a genealogical analysis of ecofeminism. In particular, Moore critically discusses the damaging effects of critiques of essentialism on ecofeminism. Arguably, in the desire to prove that ecofeminism is not essentialist, Moore points out that ecofeminists have inadvertently conceded that essentialism has constituted an appropriate and meaningful frame for theorizing ecofeminism, and women and nature. Moore extends Noël Sturgeon's genealogical approach, discussing the ways in which ecofeminists described ecofeminism before it became overshadowed and mired in critiques of essentialism. A key focal point of this chapter is how ecofeminists have responded to critiques of essentialism. Concluding her chapter with thoughts on the emergence of 'new materialism', Moore considers how this may be an intriguing lens through which to rethink ecofeminism.

Erika Cudworth's chapter 2 explores ecofeminist conceptualizations of human relations with non-human animals. There has not been a singular ecofeminist position on 'the animal question', although research has interrogated assumptions underpinning women's caring (or reproductive) labour, questions of animal liberation and the use of animals as food, clothing and companions. Cudworth rethinks some of these issues, arguing that whatever the differences between specific positions and perspectives, this body of work has been influential in problematizing 'the human', 'the animal' and human relations with non-human animals. Specifically, it allows Cudworth to reconsider the intersectionalized dimensions of oppression that allow us to develop powerful contemporary analyses of the ways the social system of gender relations is co-constituted through ideas and practices around 'nature' and species relations. Cudworth's chapter contributes to this field of study by advocating a particular feminist theorization of human relations with non-human animals within the frame of 'critical animal studies'.

Mary Phillips's chapter 3 explores the inertia of Western governments, business and the public to make the transformative changes needed to live more sustainably. Phillips argues that we are physically and emotionally distant from the ways we impact on nature, which presents ecofeminism with a formidable challenge. Confronting the twin problems of inertia and estrangement, Phillips proposes that ecofeminism can help us to embrace our organic embeddedness in nature. Recognizing that ecofeminism falls short of suggesting how body/nature awareness can be stimulated and translated into action, she combines ecofeminist philosophy with the work of French feminist Hélène Cixous in order to support a revaluation and rewriting of the body which can subvert patriarchal logic. To this end, Phillips draws on poetic writing in and of the body as a resource and form of activism that can help overcome our current inertia.

Adelheid Biesecker and Uta von Winterfeld's contribution (chapter 4) starts from the position that the capitalist world is experiencing what has been conceptualized as a multiple crisis: a term used to highlight how the global economic or financial crisis is also an ecological crisis of climate and natural resources, a social crisis involving the retreat of welfare states and social coherence, and a political crisis of governance. Biesecker and von Winterfeld focus on the crisis of work, understood as integrating the 'productive' work included within the market and 'reproductive' work that takes place outside. Deriving insights from feminist Carole Pateman's work on the social contract and Val Plumwood's critique of the separated self, Biesecker and von Winterfeld discuss, using Germany's *A Social Contract for Sustainability* as a focal point for analysis, ecofeminist approaches to political economy and political ecology.

Rounding off Part 1, Mary Brydon-Miller and Anne Inga Hilsen (chapter 5) examine the intersections between action research, covenantal ethics and ecofeminism. Like other chapters in Part I of this book, Brydon-Miller and Hilsen's chapter builds a bridge between theory and practice. The authors extend the commitment action researchers make to work for positive social change to include recognition of our responsibility to promote environmental justice and to acknowledge the inextricable relationship between ourselves and nature. The chapter argues that where action research and covenantal ethics can make the most important contribution to ecofeminism is in our understanding of the importance of the cogeneration of knowledge. Brydon-Miller and Hilsen conclude the chapter by reviewing a strategy for engaging in ethical reflection as well presenting some practical examples that illustrate how action research can reflect the values of covenantal ethics and ecofeminism.

## Part II: Practice

The second part of the book moves toward an explicit focus on practice, examining contemporary forms of ecofeminism in action.

Trish Glazebrook (chapter 6) begins by drawing on findings from a case study of women's farming to argue for implementation of UN climate adaptation funds to support women's subsistence rather than corporate farming in the Global South. Glazebrook's chapter insists that the needs of women in the Global South are pressing ecofeminist issues, not least because of the climate change impacts documented in the Fifth Assessment Report of the Intergovernmental Panel. The chapter concludes with recommendations about how UN climate funds can support women farmers.

Ida Sabelis, Tamarisk van Vliet and Harry Wels (chapter 7) draw on empirical research conducted with game rangers' wives in South Africa in order to bring to the fore the hitherto hidden experiences of these women 'living in the wilderness'. In so doing, Sabelis et al. provide an important counterpoint to the proliferation of one-sided male and masculine accounts of living and undertaking conservation work in the wilderness. Contributing to a strand of ecofeminist thought on how the intersectionality of nature and humans is lived and experienced, they analyse the narratives of the 'bush wives', as some of their study participants call themselves, to explore if and how a more inclusive, gendered understanding of 'wilderness' emerging from their stories could enhance contemporary ecofeminist debates.

Continuing in the context of South Africa, in chapter 8 Laura Wright analyses the performative nature of the South African township tour.

Wright explores how the township tour contributes to the construction of a specific tourist mythology in regard to landscape, gender politics and racially defined social mobility in the so-called 'new' South Africa. With reference to a range of cultural artefacts such as songs, novels, sculpture and film, Wright's chapter acts as a counter to the tourism industry's potentially reductive representations not only of the South African landscape (as at once uninhabited by people but populated by 'exotic' animals), but also of township spaces and residents. Wright posits that a postcolonial ecofeminism informed by the South African philosophy of *ubuntu* can serve to help tourists more fully historicize the various social, political and cultural realities that have displaced South Africans from specific spatial environments.

Also taking cultural artefacts as objects of analysis, Greta Gaard's chapter 9 surveys climate change science fiction ('cli-fi') narratives from a variety of genres – novels for adults and for teens, environmental non-fiction, films for adults and for children. Gaard argues that, in these mainstream narratives, climate change is presented as a horror story or a problem requiring technological and scientific intervention. But data provided by artists, activists and researchers in the global movement for climate justice confirm that climate change is more than a techno-scientific problem. Gaard's chapter is a tart corrective to a narrow view of climate change as a techno-scientific problem, arguing that it is a problem of globalized injustices, and that successful efforts to mitigate and adapt to climate change futures will require equal attention to economic justice as well as environmental, gender and species justice.

Christine Katz (chapter 10) uses empirical insights derived from forestry management work in Germany to examine the linkages between gender relations and nature management. Katz avers that few extant analyses in this field of study are based on (de-)constructive theories and/or conceptualize and categorize gender as a process category. Furthermore, research rarely uses intersectional approaches focusing on the interconnection between the symbolic-discursive and material features of both nature and gender and the dominance patterns in the interactions between the two. Katz provides a nuanced, feminist analysis that takes seriously the concept of gender as a process ('doing gender') alongside a notion of 'doing nature' in her investigation of two approaches to the management of nature in German forestry.

Concluding this part of the book, in chapter 11 Ali Young and Scott Taylor critically analyse the relationship between ecofeminist principles and modernist organization practices, a fascinating but neglected area of study. Young and Taylor explore the development of two contemporary spiritual communities subscribing to ecofeminist principles: 'The Moving Centre' and 'The School of Movement Medicine'. Organizations such as these, they reason, are invariably sites of tension and contradiction because they are located within neoliberal capitalism politically, economically and socially. Drawing on and contributing to the idea and practice of 'tempered radicalism' to understand better the inevitable negotiation involved in bringing ecofeminist ideals into organized forms, they conclude by suggesting that membership of these spiritual communities can be understood as a radical act and a pragmatic means of bringing radical ideas to wider attention within the context of neoliberal capitalism.

## Note

1 Research Councils UK is responsible for investing public money in research in the United Kingdom. See http://www.rcuk.ac.uk for further details. The Research Excellence Framework is the system for assessing the quality of research in UK higher education institutions. See http://www.ref.ac.uk for further details.

## References

Alaimo, S. and Heckman, S. (eds) (2007) *Material Feminisms*, Bloomington: Indiana University Press.
Barad, K. (2003) 'Posthumanist performativity: Toward an understanding of how matter comes to matter', *Signs* 28(3): 801–831.
Böhm, S., Misoczky, M.C. and Moog, S. (2012). 'Greening capitalism? A Marxist critique of carbon markets', *Organization Studies* 33(11): 1617–1638.
Cingano, F. (2014) *Trends in Income Inequality and its Impact on Economic Growth*, OECD Social, Employment and Migration Working Papers No. 163, Paris: OECD Publishing, available from http://dx.doi.org/10.1787/5jxrjncwxv6j-en (accessed February 2015).
Cook, J. (1998) 'The philosophical colonization of ecofeminism', *Environmental Ethics* 20(3): 227–246.
Cook, J., Nuccitelli, D., Green, S.A., Richardson, M., Winkler, B., Painting, R., Way, R., Jacobs, P. and Skuce, A. (2013) 'Quantifying the consensus on anthropogenic global warming in the scientific literature', *Environmental Research Letters* 8(2): 1–7.
Cuomo, C. (2002) 'On ecofeminist philosophy', *Ethics and the Environment* 7(2): 1–11.
Doan, M.D. (2014) 'Climate change and complacency', *Hypatia* 29(3): 634–650.
Dowling, E. and Harvie, D. (2014) 'Harnessing the social: State, crisis and (Big) Society', *Sociology* 48(5): 869–886.
Ellis, L. and Bastin, C. (2011) 'Corporate social responsibility in times of recession: Changing discourses and implications for policy and practice', *Corporate Social Responsibility and Environmental Management* 18: 294–305.
Gaard, G. (1998) *Ecological Politics: Ecofeminists and the Greens*, Philadelphia: Temple University Press.
Gaard, G. (2011) 'Ecofeminism revisited: Rejecting essentialism and re-placing species in a material feminist environmentalism', *Feminist Formations* 23(2): 26–53.
Glazebrook, T. (2005) 'Gynocentric eco-logics', *Ethics and the Environment* 10(2): 75–99.
Harvey, D. (2005) *A Brief History of Neoliberalism*, Oxford: Oxford University Press.
Held, V. (2006). *The Ethics of Care: Personal, Political and Global*, New York: Oxford University Press.
IPCC (2014) *Climate Change 2014: Synthesis Report*, Contribution of Working Groups I, II and III to the Fifth Assessment Report of the IPCC, Core Writing Team, Pachauri, R.K. and Meyer, L.A., Geneva: Intergovernmental Panel on Climate

Change, available from http://www.ipcc.ch/pdf/assessment-report/ar5/syr/AR5_SYR_FINAL_SPM.pdf (accessed February 2015).

Klein, N. (2014) *This Changes Everything*, New York: Simon & Schuster.

Langley, P. and Mellor, M. (2002) '"Economy", sustainability and sites of transformative space', *New Political Economy* 7(1): 49–65.

Maibach, E., Myers, T. and Leiserowitz, A. (2014) 'Climate scientists need to set the record straight: There is a scientific consensus that human-caused climate change is happening', *Earth's Future* 2(5): 295–298.

Moore, N. (2008) 'Eco/Feminism, non-violence and the future of feminism', *International Feminist Journal of Politics* 10(3): 282–298.

Newell, P. and Paterson, M. (2010) *Climate Capitalism: Global Warming and the Transformation of the Global Economy*, Cambridge, UK: Cambridge University Press.

ODI (2014) *Zero Poverty … Think Again*, London: Overseas Development Institute, available from: http://www.odi.org/zero-poverty (accessed February 2015).

Parker, R. (1984) *The Subversive Stitch: Embroidery and the Making of the Feminine*, London: Women's Press.

Perkins, P.E. (2007) 'Feminist ecological economics and sustainability', *Journal of Bioeconomics* 9(3): 227–244.

Phillips, M.E. (2014) 'Re-writing organizational environmentalism: Ecofeminism, corporeality and the language of feeling', *Gender, Work & Organization* 21(5): 443–458.

Phillips, M.E. (2015) 'Re-ethicizing corporate greening? Ecofeminism, activism and the ethics of care', in *The Routledge Companion to Ethics, Politics and Organizations*, edited by Pullen, A. and Rhodes, C., London: Routledge, 51–66.

Plumwood, V. (1993) *Feminism and the Mastery of Nature*, London: Routledge.

Plumwood, V. (2006) 'Feminism', in *Political Theory and the Ecological Challenge*, edited by Dobson, A. and Eckersley, R., Cambridge: Cambridge University Press, 51–74

Sandilands, C. (1999) *The Good-Natured Feminist: Ecofeminism and the Quest for Democracy*, Minneapolis: University of Minnesota Press.

Sturgeon, N. (1997) *Ecofeminist Natures: Race, Gender, Feminist Theory and Political Action*, London: Routledge.

Thompson, C. (2006) 'Back to nature? Resurrecting ecofeminism after poststructuralist and third-wave feminism', *Isis* 97(3): 505–512.

Twine, R.T. (1997) 'Masculinity, nature, ecofeminism', *Ecofem.org/journal*, available at http://richardtwine.com/ecofem/masc.pdf (accessed April 2012).

Warren, K. (1987) 'Feminism and ecology: making connections', *Environmental Ethics* 9(1): 3–20.

Warren, K. (1997) 'Taking empirical data seriously: an ecofeminist philosophical perspective', in *Ecofeminism: Women, Culture, Nature*, edited by Warren, K., Bloomington: Indiana University Press, 3–20.

Warren, K. (2000) *Ecofeminist Philosophy: A Western Perspective on What It Is and Why It Matters*, Lanham, MD: Rowman & Littlefield.

World Wildlife Fund (2014a) *Living Planet Report*, available from http://assets.world wildlife.org/publications/723/files/original/WWF-LPR2014-low_res.pdf?1413912230&_ga=1.230044959.269800605.1426861329 (accessed February 2015).

World Wildlife Fund (2014b) *Living Planet Report Summary*, available from https://www.worldwildlife.org/press-releases/half-of-global-wildlife-lost-says-new-wwf-report (accessed February 2015).

# Part I

# Theory

# 1 Eco/feminist genealogies

Renewing promises and new possibilities[1]

*Niamh Moore*

Ecofeminism makes such big promises!

(Lahar 1991: 28)

I first encountered the word ecofeminism in 1987 when I was a master's student doing research for a term paper in a course in feminist sociology. Freshly arrived in the big city of Toronto, which I then perceived to be completely devoid of nature (I grew up in Victoria on Vancouver Island, where nature may not have been more plentiful but was certainly bigger), I was absolutely thrilled to discover a word that already existed to represent my deepest personal and political desire, the inclusion of an environmentalist perspective in feminist theory. I craved a language that would describe my growing sense that nature must be an important consideration in any feminist political vision; I remember devouring the first ecofeminist text I encountered – *Green Paradise Lost*, I think it was – at the expense of the readings on public policy on which I was supposed to be focusing.

But the exhilaration I felt as a new convert was over quite soon, and I have never felt so strongly that I belonged in ecofeminism, despite my increasing commitment to feminist ecological politics and theory.

(Sandilands 1999: 3)[2]

Although I've been attracted to thinking at the intersections of feminism and environmentalism for years, I hesitate to call myself an ecofeminist. Indeed, I prefer to think of my work as ecological feminism, in an effort to keep the emphasis on feminism, and also to distance my approach somewhat from other work done by self-titled ecofeminists. Though I share motivations with the authors of such work, I am sufficiently critical to be uncomfortable with the label. Accordingly, in these pages, 'ecofeminism' is an umbrella term referring to forthright attempts to link some versions of feminism and environmentalism, and 'ecological feminism' refers to a specific subset of ecofeminist approaches I wish to articulate and endorse here.

(Cuomo 1998: 5–6)

Dealing with my own objections to the essentialism of some ecofeminist arguments, and the effects on my work of a widespread assumption among my academic feminist peers that such essentialisms permanently and thoroughly

tarnish ecofeminism as a political position, I have struggled with the question
of whether I would want to identify myself and my work as ecofeminist.

(Sturgeon 1997: 168)

## Confessions of reluctant eco/feminists: essential/ist concerns

Eco/feminism,[3] once described with excitement as offering such promise (see
also Warren 1990), had by the mid- to late 1990s become for many in academia
a somewhat 'reluctant confession' (Cuomo 1998: 5), or even an identification
that some wished to disown entirely. This shift from exhilaration to disavowal
speaks of an intense and fraught period in eco/feminist history. Only a few
years separate Lahar's excited, but also cautionary comment – 'Ecofeminism
makes such big promises!' – from the struggles of Sandilands, Cuomo and
Sturgeon with the term 'ecofeminism'. For them, as for many others, reserva-
tions about the spectre of essentialism came to circumscribe possible identifica-
tions with eco/feminism. Or, more precisely, their concern was that they might
be perceived as essentialist by other feminists. To be clear, Sandilands, Cuomo
and Sturgeon did not straightforwardly accept eco/feminism as essentialist.
Indeed, they all robustly provided accounts of eco/feminism as that which
cannot be reduced to essentialism. And, whatever label they might choose,
all resolutely continue to work at the interfaces of 'women' and 'nature',
feminism and environmentalism. Nonetheless, the weight of essentialism
marks the work of these and many other eco/feminists.

My 'confession', or as I would prefer, *affirmation* (following Bell 1999), is
that I am, *still*, a passionate eco/feminist. It is true that I write some years
after Sandilands, Cuomo and Sturgeon, and the present moment is a different
time in which to make an affirmation of eco/feminism – albeit that accusations
of essentialism might still be forthcoming – and (my) writing remains marked
by the intractable nature of the debate. In 1997 Sturgeon (1997) reported
encountering audiences that anticipated (or even demanded) either essentialism or anti-essentialism, and she reflected on her attempts to confound both
expectations. I have sometimes experienced something slightly different – a
sense of puzzlement about why I still feel mired in a debate that others possibly
perceive as anachronistic. This perception suggests a failure to appreciate the
damage caused by the critique of essentialism. The disavowal of eco/feminism,
by feminists and by eco/feminists themselves, might be understood as one
consequence of this critique. Eco/feminism thus offers a particularly useful
site for an examination of the devastating impact of the accusation of essentialism, as well as of an insistent anti-essentialism, on feminist theorizing and
activism. By the late 1990s talking about eco/feminism (in an academic context
at least) had become difficult, unless one also addressed, and clearly rejected,
the inevitable question/accusation of essentialism.

In the context of the hyper-politicized 'nature' of essentialism, eco/feminists
have been frustrated that their research and politics have been dismissed as
essentialist and that others have doubted their feminist credentials. For

instance, in *Ecofeminist Natures*, Noël Sturgeon (1997: 167) wrote, 'Some ecofeminists have argued that there is an "establishment feminist backlash" against ecofeminism, resulting in a lack of ecofeminist writing in prominent feminist journals such as *Signs*, as well as the invisibility of ecofeminist theory in important academic feminist conferences and anthologies'. Offering examples from her own career, Sturgeon (ibid.: 6, 167–68) recalled that a feminist mentor advised her to delete 'ecofeminism' from the title of one of her papers, and that another suggested that her job applications should not mention her editorship of the *Ecofeminist Newsletter*. Such anecdotal accounts of feminist distancing of eco/feminism, together with eco/feminists' sense of rejection and unjustified exclusion from the feminist sisterhood, are evidence of just how much has been at stake for eco/feminists.

In this chapter, I trace the damaging effects of critiques of essentialism on eco/feminism, taking the palpable disappointment of the 1990s onward as a departure point for an exploration of histories of, and possible futures for, eco/feminism. In doing this, I draw on and develop Noël Sturgeon's genea-logical approach, which has offered one of the clearest accounts of the consequences of critiques of essentialism for eco/feminism. Necessarily, in the process I construct my own – interested – genealogy of eco/feminism. Extending Sturgeon's work, I pay attention to the ways in which eco/feminists described eco/feminism before the critique of essentialism became prevalent, pointing to accounts of eco/feminist diversity and the centrality of stories of global grassroots activism. I focus on how eco/feminists have responded to feminist critiques of essentialism, through juxtaposing the figures of Françoise d'Eaubonne and Vandana Shiva, in her role popularizing the Chipko Movement. The attribution of the naming of 'ecofeminism' to d'Eaubonne has appeared as problematic when compared with the promi-nence once accorded to the Chipko movement. In conclusion, I turn to the emergence of 'new materialism' as an intriguing site through which to reflect on eco/feminism today.

## Disowning eco/feminism: the critique of essentialism and the practice of typologizing

Sturgeon termed her account of eco/feminism 'not so much a history as a genealogy' (1997: 4). Her take-up of the possibilities afforded by genealogy offered a more complex account of what has been at stake in different mani-festations of eco/feminism than others thus far, and in doing so she made an invaluable contribution to understandings of eco/feminism:

> [m]y version of the history of the origins and development of ecofemin-ism is thus not so much a coherent narrative of the even, dependable growth of an independent political position as it is several snapshots of scattered, uneven, and in many ways disconnected beginnings, retreats, dormancies, and proliferations imbedded within several different

political locations. This is a genealogy rather than a history, and as a
result, I am not following one unitary subject (ecofeminism) through
different historical moments. Instead I am articulating relationships,
legacies, simultaneous births of related entities, discontinuities, renamings,
mutations, throwbacks.

(Sturgeon 1997: 3–4)

Sturgeon traced the emergence of eco/feminism through its appearance
across a range of sites; academic, activist, organizations, and writings of all
kinds. Sturgeon's careful attention to ways of describing and defining eco/
feminism is instructive. Her final chapter of *Ecofeminist Natures* offers a
powerful account of the limits of the practice of creating typologies of eco/
feminism, whether relying on existing categories such as radical, cultural or
socialist ecofeminisms, or creating new terms such as 'feminist ecological
politics', 'ecological feminism' and 'environmental feminism'. She clearly
identified typologizing as an exercise in naming and exclusion, as enabling
the disavowal of certain aspects of eco/feminism by carving it up, disowning
'essentialist' varieties and renaming 'good' (non-essentialist) ones. In this
process, she demonstrated that the search for a new descriptor for eco/feminism
was bound up with a desire to create a term which was purified of any taint
of essentialism.

Sturgeon identified two common effects of typologizing in eco/feminism.
First, she pointed out that feminisms of colour are frequently ignored.
Second, citing Chela Sandoval (1991), she noted that superior and inferior
types of feminism are implicitly constructed, making coalitions between
activist and academic feminisms difficult. Sturgeon argued that:

the critique of essentialisms of various kinds has been a prominent tool
in creating various types of typologies of feminisms, usually to support
an 'agonistic narrative structure' (de Lauretis) in which certain feminist
theories (usually socialist feminism or poststructuralist feminism) come
out to be the winners in the contest for the most politically useful feminist theory. That these winners in the anti-essentialist competition have
also been the feminist theories most embedded in the academic contexts
is suggestive.

(Sturgeon 1997: 16)

Sturgeon's analysis offers ways of understanding much about eco/feminism's
current state. I want to push her genealogical approach further, to see what
might be learned from applying it to other ways of describing eco/feminism.

## Diverse eco/feminisms?

Typologizing has not been the only approach to defining eco/feminism.
During the late 1980s and early 1990s, the emerging and overlapping

academic and activist literatures commonly described eco/feminism by stressing its diversity. For instance, Elizabeth Carlassare wrote:

> Ecofeminism does not lend itself to easy generalization. It consists of a diversity of positions, and this is reflected in the diversity of voices and modes of expression represented in ecofeminist anthologies. The eco-feminist anthologies, *Reclaim the Earth*, and *Reweaving the World*, and the issues of *Heresies* and *Hypatia* on feminism and ecology include the work of different women from different countries and social situations, and their work does not adhere to a single form or outlook. Poems, art, photographs, fiction, prose, as well as theoretical/philosophical/'academic' works are included. Ecofeminism's diversity is also reflected by its circulation in a variety of arenas, such as academia, grass-roots movements, conferences, books, journals, and art.
>
> (Carlassare 1994: 220–221)

This range – of positions, of voices, of forms, of locations – was generally viewed positively, as suggesting that eco/feminism was not dogmatic and could embrace difference, an important value in feminism during the early 1990s. With such an emphasis on diversity, anthologies and special issues of journals, which allowed for a variety of voices and forms, were the preferred publication formats at the time. Even so, their editors sometimes felt the need to point out their limitations, as in Judith Plant's introduction to the collection *Healing the Wounds: The Promise of Ecofeminism* (1989b: 4): 'This anthology in no way fully represents the wide spectrum of thought that is ecofeminism.'

However, some commentators suggested that this emphasis on diversity might create confusion. Stephanie Lahar (1991: 28) observed that 'the newness of the movement, the breadth of issues it encompasses, and the diversity of people thinking and writing about eco/feminism have resulted in considerable confusion about what eco/feminism actually is, who eco/feminists are, and what they have to say'. Thus, though diversity was prized, making sense of eco/feminism's sheer variety constituted something of a challenge, and one feature came to be foregrounded – the emphasis on diverse locations all over the world.

The importance of the global dimensions of eco/feminism are particularly clear in the anthologies *Healing the Wounds* (Plant 1989a), *Reweaving the World: The Emergence of Ecofeminism* (Diamond and Orenstein 1990b), and *Reclaim the Earth: Women Speak Out for Life on Earth* (Caldecott and Leland 1983). All three stressed the importance of global activism. As Caldecott and Leland (1983: 5) explained, 'In many countries all over the world, women are taking an increasingly prominent role in political struggles: in the peace, anti-nuclear, health and ecology movements.' Diamond and Orenstein stated,

> This volume, with its chorus of voices reflecting the variety of concerns flowing into ecofeminism, challenges the boundaries dividing such

genres as the scholarly paper and the impassioned poetic essay. In so doing, it acknowledges poetic vision as a form of knowledge and as one of the important steps in the process of *global transformation*.

Ecofeminist philosophy and creation have brought about changes in consciousness, political action, and spiritual practice. This collection is composed of writings by poets, novelists, scholars, scientists, ecological activists, and spiritual teachers, many of which were first presented at the conference, 'Ecofeminist Perspectives: Culture, Nature and Theory', held at the University of Southern California in March 1987 and sponsored by the California Council for the Humanities. We also invited others who did not attend the original conference to contribute to the volume, thus making a more comprehensive statement about *the global emergence of ecofeminism*.

We hope to dispel the notion that poetry and politics, spirituality and activism, scholarship and vision are to remain forever divided, either from each other, or within the same person. The writers and activists represented here share *a multicultural and diversified global vision of healing for life on Earth*. Their voices have been inspiring to us, and our fervent wish is that this volume will be a catalyst for further change.

(Diamond and Orenstein 1990a: vii, emphasis added)

In her foreword to *Healing the Wounds*, Petra Kelly wrote:

This is a book about global ecological sisterhood! ... This is not a time for complacency. It is a time for continuing to link arms as sisters – like the women in the Chipko movement in India; like the women at Greenham Common, in England, who are not giving up the struggle against militarization; like the women of the Western Shoshone Indian Nation in Nevada who opposed nuclear testing by encircling the test grounds; like the women in the Pacific struggling for a nuclear-free future to prevent babies being damaged through French atomic bomb tests; like the women in the Krim Region of the Soviet Union demonstrating courageously against a new nuclear power plant.

(Plant 1989a: ix–x)

Frequently, eco/feminism was made manifest through listing places or organizations where it was understood to be emerging. Introducing eco/feminism by providing a list of global grassroots activisms was common in the late 1980s and early 1990s (see, for example: Mellor 1992: 50; Merchant 1992: 184; Baker 1993: 2; and Gaard and Gruen 1993: 1). The diversity of locations in which the activism took place was as significant as the activism itself. Eco/feminists liked to say that the movement emerged at the same time in many parts of the world: Salleh (1997: 17) wrote of 'the word "ecofeminism" turning up spontaneously across several continents during the 1970s'. Thus eco/feminists lauded women's grassroots *activism* around the world, but particularly in the Global South.

Perhaps following Lahar's observation that the diversity of eco/feminism seemed to produce confusion, holding on to diversity became too challenging, with the result that one instance – the Chipko Movement – emerged as iconic. Chipko was a movement of Indian women in the Garwhal Himalayas who publicly hugged trees to protest commercial logging. It was brought to prominence for eco/feminists by scholar and activist Vandana Shiva, through her book, *Staying Alive: Women, Ecology and Development* (1989), and also through her numerous presentations at international policy and activist conferences.

The turn to typologizing, the concomitant reification of Chipko, and the reduction of eco/feminism to the Chipko Movement might then be understood as responses to the challenges posed by its diversity. Yet all these accounts – of diversity, of simultaneous emergence around the world, and of Chipko as exemplary – exist in tension with another account, one that is often visible only in the footnotes of eco/feminist texts. In the late 1990s, when Sturgeon (1997: 167–96), Cuomo (1998) and Gaard (1998: 12–15) echoed each other in asking 'What's in a name?', they were referring to the various names that were being created to describe typologies of feminism and environmentalism. The coining of the term 'ecofeminism' by French feminist Françoise d'Eaubonne also received significant attention; however, this attention was often relegated to footnotes

## Françoise d'Eaubonne and the origins of the term 'ecofeminism'

The first use of the term 'ecofeminism' (as *'ecoféminisme'*) is commonly attributed to Françoise d'Eaubonne in her book *Le Féminisme ou la Mort* (1974). D'Eaubonne has been widely cited in the eco/feminist literature from the mid-1980s onward, as if this fact could provide some anchorage, when faced with the multitudinous protests, books, courses, workshops, conferences, poems and rituals that have come to constitute eco/feminism. The ritual and obedient citation of d'Eaubonne's act of naming testifies to the power of this moment for academics in particular. Yet, despite the fact that d'Eaubonne's act of naming has been accorded some prominence in eco/feminist literature, at the same time this recognition often appears ambivalent, sometimes afforded only a brief passing reference, or relegated to a footnote. It is as if in acknowledging d'Eaubonne, she might be credited with sole authorship, or ownership, of the new phenomenon, which would implicitly threaten accounts which stressed the grassroots, internationalist and activist basis of eco/feminism itself – as well as the authorship rights of others. In addition to efforts to diminish the significance of d'Eaubonne's act of naming, her importance has been disputed in a number of other ways. Some, such as Sturgeon (1997: 202 n8) and Gaard (1998: 13), have looked for the first instance in which d'Eaubonne was cited as the originator of the term 'ecofeminism' and identified Karen Warren's (1988) paper 'Towards an ecofeminist ethic' as the source. Gaard (1998: 13) suggested that 'from that point forward, many writers cited this attribution without verification', with this apparent lack of corroboration working to undermine claims that the term 'ecofeminism' originated in d'Eaubonne's work.

Given that *Le Féminisme ou la Mort* was not translated into English until much later, some have argued that its influence on the development of eco/feminism in the United States would have been negligible (Sturgeon 1997: 202 n8; Heller 1999: 65; Sandilands 1999: 6). The relief at finding this resolution to the dilemma of authorship was almost palpable in one overview of eco/feminism:

> Françoise d'Eaubonne's *Le Féminisme ou la Mort?* (1974) is often credited for the first usage of the word 'eco-feminism' but as Ariel Salleh has pointed out in *Hypatia*, Vol. 6, No. 1 (Spring 1991), pp. 206–214, esp. 206, the text was not translated into English until 15 years later, so it would have had little effect on those articles and texts published before 1989. The spontaneous appearance of the word or the concept of 'eco-feminism' across several continents would indicate that it arose out of a real, internationally observable phenomenon rather than the influence of a single writer.
>
> (Gaard and Gruen 1993: 1)

The chronology of translation often plays an important role in these accounts. Although a short extract from d'Eaubonne's book was published in English in 1980 as 'Feminism or death' (d'Eaubonne 1980), it did not contain the word 'ecofeminism', a fact that simply reinforced arguments about d'Eaubonne's lack of influence on early eco/feminism in the United States. Heller (1999: 65 n20) cited 1994 as the date when d'Eaubonne's work became available to English-speaking audiences; in that year, a chapter from *Le Féminisme ou la Mort*, which did include the word 'ecoféminisme', was finally translated and anthologized in a collection edited by Carolyn Merchant (d'Eaubonne 1994).

However, relying on matters of translation to determine d'Eaubonne's influence assumes that no one outside France is capable of reading French, and that little cross-cultural exchange occurs. Gaard (1998: 13) noted another route for d'Eaubonne's work, acknowledging that 'others, such as Carol Adams, claim that they had learned the term "ecofeminism" from Mary Daly, whose work *Gyn/Ecology* had used it in 1978 and whose classes included a study of Françoise d'Eaubonne's text in the original language'. In *The Sexual Politics of Meat*, Carol Adams (1991: 89) pointed out that d'Eaubonne's text was introduced 'to scores of feminists who took Mary Daly's feminist ethics class at Boston College' just after it was published in 1974. Furthermore, Daly (1978: 9) explicitly referred to d'Eaubonne in discussing the naming of *Gyn/Ecology*, which was first published in 1975. Adams (1991: 89, 218 n12) attributed the appearance of her own book, as well as Collard and Contrucci's *Rape of the Wild* (1988), to Daly's influence, Collard being a close friend of Daly. She also pointed to the broader influence of *Le Féminisme ou la Mort*

and of eco/feminist ideas linking feminism, animals and nature on discussions in the Cambridge-Boston women's community. The books by Daly
(1978), Collard and Contrucci (1988) and Adams (1991) are among the early
texts of eco/feminism, and Daly's *Gyn/Ecology* was also a central text for
many feminists at the time. This suggests that d'Eaubonne's work did have
both a significant audience in the English-speaking world and an appreciable
impact on the literature of eco/feminism, despite the continuing lack of an
English translation. However, this hardly equates with attributing eco/feminism
per se to d'Eaubonne alone, and does not necessarily challenge claims for
eco/feminism as a grassroots phenomenon that emerged in various parts of
the world. It is perhaps more an indication of the significance of Mary Daly
in the genealogy of eco/feminism.

Furthermore, the attention to translation glosses over what was perhaps
Salleh's main concern. Writing of the spontaneous rise of eco/feminism
across the world, she made the point that 'for politico-economic reasons
then, eco/feminists working from more visible niches in the dominant English-
speaking culture have tended to get their views broadcast first – even feminism
is touched by its imperialist context'. Salleh's (1991: 206) note that 'the
lonely appearance in Paris of Françoise d'Eaubonne's *Le Féminisme ou la
Mort* (1974) is an exception whose lack of an English translation some fifteen
years later, more or less proves the rule' appears intended to highlight the
dominance of the English-speaking world and the rarity of eco/feminist texts
in a language other than English (see also Gates 1998).

Sandilands (1999: 6) astutely pointed to the need to recognize that 'd'Eaubonne's writing circulated in a different and particular context'. The context
she had in mind was that of French politics, especially French feminism in
the early 1970s, which is evident in the title of the collection in which the first
English translation of d'Eaubonne's work appeared – *New French Feminisms*
(Marks and De Courtivron 1980). Nonetheless, Sandilands' comment limits
the possible influence of d'Eaubonne and risks suggesting that her work had
little diffusion or meaning outside France.

Others have produced alternative origin stories for eco/feminism in the
USA, countering claims about d'Eaubonne and pointing to the work of
Ynestra King. According to Chaia Heller (1999: 53), 'In 1978, the Institute
for Social Ecology (ISE), which Bookchin co-founded in 1974, invited Ynestra King to develop what would become the first curriculum in a feminist
approach to ecology, thus coining the term ecofeminism.' Sturgeon and
Sandilands also referred to the work of King. Sturgeon (1997: 32) stated that
'the first classes in ecofeminism in the United States were taught by King at
ISE [Institute for Social Ecology, Vermont] in 1978', and Sandilands (1999:
213) wrote that King 'disputes this "first" [d'Eaubonne's naming of eco-
feminism], and was certainly active in the mid-1970s developing ecofeminism
at the Institute for Social Ecology'. Heller (1999: 65 n20) explained her
attention to narratives of eco/feminism, her decentring of d'Eaubonne, and
her stress on the role of King by asserting that:

examining the lineage of the term is a way to explore the specific historical context in which ecofeminist theory and action emerged. Attempts to trace the ecofeminist movement itself back to d'Eaubonne obfuscate the historical continuity between ecofeminist curriculum and writing that emerged at the ISE (Institute for Social Ecology, Vermont) by King, and the wider context of the US New Left made up of activists involved in the radical feminist movement, the feminist peace movement, the anti-war movement, and the anti-nuclear movement.

Despite this apparent curiosity about trails of footnotes, citations and translations, there is little evidence of critical reflexivity about academic eco/feminists' fascination with d'Eaubonne – a fascination that continued with her invitation to a 1998 eco/feminist conference held in Montana.[4] Perhaps inadvertently, a comment by Greta Gaard on claims of d'Eaubonne's strong influence on eco/feminism in the United States is revealing:

> What none of these defenses of d'Eaubonne addresses is the different political implications of attributing the origin of the term (and, by implication, the movement and ideas behind it) to a lone, white, first world scholar – or to the 'spontaneous combustion' of many women around the globe ... It would seem that the dispute over the lineage of 'ecofeminism' has been to some extent a class war over whether the idea was born from a single woman labouring alone in the library or from many women labouring in the forests, the military bases, and the nuclear power plants. For ecofeminists who want to open up the movement in such a way that activists themselves will claim the term, a more populist origin for the word would seem to have more strategic appeal.
>
> (Gaard 1998: 13–14)

Disarmingly, Gaard (ibid.: 14) concluded 'fortunately it's also true' – that the term 'ecofeminism' emerged from grassroots activism. Despite her intimation regarding the vested interests of academics, Gaard retreated from a critical examination of the stakes that white Western eco/feminists in the academy might have had in representing eco/feminism as an international grassroots movement. In addition, though Gaard may have been wary of crediting an individual such as d'Eaubonne with the emergence of eco/feminism, there is a suggestion that her stance was taken not only because of a desire for a collective narrative of its origins. Commenting on the repeated references to d'Eaubonne, she noted that 'the cumulative force of so many citations angered some and puzzled others, who felt certain that they had learned the term elsewhere'. Writing of her first meeting with other eco/feminists at the National Women's Studies Association (US) convention in 1989, Gaard (ibid.: 13) recounted that 'it was both humorous and frustrating to discover that so many of us, working alone in our separate parts of the country, thought we had invented these ideas ourselves'.

Thus, though d'Eaubonne is as ubiquitous as Shiva and the Chipko Movement in examinations of eco/feminism, Shiva and Chipko dominated the limelight, whereas d'Eaubonne was often relegated to a brief footnote. The point of this discussion is not to provide a corrective, to defend or reassert the importance of d'Eaubonne's work, nor to suggest the greater significance of another author. Instead, I pose the question of what is at stake in the awkward circumlocutions around the attribution of the naming of eco/feminism to a French feminist. There is no reason why d'Eaubonne's use of the term 'ecofeminism' could not be seen as just another example of eco/feminism's internationalism were it not for the emphasis on the written, and on the ownership of ideas, in academia, compounded by the Western-centrism of much academia. Clearly, *Le Féminisme ou la Mort* alone does not account for women's environmental activism of recent decades or even for the consolidation of a specifically eco/feminist theory. At the same time, as a French writer and a European, d'Eaubonne is not quite international enough to be able to stand as evidence of eco/feminism's global emergence. Thus the academic convention of citing sources and origins acknowledges her as author of the term, but by confining this information to a footnote or a passing reference, her significance is undermined, suggesting that she cannot be understood to author(ize) the movement. At the same time, the more overt references to Chipko provide proof of eco/feminist activism, but equally Chipko itself does not offer an intellectual foundation. Furthermore, as controversies over difference, race and global sisterhood raged in feminism, eco/feminism faced growing criticisms over the citation, or appropriation, of Chipko, especially from feminists in the field of gender and development (see Moore 2008, 2011).

## Eco/feminist responses to critiques of Chipko

Celebratory accounts of global activism, and of Chipko in particular, rapidly gave way to more critical reflections. Discussions of Chipko, and of the place of activism in the developing world, have often focused on the anthologies mentioned earlier – Plant (1989a) and Diamond and Orenstein (1990b) contain chapters by Shiva on Chipko as well as other chapters that refer to it. Sandilands (1999: 54) offers one example of such a critique in her account of these anthologies: 'The inclusion of race was not especially analytical; it did not in most cases, suggest ways in which women may have different relations to particular ecological issues or problems, and it did not look deeply at the ways in which these traditions have themselves been lost or reconstructed in particular social contexts.' She elaborated on the characterization of indigenous cultures as 'somehow pure, somehow dissociable from what colonization has done to those different cultures and social practices. Also problematic was their general assumption that all 'women's practices in nature are (at their core at least) benign, caring and respectful'. Sandilands (ibid.: 55–56) concluded her discussion on a relieved note: 'But (I'm very happy to say) this mode of discussion is no longer predominant in ecofeminist literatures that question racism and colonialism.'

Others offered different resolutions to the apparent problems posed by these texts. One route was turning to research on women in the West, in the so-called developed world. Chris Cuomo (1998: 8–9) wrote that 'while there is a tendency in Western ecofeminist theory to describe the work of rural Third World women as paradigmatic ecofeminist activism, one sees little effort (in the literature) to develop specific models that examine the politics of "first world" megaconsumption on ecofeminist grounds'. Cuomo's suggestion was taken up by Sherilyn MacGregor (2006: 128) in accounting for her own research with women in Ontario: 'I am making the point that the experiences and ideas of urban-dwelling women in the overdeveloped world are as interesting and informative to ecofeminist thought as those of "peasant" women in developing countries.' Examining the activism of women in the West is, I think, understandable and necessary – indeed, my own research thus far has been based in Canada or the UK (Moore 2001, 2004, 2011, 2015; Moore et al. 2014) – but this strategy brings problems of its own, not least erasing existing references to Western movements already commonly cited, including Greenham Common, the Seneca Women's Encampment, the Women's Pentagon Actions, the strong anti-toxics movements in the United States, and the Women's Environmental Network. Many organizations and actions in the developed world have focused intensely on (over)consumption and its impact elsewhere. Such a resolution may also imply that (Western) eco/feminists can have nothing to say regarding women and the environment in the Third World. It also ignores ways in which Third World women can speak and be seen and heard by Western eco/feminists. Most significantly, it belies the myriad ways in which North and South are intimately interconnected through histories of colonialism and slavery, through patterns of trade and the effects of environmental degradation, and through the movements, both real and virtual, of activists. All of these connections are manifest in the work of many eco/feminist organizations. Some, such as Women for an Independent and Nuclear Free Pacific, are alliances between women in the North and South. Thus, shifting one's focus from the South to the North requires careful attention to the specificities and contexts of histories and transnational connectivities.

Questions of race and indigeneity were also central for Noël Sturgeon (1997: 116), who identified Plant (1989b) and Diamond and Orenstein (1990b) as 'the most prominent representatives of the diversity within ecofeminism'. In focusing on discourses that 'center on the idealization of "indigenous" women as symbolic representatives of ecofeminism', Sturgeon (1997: 113–114) critically summed up some of the assumptions embedded in such accounts of indigenous women: that non-industrialized cultures are seen as more ecological, as not enacting a Western separation of nature and culture, and possibly as embodying more egalitarian gender relations. Nonetheless, I want to revisit some of the criticisms of the anthologies. For instance, Sturgeon (ibid.: 121) appeared dismissive of Plant's apparent reliance on Native American rituals in her contribution to the collection *The Circle Is Gathering*. Yet this becomes more complicated when one attends to Plant's location in British Columbia – her discussion drew on specific First Nations cultures and her embeddedness in particular communities, rather than on generalized ideas of 'Native Americans' as such. I do not wish to fuel Canadian exceptionalism or to ignore the fact that the indigenous people of North America have their own approach to national boundaries – my point is that Sturgeon's argument may rely on reading a specific First Nations iconography as a generalized indigeneity. Plant's ongoing commitment to bioregionalism may also contribute to the intentionality and specificity of her account and the imagery in her chapter and in her approach to the anthology. When *Healing the Wounds* was published in the United Kingdom, its cover was changed, perhaps in recognition that it invoked a specific indigeneity that might not be understood in the UK context; the new cover featured a crystal that diffracts light in a rainbow of colours. Furthermore, critiques of the anthologies have tended to attribute agency to their editors but have paid much less attention to the intentionality of the contributors. One is left with the prospect that the women of colour whose essays appeared in these supposedly essentializing, universalist collections were naive romanticizers of their own cultures. If this was so, how could we make sense of the inclusion of black, developing world, and indigenous women who explicitly critique these kinds of discourses? I speculate that it is not only a case that editors wanted to be inclusive, but that authors may also have wanted to be included in these collections, no matter how problematic they might seem. Perhaps this desire was in part due to the persistence of eco/feminism's orientation to global and transnational interconnections, as well as to environmentalism and spirituality. Over time, Chipko and other movements slowly disappeared from the literature or became the focus of criticism, allowing authors to demonstrate the theoretical sophistication of their feminism by publicly distancing themselves from such movements. Thus Carlassare's (1994) overview of eco/feminism was perhaps the last moment when claims about diversity could easily be made. While Greta Gaard (1998: 3) once declined an invitation to write a monograph on eco/feminism, believing that it 'would not do justice to such a multivocal grassroots movement',[5] by the mid- to late 1990s, collective polyvocal texts such as anthologies and special issues of journals had been largely superseded by the monographs of white authors, most of whom were North Americans. This irony leads me to question whether the assumptions of essentialism and universalism have been sufficiently and empirically worked through.

## From diversity to typologies

Developing Sturgeon's genealogical approach and attending to other (apparently incommensurate) ways of accounting for eco/feminism can be revealing. Concerns about naming, authorship, knowledge production and political action suggest an ongoing tension about the relationship between academia and activism. In Sturgeon's (1997: 169, emphasis added) analysis of typologies, her stated aim is 'to interrogate the anti-essentialist tangent within feminist theory (and, by extension, ecofeminist theory) that *created* a division between feminist theory and feminist activist practice'. By extending Sturgeon's genealogical approach and exploring other sites of the naming and defining of eco/feminism, I make apparent that the tension between theory and activism pre-dated the turn to anti-essentialism, and that the latter simply exacerbated the tension. Before typologizing came to dominate, theory, activism, spirituality and much more co-existed, jostling alongside each other in accounts of eco/feminism. The turn to typologizing could also be understood as a response to the increasing difficulty of managing diversity, and in particular the tensions between theory and activism, and as an attempt to avoid accusations of essentialism. Typologizing signals those moments when the insistence on the entanglement of theory, ritual, poetry, literature, food, activism, spirituality and philosophy was abandoned, and when eco/feminism became defined through, and in relation to, the dualism of essentialism/anti-essentialism – rather than as an anti-dualistic philosophy and practice. Thus typologizing marks a significant change in *how* we might know and understand eco/feminism. Against diversity, typologizing is a process of categorization, an attempt to manage the range of meanings of eco/feminism.

Yet, as Sturgeon very thoroughly illustrates, typologies of eco/feminism have proliferated. I suggest that we might perversely understand the sheer variety of typologies as signalling the re-appearance of eco/feminism's diversity. The multiplying of typologies can be understood to demonstrate the failure of the binary of essentialism and anti-essentialism to fix eco/feminism in place.

## From eco/feminism and essentialism to eco/feminism and the question of nature

In the desire to prove that eco/feminism is not essentialist, that it is resolutely anti-essentialist or can be recuperated as strategically essentialist, eco/feminists have implicitly, if perhaps unintentionally, conceded that essentialism has indeed constituted an appropriate and meaningful frame for theorizing eco/feminism, and women and nature. I suggest that the shift to typologizing – including by eco/feminists themselves – marked the moment when eco/feminist academics succumbed to narratives of eco/feminism's essentialism and lost their earlier optimism regarding eco/feminism and its radical diversity. In this process eco/feminist academics ceded much of eco/feminism's radical anti-dualistic potential to essentialism. Sturgeon's (1997: 168) plaintive question – 'What has the ecofeminist movement done or not done to deserve its exclusion from certain feminist circles?' – is indicative of some eco/feminists' bewilderment over the failure of other feminists to recognize their feminism. I think it is fair to say that neither anti-essentialism nor strategic essentialism has succeeded in proving eco/feminism's feminism to (other) feminists. Arguably eco/feminists have been caught up in defending themselves against the implicit or explicit charge of essentialism, constraining the possibilities for theorizing. In this process examining 'women' and 'nature' was oddly displaced from the centre of inquiry.

I suggest that the challenge for eco/feminists now is to ask the question anew: to shift focus from the supposed question of essentialism and to take up again the question of women and nature. This is, I suggest, an interesting and intriguing moment to pursue this project – after all, in the meantime other feminists have begun to write about 'nature' in some guise. Donna Haraway of course always did; but more recently there has been the emergence of what is variously termed 'new materialism', 'feminist materialism', 'material feminisms' (for example: Alaimo and Hekman 2008; Barad 2003; Coole and Frost 2010; Grosz 2005). Yet these writers appear to proceed without the taint of essentialism – this is in itself an interesting puzzle, how do they manage this? Perhaps there is something for eco/feminists to learn – or to contribute?

Both Sara Ahmed and Maureen McNeil (Ahmed 2008; McNeil 2010) focus on new materialism's explicit abandonment of critique in favour of a more affirmative approach, and in particular a positive approach to biology. This convergence of a rejection of critique with a renewed focus on matter, biology and nature is indeed provocative in the context of eco/feminism, and is suggestive of one of the ways in which such theorists avoid the critique of essentialism or even anti-essentialism. Rather than a defence of anti-essentialism, Grosz and others offer an assertion of feminism's need to pay attention to biology. However, as Ahmed notes, this assertion is made possible only by forgetting a vast amount of feminist work on biology and, I might add, intense critique of essentialism. This, as McNeil terms it, 'affirmative post-millennial feminist theory' appears to avoid the 'critique' of essentialism by seeming to forget that there ever was an extensive feminist conversation about biology, and nature, through its radical proclamation of the 'new'. Both Ahmed and McNeil share an understanding of critique as a close and generous engagement with other feminists, but it is not clear that this is Grosz's understanding of critique. Ahmed is explicit that her concern is about the routine production of feminism as anti-biological, particularly as a founding gesture of a 'new materialism'. She is clear that there is much that is exciting in this work. Her concern is that this gesture 'would have problematic consequences for our understanding of the genealogy of feminist thought' (Ahmed 2008: 24). Although, interestingly, Richard Twine makes an analogous point about Ahmed's own work: 'whilst Ahmed criticizes the new materialists for inadequately acknowledging feminist work on the biological, neither she nor most of the new materialists acknowledge ecofeminist scholarship' (Twine 2010: 402). Nonetheless, Twine optimistically suggests that 'the emergence of a feminist new materialism ought to usher in a renewed conversation between feminism and ecofeminism due to shared interests' (Twine 2010: 402). It is not, however, clear to me whether new materialists might recognize shared interests, or shared natures. The new materialism serves as a potent reminder that while nature and essentialism are often aggregated in feminist theory, this is not always the case, a point easy to forget from an eco/feminist perspective. Ahmed reminds us not to lose sight of 'how matter matters in different ways, for different feminisms, over time' (Ahmed 2008: 36), and would likely not object to the same being said of 'nature'. Ahmed's attention to the genealogy of feminist thought is key here, and returns me to Sturgeon. Sturgeon's genealogical critique of the practice of constructing typologies may remain pertinent – after all, these post-millennial feminist theorists do not necessarily write so much about activism or spirituality, raising the question of what (else) these approaches might have had to forget in order to resist critique and avoid the accusation of essentialism. Paying attention to which biologies and natures are remembered and which are forgotten may be crucial. At the same time, feminist *critiques* of essentialism and anti-essentialism might begin to offer some alternative tools, including genealogical methodologies attentive to shifting biologies and natures, to eco/feminists who wish to escape the tri-partite schema of essentialism, anti-essentialism and strategic essentialism, and to think diversity/diverse natures again. All of which suggests that eco/feminism may yet have much (to) promise.

## Notes

1   Many thanks to readers of previous drafts of this chapter, including Bridget Byrne, Isabelle Darmon, Joan Haran, Maureen McNeil, Kate O'Riordan. This chapter is revised and reprinted with permission of the publisher from *The Changing Nature of Eco/feminism: Telling Stories from Clayoquot Sound*, by Niamh Moore, copyright University of British Columbia Press, 2015. All rights reserved by the publisher. And from material also presented in Moore, N. (2011) 'Eco/feminism and Rewriting the Ending of Feminism: From the Chipko Movement to Clayoquot Sound', *Feminist Theory* 12(1): 3–21.
2   Though note Sandilands' account in Gaard (2011: 45 n6): 'I have identified as an ecofeminist consistently since I first read the term'.
3   I use 'eco/feminism' to gesture towards the sometimes fruitful, sometimes unproductive relationship between ecofeminism and feminism. Eco/feminism is both 'of feminism' and simultaneously offers a critique of it. This is not unusual, as feminism has often been defined by such tensions. There has been a proliferation of feminism as critiques have been made by lesbian feminists, black feminists and the disability movement, to name a few of the most salient. I hold on to this label of eco/feminism as productive at this ongoing juncture in feminism, to signal a specific constellation of interests that cannot be assumed under the rubric of 'feminism' alone (Moore 2004).
4   Titled 'Ecofeminism: A Practical Environmental Philosophy for the 21st Century,' the conference was held at the University of Montana, Missoula, 2–5 April 1998. See http://www.cep.unt.edu/news/mt.html.

5 Gaard's first book on ecofeminism was the anthology *Ecofeminism: Women, Animals, Nature* (1993); although later she did publish her first monograph, *Ecological Politics*, in 1998. Perhaps by that time, monographs did do justice to eco/feminism as it had become.

# References

Adams, C. (1991) *The Sexual Politics of Meat*, New York: Continuum Press.

Ahmed, S. (2008) 'Imaginary prohibitions: some preliminary remarks on the founding gestures of the "new materialism"', *European Journal of Women's Studies* 15(1): 23–39.

Alaimo, S. and Hekman, S. (eds) (2008) *Material Feminisms*, Bloomington: Indiana University Press.

Baker, S. (1993) *The Principles and Practice of Ecofeminism: A Review*, Rotterdam: Risbo.

Barad, K. (2003) 'Posthuman performativity: towards an understanding of how matter comes to matter', *Signs* 28(3): 801–831.

Bell, V. (1999) *Feminist Imagination: Genealogies in Feminist Theory*, London: Sage.

Caldecott, L. and Leland, S. (eds) (1983) *Reclaim the Earth: Women Speak out for Life on Earth*, London: Women's Press.

Carlassare, E. (1994) 'Essentialism in ecofeminist discourse', in *Ecology: Key Concepts in Critical Theory*, edited by Merchant, C., Atlantic Highlands, NJ: Humanities Press.

Collard, A. and Contrucci, J. (1988) *Rape of the Wild: Man's Violence Against Animals and the Earth*, London: Women's Press.

Coole, D. and Frost, S. (eds) (2010) *New Materialisms: Ontology, Agency, and Politics*, Durham, NC: Duke University Press.

Cuomo, C. (1998) *Feminism and Ecological Communities: An Ethic of Flourishing*, London: Routledge.

Daly, M. (1978) *Gyn/Ecology: Towards a Metaethics of Radical Feminism*, London: Women's Press.

Diamond, I. and Orenstein, G.F. (1990a) 'Introduction', in *Reweaving the World: The Emergence of Ecofeminism*, edited by Diamond, I. and Orenstein, G.F., San Francisco: Sierra Club Books.

Diamond, I. and Orenstein, G.F. (eds) (1990b) *Reweaving the World: The Emergence of Ecofeminism*, San Francisco: Sierra Club Books.

d'Eaubonne, F. (1974) *Le Féminisme ou la Mort*, Paris: Pierre Horay.

d'Eaubonne, F. (1980) 'Feminism or death', in *New French Feminisms: An Anthology*, edited by Marks, E. and De Courtivron, I., Amherst: University of Massachusetts Press.

d'Eaubonne, F. (1994) 'The time for ecofeminism', in *Ecology: Key Concepts in Critical Theory*, edited by Merchant, C., Atlantic Highlands, NJ: Humanities Press.

Gaard, G. (ed.) (1993) *Ecofeminism: Women, Animals, Nature*, Philadelphia: Temple University Press.

Gaard, G. (1998) *Ecological Politics: Ecofeminists and the Greens*, Philadelphia: Temple University Press.

Gaard, G. (2011) 'Ecofeminism revisited: rejecting essentialism and re-placing species in a material feminist environmentalism', *Feminist Formations* 23(2): 26–53.

Gaard, G. and Gruen, L. (1993) 'Ecofeminism: towards global justice and planetary health', *Society and Nature* 2(1): 1–35.

Gates, B.T. (1998) 'A root of ecofeminism: ecoféminisme', in *Ecofeminist Literary Criticism: Theory, Interpretation, Pedagogy*, edited by Gaard, G. and Murphy, P., Urbana: University of Illinois Press.

Grosz, E. (2005) *Time Travels: Feminism, Nature, Power*, Durham, NC: Duke University Press.

Heller, C. (1999) *Ecology of Everyday Life: Rethinking the Desire for Nature*, Montreal: Black Rose Books.

Lahar, S. (1991) 'Ecofeminist theory and grassroots politics', *Hypatia* 6(1): 28–45.

MacGregor, S. (2006) *Beyond Mothering Earth: Ecological Citizenship and the Politics of Care*, Vancouver: University of British Columbia Press.

Marks, E. and De Courtivron, I. (eds) (1980) *New French Feminisms: An Anthology.* Amherst: University of Massachusetts Press.

McNeil, M. (2010) 'Post-millenial feminist theory: encounters with humanism, materialism, critique, nature, biology and Darwin', *Journal of Cultural Research* 14(4): 427–437.

Mellor, M. (1992) *Breaking the Boundaries: Towards a Feminist Green Socialism*, London: Virago.

Merchant, C. (1992) *Radical Ecology: The Search for a Livable World*, London: Routledge.

Merchant, C. (ed.) (1994) *Ecology: Key Concepts in Critical Theory*, Atlantic Highlands, NJ: Humanities Press.

Moore, N. (2001) 'Paths to ecofeminist activism: life stories from the North East of England', in *The Roots of Environmental Consciousness: Popular Tradition and Personal Experience*, edited by Hussey, S. and Thompson, P., London: Routledge.

Moore, N. (2004) 'Ecofeminism as third wave feminism? Essentialism, activism and the academy', in *Feminism in the 21st Century: Third Wave?*, edited by Gillis, S., Howie, G. and Munford, B., London: Palgrave Press.

Moore, N. (2008) 'The rise and rise of ecofeminism as a development fable: a response to Melissa Leach's 'Earth Mothers and Other Ecofeminist Fables: How a Strategic Notion Rose and Fell', *Development and Change* 39(3): 461–475.

Moore, N. (2011) 'Eco/feminism and rewriting the ending of feminism: from the Chipko Movement to Clayoquot Sound', *Feminist Theory* 12(1): 3–21.

Moore, N. (2015) *The Changing Nature of Eco/feminism: Telling Stories from Clayoquot Sound*, Vancouver: UBC Press.

Moore, N., Church, A., Gabb, J., Holmes, C., Lee, A. and Ravenscroft, N. (2014) 'Growing intimate privatepublics: everyday utopia in the naturecultures of a young lesbian and bisexual women's allotment', *Feminist Theory* 15(3): 327–343.

Plant, J. (ed.) (1989a) *Healing the Wounds: The Promise of Ecofeminism*, Philadelphia: New Society.

Plant, J. (1989b) 'Toward a new world: an introduction', in *Healing the Wounds: The Promise of Ecofeminism*, edited by Plant, J., Philadelphia: New Society.

Salleh, A. (1991) 'Review of Vandana Shiva's *Staying Alive: Women, Ecology and Development*', *Hypatia* 6(1): 206–214.

Salleh, A. (1997) *Ecofeminism as Politics: Nature, Marx, and the Postmodern*, New York: Zed Books.

Sandilands, C. (1999) *The Good-Natured Feminist: Ecofeminism and the Quest for Democracy*, Minneapolis: University of Minnesota Press.

Sandoval, C. (1991) 'U.S. third world feminism: the theory and method of oppositional consciousness', *Genders* 10: 1–24.

Shiva, V. (1989) *Staying Alive: Women, Ecology and Development*, London: Zed Books.

Sturgeon, N. (1997) *Ecofeminist Natures: Race, Gender, Feminist Theory and Political Action*, London: Routledge.

Twine, R. (2010) 'Intersectional disgust? Animals and (eco)feminism', *Feminism & Psychology* 20(3): 397–406.

Warren, K. (1988) 'Towards an ecofeminist ethic', *Studies in the Humanities* 15: 140–156.

Warren, K. (1990) 'The power and promise of ecological feminism', *Environmental Ethics* 12(2): 125–146.

Warren, K. (ed.) (1997) *Ecofeminism: Women, Culture, Nature*, Bloomington: Indiana University Press.

# 2 Ecofeminism and the animal

*Erika Cudworth*

## Introduction

For many ecofeminist scholars and activists, and for those working in human–animal studies across the humanities and social sciences, our world is co-constituted with myriad species. Whilst some of these species are utterly alien to us, many mammals are both familiar and similar to human animals. Ecofeminist understandings of human relations with non-human animals constitute a prolific body of work. Some, such as Plumwood (1996), have been interested in the treatment and status of 'wild' animals, while others have been more focused on domesticated species. With respect to the latter, work has focused on the ethics of care, reproductive exploitation and intersectionalized oppression in both material and cultural formations (Adams 1990; Cudworth 2011c; Deckha 2012; Gaard 2012). Other research has problematized the human–animal binary and sought to destabilize the certainties around these socially constituted categories. There has not been a singular ecofeminist position on 'the animal question', however, and disputes have revolved around the assumptions underpinning women's caring labour, questions of animal liberation, and the use of animals as food, clothing and companions (see Adams 1993; Diamond 2008; Donovan 2006; Haraway 2008; McHugh 2012; Plumwood 2004; Weisberg 2009). This work has been influential in problematizing 'the human', 'the animal' and human relations with non-human animals. These approaches provide a powerful analysis of the ways the social system of gender relations is co-constituted through ideas and practices around 'nature' and species relations.

This chapter begins by considering a range of ecofeminist approaches, the ways in which these have developed, and sites of debate and conflict on 'the question of the animal'. Feminist approaches to species relations have rarely been included in discussions of the development of human–animal studies scholarship (Wilkie 2013). The chapter proceeds to set out the development of critical animal studies (CAS) scholarship and the tensions and intersections between this and feminist animal studies (FAS). My own contribution to theoretical debates on human–animal relations draws on elements of both CAS and FAS, and on the recent use of complex systems approaches within sociology. The middle section of this chapter outlines my particular theorization of human relations with non-human animals, illustrates this with examples from a current empirical project on companion animals, and draws on data that focus on the theme of cultures of aggressive masculinity.

## Ecofeminism and concern for non-human animals

Ecofeminism emerged from a critique of both sexism in the green movement (Doubiago 1989) and an absence of awareness about 'environmental' questions in feminist politics (Plumwood 2004: 43; Salleh 1984). Ecofeminists draw on and develop various elements of both ecological and feminist politics, however, and understand the domination of nature to be interrelated with intra-human social hierarchy and difference based on gender, race and class amongst other formations (Cudworth 2005). Here they are influenced by left critiques of capitalism (Mellor 1992) and postcolonial scholarship (Shiva 2007), and reflect postmodern influences in critical theory (Salleh 1997). The influence of feminist politics is perhaps the strongest, as ecofeminists deploy concepts of gender domination and inequality in thinking about labour, production, knowledge and what it means to be human.

A key strand of ecofeminist critique is the interrogation of dualisms. In works from the 1970s onwards, the dominant worldview of Western modernity was characterized as problematic in that it was based on dualistic categories such as man/woman, culture/nature, mind/body and human/animal. In such a dualistic worldview, what is 'essentially human' is understood to be separate from 'nature'. The critique of dualism is embedded in all ecofeminist writing, whether examining the linked oppression of animals and women (Adams 1990), or disturbing the boundaries between the dualist categories themselves (Haraway 1989, 2008). The critique of dualism has been an important way in which ecofeminist thinking has contributed to debates on the interlinking of different forms of oppression. In Plumwood's (1993) words, 'inferior orders' of humanity (colonized, native, female) are categorically separated from the 'order of reason' and fail to come up to the dominant Western ideal of the human. The ways in which these categories are discursively constituted may be overlapping; for example, native peoples specifically, and those more generally gendered female, may be more strongly naturalized and animalized.

Closely linked to the debates on dualisms and overlapping oppressions are ecofeminist contributions to our understanding of human relations with non-human animals. In early works, some claimed that women's social practices of care mean they are more likely than men to oppose practices of harm against animals (Salamone 1982); or that women may empathize with the sufferings of animals as they have some common experiences. For example, female domestic animals are most likely to be 'oppressed' via control of their sexuality and reproductive powers (Benny 1983: 142). Joan Dunayer (1995) has examined the speciesism of linguistic practices and the links between this and our gendered and racialized use of language, while Carol

Adams (1990, 2003) argues that social practices such as meat eating are gendered and sexualized, and that popular culture is saturated with interpolations of gendered nature, and natured gender. There have been disputes, however. For example, Plumwood (2004) has critiqued the 'ontological veganism' of Adams (1990), which advocates individual abstention from all use of animals, as universalist and ethnocentric. Plumwood also argues that ontological veganism confirms the view that, unlike other species, humans can place themselves outside or above nature in avoiding the use of animals that is part of the human condition as ecologically embedded beings. As an alternative, she proposes 'ecological animalism', wherein a critique of the human exploitation of animals is combined with respect for different cultural meanings of certain practices (such as the hunting and eating of animals). Whilst in some ways ecological animism can be seen as more reflective of intersectionalized understandings of the world, Plumwood unfortunately reproduces the naturalization of behaviour (in this case the use of animals) and the dualism between human and animal that has been the subject of ecofeminist critique.

Feminist influence is particularly evident in the wealth of ecofeminist writing on gender roles, an 'ethic of care' and concern for non-human species. A key theme here is the reproduction of gendered values through socialization and a different placement in the public and private division of labour. In ecofeminist writings of the 1980s, this involved some claims that female socialization inculcates characteristics of nurturance, sympathy, empathy and 'feeling the life of the other' (Plant 1989: 1). This understanding has been strongly criticized from socialist feminist perspectives (Segal 1987), and from within ecofeminism. For Mary Mellor, the patriarchal division of the human Western world into feminized private and masculinized public spheres involves 'placing on women the major responsibility for nurturing and caring values and activities' (1992: 251). This is an 'imposed altruism' and does not foster a particular relationship to the environment, or other animals by extension of empathy beyond family members. While the public face of capitalist production takes as its premise an autonomous individual, the nurturing private world 'which has its material base in women's time and work' remains invisible (Mellor 1997: 174). Women's imposed altruism means that they are not quite so embedded, compared with most men, within advanced capitalist time, 'a sphere of false freedom that ignores biological and ecological parameters' (1997: 173). Rather, in their closer links to reproductive labour, women are influenced by biological time.

Josephine Donovan (2006) suggests that such critics have misunderstood ecofeminist care theory. Discussing the case of non-human animals as subjects of feminist concern, Donovan argues that it is not

> a matter of caring for animals as mothers (human and non-human) care for their infants as it is one of listening to animals, paying emotional attention, taking seriously – caring about – what they are telling us.
> (Donovan 2006: 305)

This need to pay attention to the being and lifeways of other species has strong similarities to Marc Bekoff's (2002) notion of 'minding animals', wherein non-human species are understood to be 'minded' (creatures with interests, thoughts, feelings and views about the world) and deserving of treatment respectful of this and of animal lifeways. For Donovan, however, understanding the 'qualitative heterogeneity of life forms' implies dialogical reasoning and the articulation of a non-human standpoint by feminist animal advocates (2006: 306–7). Whereas utilitarianism and animal rights theory has often scorned empathy and compassion as ethically irrelevant (Singer 1990), or as an unstable basis for ethical claims (Garner 2005), Donovan is sceptical of the deployment of enlightenment rationalism in the development of a universal ethics for the human treatment of non-human animals. Rather, it is via our attentive observation and our compassion, even for creatures that might appear alien to us, that we might enter into 'dialogue'. Donovan makes clear that attention and empathy must be accompanied by political engagement through an analysis rooted in intersectional understandings of power, and through advocacy which resists the objectification of animals and asserts their likely 'point of view'. This critical engagement and position of advocacy has latterly impacted on the politics of animal liberation.

## The rise of critical animal studies and intersectionalized emancipation

Peter Singer is a name that remains heavily associated with the contemporary animal advocacy movement. His *Animal Liberation*, first published in 1975 (Singer 1990), argued for the irrationality of 'speciesism', a prejudice which licenses all forms of exploitative and oppressive practices that harm sentient beings. On the basis of utilitarianism, Singer argued we should account for the interests of animals, restrict the harms we subject them to and maximize their welfare. Objecting to Singer on the grounds that non-human animals have an interest in not being used for human ends, Tom Regan (1983) developed a rights-based approach to our relations with other species, claiming that many higher animals should be free from human abuse, use and interference on the grounds that they are 'subjects-of-a-life' (with interests, desires, a sense of themselves over time and so on) and thereby had rights. As Alasdair Cochrane (2012: 7) remarks, the debate over animal interests versus animal rights has been focused on and polarized by this Singer/Regan debate.

Feminism was engaged politically, both theoretically and practically, with issues of human relations with non-human animals from the early second wave of feminist activism in the 1970s (for example, Adams 1976). The feminist critique of animal rights debates maintained that they failed to attend to the overlapping of intra-human forms of oppressions and exploitation with those in which non-human animals were caught. While Greta Gaard (2012) is right to observe that the intersectionalized observations of ecofeminist scholarship were ignored by much work in human–animal studies for 25 years, there is now increasing discussion of 'entanglements' of oppression (Nibert 2002). We have seen the development of CAS, which has linked scholars and activists, and promoted the awareness of interlinked forms of domination, inequality and hierarchy, alongside a need for advocacy (including direct action for animal liberation) (Best 2007). This has been hostile to *uncritical* approaches in human and animal studies which might critically discuss the problematic boundaries of human and animal, but tend not to problematize the systemic relations of social power which profoundly shape the lives of non-human animals. A case in point here would be Donna Haraway, whose work Zipporah Weisberg (2009) has criticized for its 'intricate word play' that pays lip service to the problematics of the human/animal binary, eschews activism opposing animal exploitation, and continues to justify exploitative practices. There are divergent perspectives in the nature and quality of scholarly engagements with activism, with some more keen than others to promote synergies (respectively, Best et al. 2009; McCance 2013; Nocella et al. 2014; Taylor and Twine 2014). Despite this, the notion that scholarship be critically engaged with undermining institutions of animal oppression has brought a wide range of research across different disciplines under the banner of CAS, which challenges the 'intricate interrelationship' of 'hierarchical power systems' within which humanity and the 'natural world' are exploited (Best 2007: 3).

While I situate my own work within CAS, I am aware that my sympathies for the work of a range of human–animal scholarship makes me less 'critical' than some CAS affiliates might be comfortable with. Some feminist work has allied itself strongly with a politics of animal rights and a stance of 'total liberation' (Best 2010). But within FAS there tends to be more tolerance of a diversity of theoretical perspectives and practical political engagements. As the recent special issue of the journal *Hypatia* on 'Animal Others' illustrates, there are a variety of positions, some of which are more closely allied to radical perspectives (Gaard 2012) and others to postmodernism (Stanescu 2012). What binds them is the appreciation of the precarious nature of animal lives, embodied materialism and a commitment to intersectional analysis. Whereas CAS has until recently marginalized feminist accounts, and often prioritizes the impact of capitalism in apparently intersectional analyses (Nibert 2002; Torres 2007), FAS has produced rich accounts of the gendering of species, albeit underplaying other elements such as the importance of race and culture in structuring species-based oppression (Deckha 2012).

Ecofeminist/feminist animal studies scholarship may well be more tolerant of diversity not just because of the plethora of feminisms, but also because there has been a concerted attempt to disturb the human/animal binary through a critique of liberal humanism and the articulation of different kinds of positions on embodiment and materiality. This is a very different trajectory from that of animal rights/liberation, which has tended to try to empty moral theory of its humancentric biases, whilst still holding fast to anthropocentric humanisms and moral and methodological commitments to reason (Diamond 2008). A further difference between feminist and non-feminist critiques of human–animal relations is that feminism has been far more attentive to the ways in which anthropocentric humanism, ironically, influences debate on what emancipation for other animals might mean. Thus abolitionists such as Gary Francione (2000) argue that liberation means that domesticated animals must cease to be, having been bred into a state of dependency and indignity, lacking any viable ecological niche. For Plumwood (2004), however, humans have always been part of co-constitutive relations with other species. The Francionist position articulates the problematic dualism of civilization and wilderness. Herein, the liberal humanist frame of liberation is not about freedom from constraint but about re-situating humans as ecologically embedded and embodied subjects of interspecies communities.

Feminist animal scholarship has always been interested in domesticated animals and articulated an embodied, affective, relational ontology. Susan McHugh (2012: 616), in a discussion of feminist dog-writing, claims feminist animal scholarship 'reframes feminist politics as intra-active, trans-species and from the ground up'. Critical animal studies has drawn closer to feminism in making clear and compelling cases for intersectionality as a framework for radical approaches to human–animal relations, yet it remains resistant to other feminist claims about our co-constituted and embodied condition with non-human animals. My own work uses intersectionality as a framework to develop a CAS approach to understanding the human domination of non-human animals. However, as will be seen below, my position is very much shaped by feminist concerns to understand human relations with other animals as those of differentiated power. What follows paints a picture of a large-scale and often extreme level of human violence towards domesticated animals, but also understands our relations with domesticated species as complex and contradictory, and open to other possibilities.

## Human domination in species relations

My own preoccupation in FAS has been with developing sociological frameworks for the understanding of human–animal relations, elaborated by empirical studies of domesticated animals used for food and companionship. I conceptualize human relations with other species as constituted by and through social institutions and processes; and these can be seen as sets of relations of power and domination which are consequential of normative practice. These sets of relations intersect to form a social system of human domination that I refer to as 'anthroparchy' (Cudworth 2005, 2011c). Humans have socially formed relational power over other species, but species relations are intrinsically co-constituted with other kinds of complex forms of domination (such as patriarchy, capitalism and colonialism) and consequently assume specific spatialized and historical formations.

Such systems of social domination exist within a relational matrix, inter-meshing and coalescing in a particular pattern, articulated in different ways, in different times, places and spaces. Human domination therefore is differ-entiated, and there are different degrees of domination of other animals by humans. I use the concepts of oppression, exploitation and marginalization in order to describe this. I use the term 'domination' as a general descriptor for systemic relations of power which inhibits the potential of an individual organism, group, micro- or macro-landscape to 'flourish'. 'Oppression' describes a harsh degree of relations of dominatory power and its application is species-specific: some species can be oppressed (such as farmed animals) and others cannot (such as intestinal flora). Exploitation refers to the use of something as a resource, and this can apply broadly, including for example the exploitation of farmed animals for labour, skin, fur, flesh and other products, or the use of animals in guarding and herding. Marginalization is the rendering of something as relatively insignificant and decentred, and has a similar meaning to humancentrism. There is diversity in the form and degree of human domination. For example, intensive forms of production in animal agriculture can be seen as extreme or strongly oppressive institutional sites. It is unlikely that all animals 'used' by humans experience domination in the same way, although there are strong similarities in the ways in which processes of domestication affect both companion and farmed animals. The oppressive experiences of farmed animals may be very different from those of prized 'working animals', such as those providing assistance for humans who are blind or deaf, for example. The lives of animals kept as 'pets' are often very different from those of farmed animals, but there is also evidence of cruelty, neglect and abandonment of animals by their human 'companions' (Cudworth 2011a). The industries that have emerged around pet-keeping in the West involve intensive breeding and also strong genetic selection for the reproduction of desirable breed (and other) traits.

The domination of non-human animals in contemporary Western societies can be understood as constituted through groups of social relations which can be found in particular arenas such as production, domestication, violence, polity and culture. For example, animal agriculture is an institutional system and a set of production relations endemic to human domination. The con-dition of domestication may involve physical confinement, the appropriation of labour and fertility, and incarceration, which are foundational for the farming of animals. Huge numbers of a limited range of species are essential forms of property and/or labour. Animals are a specific form of embodied property, however, and it is the distinction of human from non-human life that is *a priori* for such commoditization. Animals produce commodities in terms of offspring, milk and eggs, which become human food. These social relations are framed by law, culturally mediated and politically supported or contested.

Anthroparchal cultures marginalize non-human animals or present them in ways that are framed by human interests, and re-inscribe the norms of human domination. If we again refer to the example of 'meat', the hier-archical ordering of the Western diet is reproduced in the popular culture of cooking and eating in which the eating of animals is constituted as normative. This process of reproducing food cultural norms is also shaped by various kinds of intra-human difference in addition to the distinction of species that enables 'meat' to be eaten (Adams 1990; Cudworth 2010). Animal foodways have been relatively stable, despite significant social change, and in the West our representative regime of animals-as-meat continues to be framed by inter-sected discourses of difference and power, in particular those constitutive of formations of gender, sexuality and nation.

Institutionalized violence is also systemic, and for species with greater levels of sentiency, this operates in similar ways to violences affecting humans. For exam-ple, animals raised and killed for food may experience pain and fear. The lives, deaths and dismemberments of animals for 'meat' articulate a range of forms and degrees of physical violence and in some cases, psychological harm, and reflect the complex intersections of relations of social power (Cudworth 2008). I want to now examine the arena of violence in which the intersectionalized relations of species are played out. I concentrate here on the ways in which the human/animal binary is reproduced with respect to species violence, concentrating particularly on domesticated animals. The following two sections consider, in turn, species violence in relation to agricultural animals raised for food, and species violence in relation to animals kept as companions in the home.

## Intersectionalized violence and animal sacrifice

Globally, 99 per cent of all domesticates are commodities in animal agri-culture (Williams and DeMello 2007: 14) to be killed and transformed into food products. The statistics are of staggering proportions. At least 55 billion land-based non-human animals are killed in the farming industry per year (Mitchell 2011), with almost 10 billion of these killed for food in the USA alone. Figures are projected to increase substantially, with an extra 360 million cattle and buffaloes, 560 million extra sheep and goats, and 190 million extra pigs needed by 2030 to match growing consumer demand (FAO 2002). There has been a phenomenal increase in the populations of farmed animals in poorer countries of the Global South, where the intensive production of stock is set to become the model for agricultural development. On current trends, 120 billion farmed animals are likely to be killed annually by 2050 (MacDonald 2010: 34).

Feminist work on gender-based violence in situations of armed conflict has painted a frightening picture of what happens to humans in circumstances where routine violence and killing becomes a 'runaway norm', unravelling the legal and cultural taboos that police intra-human violence (Leatherman 2011: 9). In these situations, human beings find, disturbingly, that 'we are all, after all, potentially animals before the law' (Wolfe 2013: 105). The racialized animali-zation of humans (as 'vermin', for example, in the well known cases of Nazi Germany where Jewish people were referred to as rats and lice, or the

Rwandan genocide in which Tutsis became cockroaches) has been an effective means of suspending prohibition on violence against humans and legitimating mass killing. For non-humans, however, different moral status enables mass killing to be routine rather than exceptional, and to be normalized.

For Cary Wolfe, this is because animals are 'before the law'. This has a dual meaning. In one sense, this involves standing before legal judgment; we are 'before', or subject to, legal judgment. In addition, animals are subjected to 'originary violence' in the sense that the human/animal distinction precedes the development of the law and thus is taken for granted by it (Wolfe 2013: 9). This invites parallels with the treatment of others seen as outside the frame of law in certain periods and cultures (women in Western modernity, for example). Wolfe suggests not only that animals therefore cannot be protected by law, but that the human/animal distinction is continually reinforced by the 'violence of sacrifice'; that is, animals are sacrificeable whereas humans, most usually, are not. Here he draws on Jacques Derrida's notion that 'beasts' (non-human animals and animalized humans) fall below the law (Derrida 2009: 20–21) and thus might be subjected to a routine 'non-criminal putting to death' (Derrida 1991). This routine killing, for both Wolfe and Derrida, enables the law to disavow its own contingency. Rather, as Wolfe notes following Foucault, the law is able to 'make live' and to 'let die' by permitting the breeding, exploitation and killing of some animals for food, whilst redefining the frame of who is 'in' and who is 'out' by granting others, such as great apes, some basic human rights (2013: 11).

The animals we farm for food in the West are self-aware, emotional beings with views about the world (Masson 2004). Whilst there have undoubtedly been moves to improve 'welfare' in the short lives of some farmed animals in the West (Bock and Buller 2013), farmed animals are made to live and let die through institutional and relational systems that involve an almost totalized system of oppressive relations. The institutions of animal agriculture, from breeding and growing to killing, are institutions of violence that are for the most part normative and legitimate. These involve the butchery of animal bodies post-killing, reproductive violences including rape, forced confinement, and the inability to express species-life behaviours. Most extreme, yet entirely normative, are the violences of slaughter involving shooting, electrocution, strangulation and throat-cutting.

These institutionalized practices of violence are gendered. In my research into animal farming and the journeys of animal bodies becoming meat, I found farmed animals to be disproportionately female and usually feminized in terms of their treatment by predominantly male human agricultural workers. Farmers disproportionately breed female animals so they can maximize profit via the manipulation of reproduction; and some animals (cattle, pigs, sheep) are bred for distinctly gendered traits such as docility and mothering ability in females, and strength and virility in males. Female animals that have been used for breeding can also be seen to incur the most severe physical violence within the animal food system, particularly at slaughter (Cudworth 2008).

Female and feminized animals are bred, incarcerated, raped, killed and cut into pieces, in gargantuan numbers, by men who are often themselves sub-jected to highly exploitative working conditions. These working conditions are structured by the gendered division of labour and characterized by a culture of machismo (Cudworth 2008).

Operations of local, regional and global networks of relations shaped the development of animal food production, and the production and consump-tion of animals as meat was a historical process in which systemic relations of species are constituted with and through relations of colonialism. In the eighteenth and nineteenth centuries, European countries established the global international system of meat production. Britain and Germany in particular invested heavily in land and factories in South America, primarily in Argentina in the eighteenth century, and in Brazil in the nineteenth (Velten 2007: 153). The colonial model of meat production was further enabled by the development of refrigerated shipping, which made it possible to ship 'fresh' meat to Europe from the USA, South America and Australasia (Franklin 1999: 130). This enabled Europeans to consume greater quantities of meat, but in order to make best use of the potential market in Europe the price had to be minimized by intensifying production and saving labour costs – typically through increased processes of mechanization which led to the development of intensive agriculture in Europe and the USA. Indeed, models of production now spread across the globe with corporate interventions in Asia, Africa and the Caribbean (Cudworth 2011b).

Finally, we must also consider the impact of farmed animal agriculture on the worlds of other species and things. As is becoming increasingly recog-nized, industrialized animal agriculture is a driving force behind pressing environmental problems such as deforestation, water scarcity, air and water pollution, climate change and loss of biodiversity (Steinfeld et al. 2006). Thus, whilst farmed animal agriculture is an integral element of a social system of species relations in which domesticates are oppressed, it is also constituted by relations of capital, colonialism and patriarchy, and shaped in important ways by intra-human difference.

## When domination meets affection?

For Yi Fu Tuan, the creation of the 'pet' emerges when domination is 'combined with affection' (Tuan 1984: 2). This, for Tuan, is clearly an exercise of power over those who, in different times and places, are viewed as not capable of being human. Thus children, women, slaves, dwarves and fools, as well as plants and non-human animals, might be kept for pleasure, enter-tainment or convenience. Given its long relation with humans and the extensive ways in which we have modified various breed types, Tuan sug-gests that 'the dog is the pet par excellence' (1984: 102). For Tuan, as for much CAS scholarship, the role of the pet is rarely beneficial for those so kept. As Bob Torres points out, the legal ownership of companion animals such as dogs makes them incredibly vulnerable, so that they might be euthanized at the whim of the owner, or abandoned (2007: 156–57). The large-scale commercial breeding of companion animals relies on sophisticated marketing to boost demand, maximizes profits through highly intensive and often cruel methods, oversupplying animals for the pet trade to the extent that, in the USA for example, 'animal shelters are forced to destroy millions of unwanted pets each year' (Williams and DeMello 2007: 15). In addition, the treatment of breeding animals mirrors the treatment of intensively farmed animals such as pigs, and is similarly dependent on gendered manipulation of fertility and sexuality and, on occasion, sexualized abuse (Dunayer 1995: 14). Furthermore, notions of breed purity and pedigree breeding narratives are constituted through strongly classed and racialized discourse (McHugh 2004: 91–95).

Human inequalities undermine the security of companion animals who may be subject, for example, to domestic violence. Some of Carol Adams' (1995) research examines how threats to harm or kill family pets are used as threats against women and children. Pets themselves become victims of battering and may be mutilated, executed or otherwise harmed by violent men (Ascione 1997). This often impacts on both battered women and animal companions that survive abuse, both psychologically and practically (Flynn 2000). Estimates by animal welfare charities in Britain and the USA indicate that numbers of companion animals abandoned, mistreated (in organized fights, by drowning, stabbing, burning or by neglect) is significant, and seems to be on the increase in times of austerity. The levels of systematic cruelty against dogs emerged in my discussions of dog 'ownership' with the 'good' and 'responsible' owners of dogs in east London and rural Leicestershire in the UK. Many had adopted dogs from rescue and rehoming centres and programmes of different kinds, and tales of various forms of human misanthropy are embedded in dog lives, as noted in the ethnographic diary I kept as part of my research project 'Walking the Dog':

> [When they got the dog] she had nightmares; she would wake up and run across the room to hide. If you raised your voice in the house, she would stand and shake and wet herself.
>
> She explains that this is her friends' dog. The dog is not socialized and attacks other dogs. She is taking him out as part of his rehabilitation. He gets better all the time. He had four years living with 'an abusive man' and a woman who was not allowed leave the house and take him for a walk.

In addition to dogs being caught up in patterns of gender violence in the household, there are specific violences that dogs are subject to as a result of their abandonment by humans, or 'bad behaviour' that deems animals incapable of being kept or being rehomed. The numbers of abandoned and apparently 'aggressive' dogs killed are staggering. For example, an estimated 6–9 million dogs were 'humanely' killed in pet shelters in the USA in 1990 alone (Palmer 2006: 171–72). Even when dogs are loved, wanted and well cared for, the institutional vulnerability of dogs as 'animals before the law' may make it incredibly difficult for human companions to afford them protection.

The Dangerous Dogs Act of 1991 in the UK is a case in point. This legislation specifies unacceptable 'dog behaviour' and covers all breeds of dog, but it is also what is known as 'breed-specific legislation'. The Act introduced a list of banned dogs and dogs of these breed and mixed-breed types that, if judged by a magistrate to have 'sufficient breed characteristics', must be destroyed (Dangerous Dogs Act 1991). The legislation was hastily passed at the height of media focus on the social problem of 'dangerous dogs', which centred on a number of attacks by one foreign interloper in particular – the American pit bull terrier. The legislation has done nothing to reverse an apparent trend in attacks on humans by dogs (Barkham and Murphy 2012). It has resulted, however, in the seizure, incarceration and killing of large numbers of 'pit bull-type' dogs. 1,152 were seized by the London Metropolitan police in 2009, and police have simply to 'believe' that a dog may be of a banned type in order to seize and incarcerate. Even if dog owners are seen to be responsible and dogs have been assessed by animal behaviourists as non-aggressive, they can still be killed.

Since the Act, animal welfare groups have observed a rise in the numbers of mixed-breed dogs, particularly the breeding of Staffordshire terriers ('Staffies' or 'Staff') with American pit bulls, and are dealing with a crisis of rehoming such dogs. Many of my interviewees in London's Lea Valley Park observed these developments and commented on the disposability of such dogs:

> I know two examples of people who have been offered, literally at the school gates, erm … a Staffie puppy for nothing.

Tales of 'dangerous dogs' and human misanthropy often are interwoven. When the River Lea was dredged, hundreds of bodies of Staffordshire terrier and Staffie-cross puppies and dogs were found. Specific cases of the abuse of these particular breeds managed to find their way into my study, as illustrated by these two excerpts from my field notes:

> In her arms, L is carrying a white Staff puppy, very small. 'Another dog?' I ask. Not exactly, says P, they have it by 'mistake'. A client she works with came across some guys about to throw it in the river and drown it. It was the runt of the litter and they couldn't get the money they wanted for it.
>
> I've been involved in calling the police up here because there were gangs with great big sticks organizing dog fights. You know, they're dog owners and they're organizing dog fights. I think that's the other side of being a dog owner. There are reasons why we have dogs, but other

people have dogs as status symbols, for earning money and having a laugh ...

Animal welfare organizations link the breeding of these 'fighting dogs' to street gang culture and the weaponizing of animals, and tales of machismo and the ownership of fighting-breed dogs as tools of intimidation pepper my diary entries and interview material:

> I work with a woman who's got a dog that she claims to be pit bull/ Shar Pei cross – Colonel. And she keeps saying 'He's a bit naughty', and I go 'What do you mean?'. She can't walk him by herself, he's too strong. He sees another dog and goes berserk, wants to attack ... You can't muzzle him because her bloke wants to walk him down the street and confront other pit bulls ... She's pregnant now, and she's petrified – what's she going to do with Colonel, who she can't control, and her baby?
>     I mean it's frightening, you know, you don't want to be attacked and you certainly don't want your dog to be attacked and y'unno I've changed, I mean I used to walk in the morning always in the park, y'unno at the back on the field but there was too many young kids going over there with ... their Staffies ... so I just didn't go in there any more.

It should not be assumed, however, that the culture of machismo operates only to further confirm identities of machismo and the (ab)use of fighting breed dogs. In one interesting account, a dog is used to prevent bullying:

> I've got three wimpy teenage boys at home, where we live's quite rough, er and I knew that having a big dog, we knew [name of dog] would be a big dog, and would give them a bit of kind of local kudos and er some kind of protection, ... and it's worked, er in spades really, the boys don't actually have to do anything, the dog just has to come out of our house attached to a big brass chain and that's it, you know, it's kind of non-verbal, mastiffs are sort of [pause] well, [laughing] he makes a huge impression on the local idiots.

So, whilst being an animal before the law means that all kinds of dogs are subject to the potentially life-threatening situation of abandonment, to different degrees of violence within the home, or to being implicated in forms of systemic violence such as domestic abuse, some breeds have been particularly caught up in intra-human violences. The weaponizing of animals has a long cross-cultural history, and the association of fighting-dog breeds with public displays of aggressive masculinity is nothing new. What is new is that these social forms be understood as persistent elements of human–animal relations, and the darker side of our co-constituted social formations with other species.

## A man without a dog

A stalwart man once sharply contested my claim to this freedom to go alone. 'Any true man,' he said with fervor, 'is always ready to go with a woman at night. He is her natural protector.' 'Against what?' I inquired. 'As a matter of fact, the thing a woman is most afraid to meet on a dark street is her natural protector. Singular'

(Perkins Gilman 1935: 72)

'[She] stops, nervous in the dark as usual, making sure she knows it's me.' So reads an entry from my diary, and one which is repeated in similar form across various encounters with women walking dogs in the dark. On a final note, an element that has shaped my work with dogs and their humans has been that the majority of dog walkers who I have seen and spoken with have been women, and that walking in public space raises issues of risk. Most of the comments about risk have been almost afterthoughts in the stories that dog walkers tell, but there is evidence that many women fear violence and police their times of walking. Many will only walk with someone else, some will only walk alone in the light, while others prefer the dark because 'in the dark you and your dog can hide'. For the early morning walkers taking dogs out before work, there is limited flexibility and there are times when women express fear of their 'natural protectors', and that fear is usually associated with doglessness:

It was really early and still quite dark, and there was this man who … wasn't dressed for walking and he wasn't with a dog … then I realised he changed direction – he'd gone under the bridge away from me and then suddenly he was behind me and normally [the dog] doesn't pay attention to people but he kept running around this man … I was glad I actually wore my wellies that morning because it meant I could go anywhere, and unless he wanted to get himself covered in muck, he couldn't, so I sort of cut back across that meadow to the car park. I was frightened …

In the following case, two women had lost 'their' dog in Ashdown forest in Sussex, and had searched for a number of hours until

… at 9 o'clock at night in December. The two of us, sliding all over the place in the mud and we couldn't see anything. And we had a squeaky toy and two heavy duty torches and we were going 'Maaudy Maaaaudy!' and sliding about, and the next thing, in the darkness, in the middle of no-where, this man appeared …
[partner interjects] without a dog.
So I thought he'd been burying somebody and she thought he was out sheep-shagging [laughing]. It shows you where our minds are really [laughing]. It was 'orrible! … He freaked us out.

Yet despite this context of risk, walking with a dog is seen as an enabling activity that functions to reclaim public space, both for women and, as the following quote illustrates, for men also:

> I saw the marshes as a dangerous place really. Somewhere that you wouldn't go, not on your own. But now I have [name of dog] I'm just here all the time. So she's opened all this up to me, the park, the marshes, I'm out there!
>
> I'd really miss not having a dog, I'd feel kind of excluded from here because of my [pause] my own sort of worry with seeing blokes without dogs wandering about – 'where's their dog? They must be a weirdo!' It's terribly unfair but er yeah I just like to get out here, and I can't really imagine feeling comfortable unless I had a dog with me.

There are always shards of light, even when what I have emphasized here is, of course, the dark side of relations between humans and animals raised as companions. In researching animal agriculture, I expected to find the grim tales and normative, everyday violences that I did. In looking at the lives of people with companion dogs, I wanted to work on something that, frankly, was more uplifting and less painful. I wanted to move away from what I call – borrowing from Catherine Nolan (2010), who in turn adopted from Ruth Behar (1996) – 'sociology that breaks your heart'. Yet researching people's lives with pets has convinced me of the intense vulnerability of the animal, both human and non-human. Living well with other animals involves an acknowledgement of the problematics of the human/animal distinction and the ways human domination shapes the lives of other animals, even those with human companions who are 'minding' of them. There are positive stories also that might be told, of companionship, of love, of spaces of community; and in searching for a heart less broken, I am in the process of telling such tales within a frame that remains critical of the dominant relational matrix of species.

## Conclusion

Ecofeminist work on human–animal relations has provided powerful analyses of the ways gender is co-constituted through ideas and practices around 'nature' and species relations. My own contribution to such debates has been to argue for an analysis of species and intersectionality in terms of complex systems of social relations. A social relational approach means that human relations with a certain species might be understood as exhibiting particular and distinct characteristics whilst at the same time being co-constituted with intra-human forms of domination and exclusion. Thus, at different times and in different places, particular groups of humans might be animalized. The relations of species are dynamic, and the binary of human/animal shifts over time so that the animalization of humans is less likely and more strongly contested. Despite moves to include animals as subjects of law, however, and in some cases to 'uplift' a few kinds of animal to quasi-human status, for much of the time the species distinction remakes itself in ways that are rarely favourable to non-human animal being and lifeways.

This chapter has focused on an arena of human–animal relations in Western modernity in which human domination has particularly harsh effects. I have suggested that the small number of species raised for meat are caught in relations of oppression. The development of Western food practices and networks of animal food production have long had global reach, and have been founded and developed through relations of colonial capital. These relationships (to farmed animals and in production) are also shaped by gender, in that various kinds of violence (such as reproductive violence or killing) are undertaken by a predominantly male labour force and involve feminized animal bodies. Such patterns of gendered human domination in production can also be found in the breeding in the West of domesticated animals to be kept as 'pets' in the home, and such animals are also vulnerable both due to their dependency on human 'care' and as creatures in relations of property ownership. Yet if we understand human relations with other animals as differentiated, not all relations are of the same intensity and quality. In my work with humans living with companion dogs, I have found many people concerned with ensuring that they 'live well' with other creatures. This is certainly not easy to negotiate in a world structured around the privileging of the human, but the hope of those of us who are concerned with 'minding animals' is that, over time, more of us will explore the art of 'living well'.

It is certainly a positive development that we have seen the expansion and, to some degree, more inclusion of CAS as an approach to human–animal studies. It is also important to note both that CAS scholarship is paying more attention to feminist analyses, and that there has been a re-assertion and invigoration of FAS. My hope is that the intersection between feminist and critical animal studies will be an increasingly productive space, raising challenges for mainstream animal studies scholarship and disturbing the exclusively human preoccupations of many academic disciplines. Both critical and feminist animal studies often bring together activism and the academy, and this is somewhat more difficult terrain. While there may be arenas for analytical agreement on what is wrong with contemporary forms of human relations with other animals, there seems little consensus on what might be appropriate responses. A creative dialogue on advocacy would be an important future step.

## References

Adams, C.J. (1976) 'Vegetarianism: the inedible complex', *Second Wave* 4(4): 36–42.
Adams, C.J. (1990) *The Sexual Politics of Meat*, Cambridge: Polity Press.
Adams, C.J. (ed.) (1993) *Ecofeminism and the Sacred*, New York: Continuum.

Adams, C.J. (1995) 'Woman battering and harm to animals', in *Animals and Women: Feminist Theoretical Explorations*, edited by Adams, C.J. and Donovan, J., London: Duke University Press, 55–84.

Adams, C.J. (2003) *The Pornography of Meat*, London: Continuum.

Ascione, F. (1997) 'The abuse of animals and domestic violence: a national survey of shelters for women who are battered', *Society and Animals* 5: 205–218.

Barkham, P. and Murphy, S. (2012) 'Bark but no bite: Dangerous Dogs Act in spotlight as attacks rise', *The Guardian* 18 January, retrieved from http://www.guardian.co.uk/uk/2012/jan/18/dangerous-dogs-act-in-spotlight (accessed 18 January 2012).

Behar, R. (ed.) (1996) *The Vulnerable Observer: Anthropology that Breaks Your Heart*, Boston: Beacon Press.

Bekoff, M. (2002) *Minding Animals: Awareness, Emotion and Heart*, Oxford: Oxford University Press.

Benny, N. (1983) 'All one flesh: the rights of animals', in *Reclaim the Earth*, edited by Caldecott, L. and Leyland, S., London: Women's Press, 141–151.

Best, S. (2007) 'Introduction', *Journal of Critical Animal Studies* 5(1): 2–3.

Best, S. (2010) 'Animal liberation, human liberation and the future of the left', http://www.drstevebest.org/RethinkingRevolution.htm (accessed 21 March 2014).

Best, S., Nocella II, A.J., Kahn, R., Gigliotti, C. and Kemmerer, L. (2009) *Introducing Critical Animal Studies*, http://www.criticalanimalstudies.org/wp-content/uploads/2009/09/Introducing-Critical-Animal-Studies-2007.pdf (accessed 10 December 2012).

Bock, B. and Buller, H.J. (2013) 'Healthy, happy and humane: evidence in farm animal welfare policy', *Sociologia Ruralis* 53(3): 390–411.

Cochrane, A. (2012) *Animal Rights without Liberation*, New York: Columbia University Press.

Cudworth, E. (2005) *Developing Ecofeminist Theory: The Complexity of Difference*, Basingstoke: Palgrave.

Cudworth, E. (2008) '"Most farmers prefer blondes" – dynamics of anthroparchy in animals "becoming meat"', *Journal for Critical Animal Studies* 6(1): 32–45.

Cudworth, E. (2010) '"The recipe for love"? Continuities and changes in the sexual politics of meat', *Journal for Critical Animal Studies* 8(4): 78–99.

Cudworth, E. (2011a) 'Walking the dog: explorations and negotiations of species difference', *Philosophy, Activism, Nature* 8: 14–22.

Cudworth, E. (2011b) 'Climate change, industrial animal agriculture and complex inequalities', *International Journal of Science in Society* 2(3): 323–334.

Cudworth, E. (2011c) *Social Lives with Other Animals: Tales of Sex, Death and Love*, Basingstoke: Palgrave.

Dangerous Dogs Act (1991), retrieved from http://www.legislation.gov.uk/ukpga/1991/65/contents.

Deckha, M. (2012) 'Toward a postcolonial posthumanist feminist theory: centralizing race and culture in feminist work on non-human animals', *Hypatia* 27(3): 527–545.

Derrida, J. (1991) 'Eating well, or the calculation of the subject: an interview with Jacques Derrida', in *Who Comes After the Subject*, edited by Cadaver, E., Connor, P. and Nancy, J.-L., London: Routledge, 96–119.

Derrida, J. (2009) *The Beast and the Sovereign* Volume 1, edited by Lisse, M., Mallet, M.L. and Michaud, G., translated by Bennington, G., Chicago and London: Chicago University Press.

Diamond, C. (2008) 'The difficulty of reality and the difficulty of philosophy', in *Philosophy and Animal Life*, edited by Cavell, S., New York: Columbia University Press, 43–89.

Donovan, J. (2006) 'Feminism and the treatment of animals: from care to dialogue', *Signs* 31(2): 305–329.

Doubiago, S. (1989) 'Mama Coyote talks to the boys', in *Healing the Wounds: The Promise of Ecofeminism*, edited by Plant, J., London: Green Print, 40–44.

Dunayer, J. (1995) 'Sexist words, speciesist roots', in *Animals and Women: Feminist Theoretical Explorations*, edited by Adams, C.J. and Donovan, J., London: Duke University Press, 11–31.

FAO (2002) *World Agriculture: Towards 2015/2030: Summary Report*, Rome: Food and Agriculture Organization of the United Nations, retrieved from ftp://ftp.fao.org/docrep/fao/004/y3557e/y3557e.pdf.

Flynn, C.P. (2000) 'Battered women and their animal companions: symbolic interaction between human and non-human animals', *Society and Animals* 8(2): 99–127.

Francione, G. (2000) *Introduction to Animal Rights: Your Child or the Dog?*, Philadelphia: Temple University Press.

Franklin, A. (1999) *Animals and Modern Cultures: A Sociology of Human–Animal Relations in Modernity*, London: Sage.

Gaard, G. (2012) 'Speaking for animal bodies', *Hypatia* 27(3): 520–526.

Garner, R. (2005) *The Political Theory of Animal Rights*, Manchester: Manchester University Press.

Haraway, D. (1989) *Primate Visions: Gender, Race and Nature in the World of Modern Science*, London: Routledge.

Haraway, D. (2008) *When Species Meet*, Minneapolis: University of Minnesota Press.

Leatherman, J.L. (2011) *Sexual Violence and Armed Conflict*, Cambridge: Polity Press.

MacDonald, M. (2010) 'Foodprints', in 'The Future of Food', special issue of *Resurgence* 259, March/April, 2–3.

Masson, J.M. (2004) *The Pig Who Sang to the Moon: The Emotional World of Farm Animals*, London: Jonathan Cape.

McCance, D. (2013) *Critical Animal Studies: An Introduction*, Albany, NY: SUNY Press.

McHugh, S. (2012) 'Bitch, bitch, bitch: personal criticism, feminist theory and dog-writing', *Hypatia* 27(3): 616–635.

Mellor, M. (1992) *Breaking the Boundaries: Towards a Feminist Green Socialism*, London: Virago.

Mellor, M. (1997) *Feminism and Ecology*, Cambridge: Polity Press.

Mitchell, L. (2011) 'Moral disengagement and support for non-human animal farming', *Society and Animals* 19(1): 38–58.

Nibert, D. (2002) *Animal Rights/Human Rights: Entanglements of Oppression and Liberation*, Lanham, MD: Rowman & Littlefield.

Nocella, A.J., Sorenson, J., Socha, K. and Matsuoka, A. (2014) *Defining Critical Animal Studies: An Intersectional Social Justice Approach for Liberation*, New York: Peter Lang.

Nolan, C. (2010) 'Geography that breaks your heart: feminist geography from/to the peripheries', Suzanne Mackenzie Memorial Lecture (sponsored by the Canadian Women in Geography group), University of Regina, 3 June.

Palmer, C. (2006) 'Killing animals in animal shelters', in *Killing Animals*, edited by The Animal Studies Group, Urbana and Chicago: University of Illinois Press, 170–187.

Perkins Gilman, C. (1935) *The Living of Charlotte Perkins Gilman: An Autobiography*, New York: Appelton-Century Co.

Plant, J. (1989) *Healing the Wounds: The Promise of Ecofeminism*, Philadelphia: New Society.

Plumwood, V. (1993) *Feminism and the Mastery of Nature*, London: Routledge.

Plumwood, V. (1996) 'Being prey', in *The Ultimate Journey: Inspiring Stories of Living and Dying*, edited by O'Reilly, J., O'Reilly, S. and Sterling, R., Palo Alto, CA: Travelers' Tales.

Plumwood, V. (2004) 'Ecofeminism', in *Controversies in Environmental Sociology*, edited by White, R., Cambridge: Cambridge University Press, 43–60.

Regan, T. (1983) *The Case for Animal Rights*, Los Angeles: University of California Press.

Salamone, C. (1982) 'The prevalence of natural law within women: women and animal rights', in *Reweaving the Web of Life: Feminism and Non-violence*, edited by McAllister, P., San Francisco: New Society, 364–375.

Salleh, A.K. (1984) 'Deeper than deep ecology: the eco-feminist connection', *Environmental Ethics* 6(4): 339–345.

Salleh, A.K. (1997) *Ecofeminism as Politics: Nature, Marx and the Postmodern*, London: Zed Books.

Segal, L. (1987) *Is the Future Female? Troubled Thoughts on Contemporary Feminism*, London: Virago.

Shiva, V. (2007) *Soil Not Oil: Climate Change, Peak Oil and Food Insecurity*, London: Zed.

Singer, P. (1990/1975) *Animal Liberation*, London: Picador.

Stanescu, J. (2012) 'Species trouble: Judith Butler, mourning and the precarious lives of animals', *Hypatia* 27(3): 567–582.

Steinfeld, H., Gerber, P., Wassemaar, T., Castel, V., Rosales, M. and de Haan, C. (2006) *Livestock's Long Shadow: Environmental Issues and Options*, Rome: Food and Agriculture Organization of the United Nations.

Taylor, N. and Twine, R. (eds) (2014) *The Rise of Critical Animal Studies: From the Margins to the Centre*, London: Routledge.

Torres, B. (2007) *Making a Killing: The Political Economy of Animal Rights*, Oakland, CA: AK Press.

Tuan, Y.-F. (1984) *Dominance and Affection: The Making of Pets*, New Haven, CT: Yale University Press.

Velten, H. (2007) *Cow*, London: Reaction Books.

Weisberg, Z. (2009) 'The broken promises of monsters', *Journal of Critical Animal Studies* 7(2): 22–62.

Wilkie, R. (2013) 'Academic "dirty work": mapping scholarly labour in a tainted mixed-species field', *Society and Animals* (online first), doi: 10.1163/15685306-12341312.

Williams, E.E. and DeMello, M. (2007) *Why Animals Matter: The Case for Animal Protection*, Amherst: Prometheus Books.

Wolfe, C. (2013) *Before the Law: Human and Other Animals in Biopolitical Frame*, Chicago and London: Chicago University Press.

# 3 Developing ecofeminist corporeality

## Writing the body as activist poetics

Mary Phillips

## Introduction

There is now overwhelming evidence that climate change is happening. More specifically, the impacts of climate change in terms of the frequency and intensity of severe weather events, as well as more insidious ecological changes, are beginning to become ever more apparent. The fifth report of the IPCC (2014) forecasts that, on current global trajectories, greenhouse gas and carbon emissions will lead to warming in excess of the 2°C increase over pre-industrial levels deemed 'safe'. Indeed it could reach 3°C or even a catastrophic 4°C. However, Western governments and businesses appear paralysed by inertia and apathy, unable to develop and implement programmes of radical change (Wittneben et al. 2012), while publics also demonstrate low levels of engagement (Doan 2014). It is difficult to make sense of the disconnect between what is known about the urgent action required to avoid ecological disaster and what political sociologist Ingolfur Blühdorn describes as society's 'adamant resolve to sustain what is known to be unsustainable' (2007: 272, cited in Doan 2014: 634).

One explanation is that in the West we have become disconnected from our bodies, and our bodies are disconnected from nature. We physically seal ourselves off from the effects of the weather and climate in our homes, offices and cars such that we are largely insulated from and cannot feel, viscerally, how weather patterns might be changing in the West as well as further afield. Moreover, we are emotionally distant from the ways in which our activities are impacting on nature and on other humans. Claire Colebrook describes this as hyper-hypo-affective disorder; an over-generation of affect stimulated by current modes of consumption accompanied by affect fatigue such that there is 'an inverse relation between the wider and wider *extension* of affective influx and the ever-diminishing *intensity* of affect' (Colebrook 2011: 45, emphasis in original). In terms of the ecological dangers that confront us, Colebrook (2011) describes how the news media contribute to the imaginary of climate change as having a cinematic quality. Severe weather events are reported in such a way that viewers experience them with a compelling frisson similar to that felt when watching apocalyptic or disaster movies. Affect is thus generated as a consumer product. However, there is no depth to such affect in that we are distanced from the event and fail to respond as we would if we recognized that our bodies are implicated in and will be affected by environmental issues; in other words, that climate change is 'real' and will impact on us. Colebrook links this lack of bodily involvement in climate change to the lack of 'panic, [or] any apparent, affective comportment that would indicate that anyone really feels or fears [this threat]' (Colebrook 2011: 53). We are thus emotionally and physically alienated from weather and from its effects.

For ecofeminist philosophers, such distancing is part of an alienation from and instrumental use of nature symptomatic of the 'logic of patriarchy'[1] (e.g. Kheel 2008; Plumwood 1993; Warren 2000). This logic is reinforced through sets of interrelated dualisms such that putative human authenticity is coterminous with idealized, hegemonic masculinity defined in opposition to what is taken to be natural, nature, or the physical or biological realm. This creates a disembodied and disengaged subject 'free and rational to the extent that he [*sic*] has fully distinguished himself from the natural and social worlds' such that 'the subject withdraws from his own body, which he is able to look on as an object' (Taylor 1995: 7). The ecofeminist project challenges such dualistic thinking in order to undermine the alienation and disconnection from nature that are its outcome. The recuperation of body and its visceral inhabitation in the world has to be part of that project. For Neimanis and Walker, it is imperative that we 'reimagine climate change and the fleshy damp immediacy of our own embodied existences as intimately imbricated' (2014: 559), where the imaginary and the corporeal are deeply entwined in 'a common space, a conjoined time [and] a mutual worlding' (ibid.: 560). If we can embrace the materiality of our bodies, that we are organic beings embedded in nature, then perhaps we can overcome our alienation and estrangement from nature. Thus the body has to be of fundamental importance in challenging the ways that nature, femininity and emotionality are cast, and beginning to reimagine them. However, ecofeminist approaches to the body which acknowledge the interrelationships between the subordination of body, nature and femininity are relatively absent, and work theorizing body/nature awareness stops short of suggesting how such an awareness can be stimulated and translated into action.

So the challenge is to develop ecofeminist thinking around the body that can lead to action, and to do this I combine an ecofeminist approach with the work of French feminist Hélène Cixous, a writer and poststructuralist philosopher[2] who strives tirelessly to disrupt the binary thinking privileging rationality and instrumentality that characterizes the logic of patriarchy. Her focus is on writing the body to find modes of representation that do not alienate us from nature. I start with a more detailed outline of one of the main elements of ecofeminist philosophy: mounting a challenge to interrelated sets of dualisms which support systems of subordination not only of nature but of all 'othered' groups and, importantly for the purposes of this chapter, the material body itself. I then argue that ecofeminism must engage with corporeality and reaffirm the importance of visceral emotion to develop an affective engagement with nature. Writing creatively in and of the body is suggested as one means to help us reflect on our organic embeddedness, and to further develop this I turn to the work of Hélène Cixous. This complements and resonates with the ecofeminist project by calling for a revaluation and rewriting of the body which can subvert patriarchal logic. Building on this, I articulate the specific contribution of this chapter by exploring how such embodied and poetic writing is a form of activism that can help overcome our current inertia, and I offer the example of activist and eco-poet Susan Richardson's work.

## The ecofeminist project

The ecofeminist project is to claim that feminism and environmentalism are inherently connected through an insistence that environmental issues require feminist analysis. It does not, however, offer a grand theory to replace current truth claims. Instead, Karen Warren, whose work has been highly influential in the development of philosophical ecofeminism, has metaphorized eco-feminism as a quilt: 'An ecofeminist philosophical quilt will be made up of different "patches", constructed by quilters in particular social, historical and materialist contexts' (2000: 66). In the same way that the borders of a quilt can contain an infinite richness of patterns, colours and designs, the parameters of ecofeminism allow for a wide range of emphases and methodologies (Cuomo 2002) that share a commitment to core values such as justice and caring for both human and non-human life. Relatedly, ecofeminism pro-motes a transformative agenda that both initiates and supports activism and engages with academic, theoretical debate.

The focus on interwoven and cross-cutting systems of domination that justify colonialism, racism, sexism and the subordination of nature is a common theme across ecofeminist philosophies that make up Warren's quilt (Cudworth 2005; Glazebrook 2005; Plumwood 1993; Warren 2000). The ecofeminist project seeks to illuminate how a 'culturally exalted hegemonic ideal' (Kheel 2008: 3, see also Gaard 1993; Plumwood 1993; Warren 2000) of masculinity is promoted through a set of interrelated dualisms such as mind/body, reason/nature, reason/emotion, masculine/feminine or human/nature. Ecofeminist philosopher Val Plumwood (1991, 1993) details how the hier-archical ordering of contrasting pairs has produced a logic of identity that has become objectified and given the status of reality. This logic operates by differentiating self from others, where others include the natural world. The dominant group, that which claims possession of what Plumwood terms 'the Master identity' and with the most power and privilege, asserts for itself those attributes which it categorizes as indicative of an active human subject. Those who are deemed not to possess the same attributes are cast as lacking in relation to the dominant group and therefore sub-standard and Other.

Non-conformance with the categories determined by the dominant group, including mind over body, reason over emotion, activity over passivity, is therefore to be considered either an inferior copy of the human, or non-human. As Plumwood points out:

> The account draws on the familiar view of reason and emotion as sharply separated and opposed, and of 'desire', caring, and love as merely 'personal' and 'particular' as opposed to the universality and impartiality of understanding and of 'feminine' emotions as essentially unreliable, untrustworthy, and morally irrelevant, an inferior domain to be dominated by a superior, disinterested (and of course masculine) reason.
>
> (Plumwood 1991: 5)

Thus a genuinely human self is one that is essentially rational and sharply differentiated from what is presented as merely emotional or as associated with the body. Such attributes are linked to what is 'natural', not to the properly human realm of reason, such that emotions, bodies and nature are construed as inferior and given instrumental value only. Those things which supposedly give humanity its defining characteristics, such as rationality, freedom and capacity for abstraction (and which are all traditionally viewed as masculine), are not shared with nature, with the body or with the feminine. Indeed, the body is something to be transcended as it is constructed as separated from the 'true' self (which might be defined as soul, mind, spirit, will, creativity, freedom) and undermines and impedes the efforts of that self to achieve self-realization (Bordo 2003). Hence the ideal human self does not include features associated with nature, but is defined as separate from and in opposition to it.

### Re-engaging the corporeal

Ecofeminists such as Plumwood and Warren have shown how the body is devalued in opposition to the mind, because the body is aligned with women and nature in the binary system that privileges reason and masculinity. However, there has seemingly been a reluctance by ecofeminists to engage with and realize the full potential of a focus on the body to subvert and disrupt the 'dead matter of the Cartesian world view' (Field 2000). This is so because ecofeminism was accused of essentialism as some of its adherents focused on what they regarded as historical, biological and experiential affinities between women, women's bodies and nature (for an overview see Sturgeon 1997). Critics argued that this risked antifeminist complicity with patriarchal ideas where the supposed disorder or anarchy of the female body is used to justify women's inherent inferiority. The superior, male/masculine mind is positioned as able to minimize, subjugate and govern corporeality's unwelcome intrusions whereas women are more completely embodied and thus innately less able to control the passions, flows and fluxes of their bodies. Moreover, as women, in general, exude blood, milk and other fluids, nurture other bodies within their own and give birth to them, the boundaries of their embodiment are mutable and precarious. Their bodies thus leak, trouble and overflow the boundaries between self and other and are perceived as a source of contagion (Grosz 1989). The dominant masculinist imaginary can thus not only justify women as inferior, but also cast them as objects of fear and repulsion. The power and tenacity of such ideas meant that many feminists were wary of engagement with a female body whose status was highly problematic (Shildrick and Price 1999; Witz 2000). Ecofeminism in particular faced accusations that it promoted a form of 'motherhood environmentalism' (Sandilands 1999: xiii), in which it was argued that woman was somehow closer to nature and which celebrated 'traditional' womanly or nurturing values while ignoring intersectional dimensions of class, ethnicity, able-bodiedness and so forth. Many ecofeminists therefore distanced themselves:

> from the 'touchy-feely', religious, and reproductive celebratory strands [of ecofeminism]; jokes about placenta-eating covens of ex-hippies became (and remain) common.
>
> (Thompson 2006: 507)

While much of the more general critique was unfair, decontextualized and inaccurate, such accusations were often used to dismiss ecofeminism as a whole (Sturgeon 1997). One outcome was that corporeality became an almost unspeakable issue within ecofeminism (for exceptions see Alaimo 2008, 2009; Field 2000; Glazebrook 2005; Twine 2001). Although ecofeminist work has focused on embodied relations of power as they relate to the impacts of environmental degradation on the bodies of women (e.g. Shiva 1989), reproductive technologies (Cudworth 2005) and the production of food (Kheel 2008), academic ecofeminism has tended to avoid engaging with potentially important contributions to ecofeminist thought provided by poststructuralist approaches to the body.

There are several reasons why ecofeminism needs to embrace the body. First, the body is an important reminder that humans are organically embedded beings whose future and wellbeing are inherently entwined with the future and wellbeing of the planet. Those members of humanity (and I include myself) who have benefited most from economic development, who have contributed most to ecological degradation and who are most remote from their physicality need to rediscover our 'earthian' place by becoming aware of and accepting our fleshiness, and the frailties that flesh lends us. For Alaimo (2009), embracing the vulnerability of the body is a recognition of precarious, corporeal openness to the material world which can foster an ecocentric ethics wherein the vulnerability of nature is also recognized. She asserts a feminist stance towards the environment that is transcorporeal and that acknowledges the substantial interconnections between human corporeality and the more-than-human world. As Alaimo points out, 'human corporeality in all its material fleshiness is inseparable from "nature" or "environment"', while the body/nature are also intertwined with 'culture'. Refusing to separate culture and nature allows us to destabilize the culture/ nature binary and to develop ethical and political positions that can contend with the ecological realities with which we are faced (Alaimo 2008: 238).

Second, we need to reaffirm the visceral emotions experienced through our bodies such that we can begin to develop the kind of affective engagement with and embodied knowledge of nature that might lead us to respond more appropriately to the ecological threats we have been so instrumental in creating. Such an engagement, however, has to be active rather than a passive consumption of affect that has been commodified. Emotion is a valuable means to learning which can challenge the veneration and mystification of knowledge that claims to be disembodied, transcendent and complete (Alaimo 2008, 2009). Glazebrook (2005) points to the importance of eco-logical emotion in developing a gynocentric eco-logics wherein we value responsive and emotional engagements alongside those that are grounded in rationality in our development of knowledge of the environment. Such an eco-logics respects the epistemological validity of knowledge that cannot be fully articulated according to the demands of objectivity, and is productive of ways of knowing guided by and responsive to the physical environment in which it is practised rather than a reductive objectivity. The third reason relates to the subversive potential of bodies, and particularly of those bodies that do not conform to what Grosz has referred to as the 'corporeal "universal"' (1994: 188) which functions as an implicit projection of a masculine norm which is reductive and damaging for those who are its others – women, differently abled, cultural and racial minorities, animals. As Twine points out (2001), the manner in which nature, femininity, emotionality and corporeality are cast and represented reveals a deep anxiety around the organic materiality of the body and around the fleshiness of those who assume for themselves the rationality and universality that inhere in the Master identity. The embodiment of others is accentuated, while that of those who claim the Master identity is downplayed. A fear of flesh and fleshy desire out of control is projected onto those others who can then be positioned as being of the body rather than the mind, and who are thus associated with animality and the corporeality of the non-human. To bring the body into focus is to challenge the power dynamics of meaning and value ascribed to this universal body – to its status as impermeable, autonomous and self-identical. Female, animal and other othered bodies are uncomfortable reminders that all bodies are permeable, leak fluids and gases, and have the potential to be disruptive, unmanageable, disordered and disordering. For Grosz, drawing on Julia Kristeva's notion of abjection, the bodily fluids produced by all bodies:

> attest to a certain irreducible 'dirt' or disgust, a horror of the unknown or the unspecifiable that permeates, lurks, lingers, and at times leaks out

of the body, a testimony of the fraudulence or impossibility of the 'clean' and 'proper'. They resist the determination that marks solids, for they are without any shape or form of their own. They are engulfing, difficult to be rid of; any separation from them is not a matter of certainty, as it may be in the case of solids ... they betray a certain irreducible materiality; they assert the priority of the body over subjectivity; they demonstrate the limits of subjectivity in the body, the irreducible specificity of particular bodies.

(Grosz 1989: 194)

Thus ignoring the body colludes in the erasure of the body from the Master identity, the elision of male corporeality and the reproductive capacities of the male body (Twine n.d.), while Field (2000) reminds us that men's bodily experiences, for example of erection or ejaculation, could also be construed as deconstructive experiences that challenge public/private, me/not me, inside/outside distinctions.

To state that there is a 'corporeal universal' is to recognize that bodies do matter (cf. Barad 2003) and that those who do not conform are forced to live with and within institutions that privilege male modes of embodiment. Social experiences are often constituted by the body one has, such that how the embodiment of women and other othered groups are represented requires challenge in order to bring about social, economic and political change. If the body is seen *only* as a cultural phenomenon, a surface inscribed by cultural signification whose naturalness and materiality is an illusion, we disembody bodiliness and abandon nature, which loses any independence from the social and political meanings that are invested in it. To deny the materiality of bodies and of nature is to perpetuate alienation from nature and to reinforce an anthropocentric and androcentric view of the world (Bigwood 1991). It elides the effects of other materialities; non-human beings, with earth, water, sky on our understanding of our being, which is imbricated within culture but is also situated in relations with the non-human. As Bigwood points out, neither body nor nature exists in some pure, pre-cultural state, but neither is there a culture that pre-exists nature.

For feminism and ecofeminism, the challenge is to find a way of articulating a recuperated corporeality such that the body is not that which has been distorted, ignored or rendered abject by masculinist logic and representation. However, this has to be achieved without sustaining the Cartesian mind/body dualism by simply reversing the terms of the dualism; instead, enabling a more positive approach that allows an active consideration of body and thought. In the next section I argue that writing creatively in and of the body can help us reflect on our organic embeddedness and materiality and develop a heightened engagement with nature and the world, and I engage with the poststructuralist, philosophical work of Hélène Cixous to demonstrate how that might be so.

## Writing bodies, writing nature

But how can we re-engage with bodies, with our fleshiness and with the senses that flesh engenders? How can we experience and tell others about our bodies as *lived*? And, from an ecofeminist point of view, how can we relate all that to nature in order to develop a more ecocentric awareness of and empathy for the non-human? This is indeed a challenge because:

> The ineffable nature of affective knowledge seems to imperfectly survive its formal representation, persuading us that there must be two quite different domains of sense in operation; one corporealised, immediate, and intimately given, and the other intellectualised, mediated, and constructively reinterpreted. Language appears to fall short of experience then because it cannot equate these two quite incommensurable ways of 'making sense'.
>
> (Kirby 1999: 19)

Kirby reminds us that language/writing is a form of abstraction which postmodern critique characterizes as an all-pervasive productive force while firmly positioning it within the confines of culture. How, then, can writing be a generative force to encourage an affective engagement with and through the world? And how can we write of the body and embodiment, and its imbrication in and through nature, without sensing that something of the materiality, fleshiness and earthiness of the body with nature has escaped?

To answer these questions I turn to the work of Hélène Cixous, a prolific writer and poststructuralist philosopher who is pre-occupied with the subversive potential of writing the body. Cixous works to overcome oppressive systems resulting from hierarchical binary oppositions that structure Western philosophies and culture, and in which the 'other' term is represented as negative and powerless. She shares with ecofeminism an argument that these have traditionally bound women and other subordinate groups into inferior positions that deny them a place or voice in socio-economic, political and historical arenas. Her vision of an embodied writing represents a move to resist the ways in which women/nature are linguistically, historically and sexually confined, and opens up the possibility of writing the body differently, particularly women's bodies, to undo binary hierarchies. It suggests how we might unsettle and shake indifference to the materiality of the body and to nature that could help us break the mould in current ways of understanding the world. Cixous invites women 'to write her body in order to discover herself. She must explore her *jouissance*, her sexual pleasure, so as to bring down phallogocentric discourse and, ultimately, change the world' (Juncker 1988: 426). A productive dialogue between an ecofeminist approach to addressing looming ecological crises and Cixous's focus on a writing that is multiplicitous and liberatory could encourage recognition that nature is intertwined with our corporeal existence. If we can recognize and *feel* this, we may be moved to act.

Cixous did not address ecopolitics directly, but she challenged the concept of nature as the other of reason or culture:

> The natural word, the word *nature*, has a sad fate ... as if 'nature' existed in opposition to 'culture', or there were such a thing as pure nature.
>
> (Cixous 1993: 128–29)

Cixous argues for a relation between subjects that respects nature, lives in immanence and is fully aware of its situatedness in an organic world. For her, it is about accepting our materiality and our connections to the rest of the natural world, for we are 'assemblings' of atoms and molecules, and at the atomic level it is far more difficult to say where one entity begins and the other ends. We are all interconnected. However, we have become estranged from our bodies because they remind us of our frailty and the fact that, like all living things, our lives will end. Her description of the work of the Brazilian writer Clarice Lispector makes this clear:

> she returns the ability not to forget *matter*, which we don't notice, which we live, which we are ... We are unable to think matter because we consider it to be invisible. We are made of assemblings that hide their truth, their atomic side, from us. We dislike matter, that is ourselves, because we are destined to matter, because anonymous matter is called: death. We repress [matter, anonymity] at any price.
>
> (Cixous 1993: 130)

We can see here that Cixous's philosophy shares much ground with eco-feminism, in particular with regard to the continuity between the human and the natural and human dependency on nature. In a world dominated by rationality, the realization that we are embodied and made of matter is threatening because the body reminds us of our material existence as organic beings who will inevitably die. At the same time, a recognition of the permeability between human flesh and the natural world should not deny or negate nature's otherness or separateness from humanity. That would be to incorporate nature, to risk perpetuating anthropocentrism and to deny nature's own agency. It is more that we should strive to make space within ourselves for that otherness, to put ourselves second at least sometimes (Cixous and Calle-Gruber 1997). As with many ecofeminist thinkers, Cixous calls for other modes of exchange and representation that pursue and celebrate differences rather than simple reversals of power relations.

For Cixous, writing that engages with matter and with bodies has subversive and transformative power that can disrupt binary thinking and explode phallocentrism. Writing from the body has the capacity to circumvent reason and is in contrast to the language we have been taught:

that speaks from above, from afar, that listens to itself, that has ears only for itself, the dead language of deafening that speaks to us in advance. We have been taught a language that translates everything in itself, understands nothing except in translation; speaks only in its language, listens only to its grammar, and we separated from the things under its order ...

(cited in Conley 1997: 126)

Thus writing from a bodily immediacy that is in touch with the world around us should challenge domains bounded and limited by rationality, which she conceives of as a sort of translation that separates and excludes us, immobilizes us, interrupts flows of giving and receiving and kills life. We 'receive what happens to us with "received feelings". We do not profit from it in any way' (Cixous and Calle-Gruber 1997: 12) – we do not feel it properly, or know how to suffer or enjoy experience. We should instead be attuned to the language of feeling that precedes translation and thus come to experience in our bodies the more-than-rational, the excessive, the emotion that could re-connect and re-embody us within nature such that we are open to the possibilities of bodies in tune with the Earth:

There are those voices that like a flame lowers, scarcely speaks, but moves still nearer, still nearer to the secrets of things, lowers all the way to the earth, lies down, touches the imperceptibly trembling soil, listens to the music of the earth, the concert of the earth with all things.

(Cixous 1979: 10)

Writing the body and writing nature provides a means to shift our understandings and move us to new perspectives:

As soon as I use it [the word 'nature'] in the domain of writing it begins to move, to twist a little, because in *writing* this is what it's all about. As soon as there is writing, it becomes a matter of *passage*, of all kinds of passages, of delimitation, of overflowing.

(Cixous 1993: 128–29)

Cixous illustrates such movements in her own writing, which is poetic, flowing and playful, with language, as we see in the following quotation where complementarities with the philosophical positions taken by ecofeminists are also evident:

It is a way of dehierarchizing – everything. ... because we are geocentric, we say: from the earth to. And the moon is the other. ... Let us change points of view. If I write 'de lune a l'autre', in this case the other would be the earth. We must play musical chairs with hierarchies, it is also because by dint of commanding without knowing, that is of being commanded in advance by language, we deprive everyone of everything. We deprive ourselves of otherness – of the otherness of the earth. ... The earth seen from the point of view of the moon is revived: it is unknown; to be rediscovered.

(Cixous 1993: 10)

Cixous argues that if we restrict ourselves to the dominant geocentric or anthropocentric perspective we are impoverished and constricted. To escape, we need to play with the hierarchies inherent in dualism, to put ourselves in the other's place, see the Earth from the Moon, and thus perceive the Earth differently. We would see the familiar with new eyes and be shifted into strangeness, a being abroad at home, that Cixous terms the *entredeux*. She also plays with language here. '*De lune a l'autre*' (from the moon to the other) could also be read/heard as '*de l'une a l'autre*' (from the one to the other), itself a departure from the idiomatic French expression '*de l'un a l'autre*' which for Cixous denies the feminine. This twists meaning further as 'the one' and 'the moon', the dominant and the other, are in a continual interplay of shifting places. This in contrast to the 'language that speaks from above' where meaning is constructed through binaries that classify, hierarchize, and appropriate or destroy the feminine and nature.

Cixous proposes and practises a writing not of mind or rationality, but of the body. It speaks of and through a body that is permeable, and that does not contain or restrict. To write in the *entredeux* is to produce texts that 'work on the difference', which strive to undermine phallocentric culture and split asunder the closure of binarism. She takes oppositions and rewrites them into differences, working in the in-between of binaries (nationalities, individuals, genders, sexualities, subject and object, human and more-than-human). At the same time, it is a matter of recognizing and respecting the boundaries, where one ends and the other begins, in a process of encounter and transformation:

> The origin of the material in writing can only be myself. I is not I, of course, because it is I with the others, coming from the others, putting me in the other's place, giving me the other's eyes ...
>
> (Cixous and Calle-Gruber 1997: 87)

This writing therefore does not envisage the obliteration of the self nor the incorporation of the other, which would merely reverse the binary, the dialectic between self and other. It requires respect for the other and self-knowledge of one's own desires, prejudices, fears and questions. Difference is thus a range of possibilities that opens up multiplicity rather than an opposition of mutually exclusive alternatives. She sets out not to efface or correct those binaries but to revel in the shifting space between the two: 'What is intoxicating, what can be disturbing, difficult – in that it is not the third term, it is not a block between two blocks; it is exchange itself' (Cixous and Calle-Gruber

1997: 53). Such writing acknowledges the self as relational, infinitely extended, in a fleeting embrace with the other.

Cixous was not referring to climate change or environmental degradation when she wrote:

> But in these feeble and forgetful times, when we are far away from things, so far from each other, very far from ourselves, in these sad and forgetful times, of feeble looks, too short, falling aside from things, far from living things, where we don't know how to read, to let senses radiate, and we are cold, a glacial air is blowing around our souls.
>
> (Cixous 1979: 46–48)

But she is writing about human estrangement from the self and from the other living things with which we share the planet. It is this inability to connect, to 'read' and understand in the widest sense of the term, to fail to embrace our embodied senses that has chilled us, such that we 'no longer inhabit in life' and have become 'unnerved anaesthetized devitalized bodies in which we circulate, metallically, mechanized and we roll along rails every same morning' (Cixous 1979: 78). But even in these days when we seem lost in darkness and solitude, bereft of the life-giving warmth of connection, Cixous's work embodies hope in the belief that a different future is possible in which we will survive our past and 'inhabit time humanly' (Cixous 1979: 76), where to be human is to rediscover how to live and think in ways that are attuned to the natural rhythms of the world. This is a radical challenge in a world where body and nature are increasingly commodified, commoditized and consumed. For Cixous, it is the medium of writing that rescues her from fearfulness, isolation and doubt to instead envision how separations can be dissolved and the ultimate connectedness of all living things affirmed, as she embraces 'the marvellous quantity of things of all kinds, of all species, human, vegetable, animal, of all sexes, of all cultures' (Cixous 1979: 110).

While Cixous fully recognizes that the ready-made laws of masculine discourses cannot be completely broken, they can be destabilized so that texts which write of and from the body are subversive and volcanic, exploding through the crust of masculine rationality, to create living spaces where humans can break out of their frozen states and re-connect with each other and the world of which they are a part. For Cixous, poetry is therefore an activist practice that reaches beyond the page to bring about change.

## Poetry as activist practice

Cixous believes that the forms of writing she espouses will bring about wider social and political changes. She refuses to separate the political and the poetic, which are equally necessary as inseparable dimensions of living; only the either/or of binary distinctions makes them appear separate. For her, working with language that uses the poetic politically and heightens the political poetically (Bammer 2003) is practice of activism; as she explains in *The Laugh of the Medusa*, 'writing is precisely *the very possibility of change*, the space that can serve as a springboard for subversive thought, the precursory movement of a transformation of social and cultural structures' (Cixous 1976: 879, emphasis in original). This is so because the materiality of the world is mediated through language, and it can therefore be transformed and de/re-constructed through language. Thus Cixous's wider project is to induce us to re-think our connection to the world, and it is exactly this re-connection that is called for by the ecofeminist project also. Poetry offers a means to embrace multiplicity, emotion and corporeal responses to the worlds in which we live, and is transformative in ways that are complementary to activism:

> The poet ... knows very well that the influence of a text is always postponed: but it does exist. The text is active, but later, and in a different way to action. Poetic gestures transform other aspects of both the soul and of human life beyond those which are modified by political action.
>
> (Cixous 2008: 89)

Thus for Cixous rage and pleasure, struggle and poetry, as suggested in her image of the laughing Medusa, are both necessary to bring about political change.

This resonates with how ecofeminist Val Plumwood describes creatively writing body and nature, which alerts 'readers to ways of challenging the experiential framework of dead and silent matter entrenched by the sado-dispassionate rationality of scientific reductionism' (Plumwood 2007: 17–18). Such writing enables us to feel our embodied connections to the natural world and to respond with emotion; to open ourselves to care. Creative work thus makes 'visible new possibilities for radically open and non-reductive ways to experience the world' (Plumwood 2007: 17). Cixous's insistence that poetry is an element of political struggle accords with the importance given by ecofeminism to the place of radical scholarship com-mitted to 'sparking consciousness-change that results in real actions' (Gaard 2011: 41) such that theory and activism combine to work for justice for all subordinated groups, including nature.

To further demonstrate how writing that is embodied can be a practice of activism, I now turn to the work of Susan Richardson, a published eco-poet (and self-identified ecofeminist) who performs her poetry and facilitates writing workshops. Richardson's poetry explores the icy environment and the mythology of the Arctic, drawing on sources such as Inuit folk stories, polar explorers' tales and Icelandic sagas together with her personal travels in northern, Arctic and sub-Arctic regions. I have selected the following example because, for me, it speaks to an embodied sense of loss and anguish that can be expressed and felt viscerally through the medium of poetry.

**Silence –**
is the wail of an iceberg with a migraine
Weeping one-sided into the sea
is the ghost bear's moan
as it runs out of swim

curses till frozen soil recoils
houses
lurch
roads subside

never bothered to learn an indigenous language
so enunciates self-interest by shouting very slow

is the howl of greenland's blistered skin
and the march of sequoias
through the arctic

is the scream of nine hundred species hurled
off the earth now they have nowhere
further north to thrive
burps
it's bloated with extinction
then drums its glutted fingers urging
the emergence of the next
Big Bang

(Richardson 2010: 77)

Silence is associated with what is not silent and absence is replaced with presence; with sounds emanating from bodies in pain, particularly where those bodies are not human, but are the ice itself, a ghost-bear, a land-mass. We feel, viscerally, the sense of loss as the ice weeps and we identify with the pain and the disturbed vision of the migraine attack which results in seeing things askew. We know that polar bear numbers are declining because the ice packs on which they depend are disappearing and that one day only the ghosts of bears will remain, but the poem ensures that we hear a particular bear's anguish as it can swim no further. The burning of the sun produces a howl of pain as Greenland's skin blisters and species are driven to extinction. But there are other levels of meaning associated with silence. There is the silence of complacency, of not speaking out, and the silence of self-interest, that does not care to hear what it is displacing, that devours all and waits for the next Big Bang, the next explosion of vested interest.

There is a wildness about poetry in that the different patterns of meanings, expressed through metaphor, rhythm, rhyme and scansion, are slippery and cannot be pinned down. Poetry, to paraphrase the poet Emily Dickinson, tells all the truth but slant and, for Cixous, escapes from the cage of the language of logic (Cixous and Calle-Gruber 1997). Poetry thus disturbs the ways in which we currently experience the world. It 'bypasses the intellect and goes straight to the heart' (Richardson, cited in Phillips 2014), and by the very discomfort it creates, it can provide new insights that impact on our engagements with nature. As Richardson notes, stepping beyond our current boundaries to imagine and be moved to act for a different future is:

> the role that poetry and the other arts have because it is very easy to feel completely disempowered, disenfranchised, hopeless and there has to be something to combat that.
>
> (personal conversation, January 2012, Cardiff)

Because such writing has an emotional impact that can inspire change, for Richardson, her work is very much an activist project:

> Other people are activists in terms of climbing ice shards and marching and I've done marches as well but I don't do direct action in that way … so I wanted to do more, so I do what I can do which is the writing and performing [of eco-poetry].
>
> (personal conversation, January 2012, Cardiff)

As an example, she recounts how she has performed her poetry to some very challenging audiences, such as members of local business organizations, who reported that they did not want to think about the effects of climate change, but who had been moved by her work to at least see the necessity for change and begin to consider how it might be achieved. Participants in writing workshops report that they want to read and learn more about climate change and do something about it. While any link between inspiration and actual behaviour change is certainly not proved by the subjective experience of one poet-activist, there is increasing interest in forms of engagement with environmental issues that draw on the power of the arts to inspire affective responses. Examples include community energy companies; environmental non-government organizations that sponsor poetry-writing workshops to win people to a cause; and scientific bodies such as the Cabot Institute at Bristol University, UK, which has worked with an artist-in-residence; and the UK Arts and Humanities Research Council, which offered funding for arts-led projects to promote more sustainable living. In Cixous's terms, poetry such as *Silence* and other creative responses challenge the 'dead language' of translation such that we re-connect with our feelings and with the world of which our bodies are a part. Such work is perhaps best thought of as a seed being planted or a passageway that opens us to the emotional ebbs and flows relevant to the ecological crises in which we are implicated.

## Concluding remarks

The aim of this chapter is to argue that ecofeminism has to engage with corporeality, and specifically with writing the body, to promote reflexive, emotional and affective engagements with nature. This engagement is one that has been largely deferred within ecofeminism, perhaps understandably given the ferocity of the charges of essentialism laid at ecofeminism's door. However, a focus on the body is necessary to remind us that we are organically embedded beings, to reaffirm the validity of viscerally felt emotions, and to undermine the disembodiment of the Master identity. Ignoring the materiality of bodies and nature ultimately colludes in an anthropocentric and andro-centric worldview that privileges reason, culture and instrumentality. I have therefore drawn on the work of Hélène Cixous to offer a way of combining poststructuralist and ecofeminisms in a contemporary perspective that fore-grounds the immanence of the body in nature. Cixous's practice of and call for a poetic writing of the body as a form of political activism that can tunnel under and through dominant discourses accords with a focus on a combined activism *and* theorizing that has always been important to ecofeminism (Gaard 2011; Sturgeon 1997).

The contribution to the 'patchwork' that is the ecofeminist project is to offer a means to challenge the ways in which nature *and* bodies, emotion and femininity, are constructed and marginalized by a masculinist logic predi-cated on instrumental rationality. I have argued that revaluing bodies and embodied experience through writing can lead to a revaluation of nature such that an embeddedness in nature is recognized and felt, rather than held at a distance. This is not an over-idealistic position that could re-cement women's position as without logic, and outside discourse and power. Cixous believes it is impossible to step outside what ecofeminism would call the logic of patriarchy, or its discourses, but she does show how it might be possible to subvert, twist and change that logic. Although we have little choice but to live in the masculine discursive spaces through which the materiality of our world is mediated, we can work to recreate those spaces as more inclusive and where difference and multiplicity, including that of nature, are valued. For Cixous, this is an imperative for otherwise we are wasting our lives in the same way that men caught in those spaces have wasted theirs (Conley 1991).

Contemporary ecofeminism is situated in the context of a history in which ecofeminism was critiqued as essentialist to the extent that feminist academics working on the intersections of gender and nature so feared contamination-by-association (Gaard 2011) that they abandoned the ecofeminist label. It will therefore require courage and passion to re-open the Pandora's box that is discussion of the body. However, writing the body to re-imagine and re-engage with nature such that it is valued for itself offers a 'practice of hope' which Ynestra King explains thus: 'to have hope … is to believe that [the] future can be created by intentional human beings who now take responsibility [for it]' (cited in Lahar 1991: 32). Without such hopeful possibility, we will remain frozen and separated from the world that ultimately sustains us.

## Notes

1 In this chapter, patriarchy refers to the social system and mechanisms that reproduce and exert the dominance of idealized forms of masculinity over other forms of masculinity and over femininity. References to masculinity in this chapter are to this hegemonic ideal (see Connell 2001).
2 Poststructuralist philosophy and theorizing focuses on making visible the constitutive power of discourses particularly in relation to subjection and desire. Emphasizing the discursive and contingent nature of identities, it engages with the production of gendered subjectivity in particular.

## References

Alaimo, S. (2008) 'Trans-corporeal feminisms and the ethical space of nature', in *Material Feminisms*, edited by Alaimo, S. and Hekman, S., Bloomington, IN: Indiana University Press, 237–264.

Alaimo, S. (2009) 'Insurgent vulnerability and the carbon footprint of gender', *Kvinder, Kon & Forskning* 3/4: 22–35.

Bammer, A. (2003) *Partial Visions: Feminism and Utopianism in the 1970s*, London: Routledge.

Barad, K. (2003) 'Posthumanist performativity: toward an understanding of how matter comes to matter', *Signs* 28(3): 801–831.

Bigwood, C. (1991) 'Renaturalizing the body (with the help of Merleau-Ponty)', *Hypatia* 6(3): 54–73.

Blühdorn, I. (2007) 'Sustaining the unsustainable: SymBolic politics and the politics of simulation', *Environmental Politics* 16(2): 251–275.

Bordo, S. (2003) *Unbearable Weight: Feminism, Western Culture and the Body*, Berkeley, CA: University of California Press.

Cixous, H. (1976) *The Laugh of the Medusa*, translated by Cohen, K. and Cohen, P., *Signs* 1(4): 875–893.

Cixous, H. (1979) *To Live the Orange*, translated by Liddle, A. and Cornell, S., Paris: Des Femmes.

Cixous, H. (1993) *Three Steps on the Ladder of Writing*, New York: Columbia University Press.

Cixous, H. (2008) *White Ink: Interviews on Sex, Text and Politics*, edited by Sellers, S., Stockfield: Acumen.

Cixous, H. and Calle-Gruber, M. (1997) *Rootprints*, translated by Prenowitz, E., London: Routledge.

Colebrook, C. (2011) 'Earth felt the wound: the affective divide', *Journal for Politics, Gender and Culture* 8(1): 45–58.

Conley, V.A. (1991) *Hélène Cixous: Writing the Feminine*, Nebraska: University of Nebraska Press.

Conley, V.A. (1997) *Ecopolitics: The Environment in Poststructuralist Thought*, London: Routledge.

Connell, R.W. (2001) 'The social organization of masculinity', in *The Masculinities Reader*, edited by Whitehead, S.M. and Barrett, F.J., Cambridge: Polity Press, 30–50.

Cudworth, E. (2005) *Developing Eco-feminist Theory: The Complexity of Difference*, Basingstoke: Palgrave Macmillan.

Cuomo, C. (2002) 'On ecofeminist philosophy', *Ethics and the Environment* 7(2): 1–11.

Doan, M.D. (2014) 'Climate change and complacency', *Hypatia* 29(3): 634–650.

Field, T. (2000) 'Is the body essential for ecofeminism?', *Organization and Environment* 13(1): 39–60.

Gaard, G. (1993) 'Living interconnections with animals and nature', in *Ecofeminism: Women, Animals, Nature*, edited by Gaard, G., Philadelphia: Temple University Press, 1–12.

Gaard, G. (2011) 'Ecofeminism revisited: rejecting essentialism and re-placing species in a material feminist environmentalism', *Feminist Formations* 23(2): 26–53.

Glazebrook, T. (2005) 'Gynocentric eco-logics', *Ethics and the Environment* 10(2): 75–99.

Grosz, E. (1989) *Sexual Subversions: Three French Feminists*, Sydney: Allen & Unwin.

Grosz, E. (1994) *Volatile Bodies: Toward a Corporeal Feminism*, Bloomington: Indiana University Press.

IPCC (2014) *Climate Change 2014: Synthesis Report*, Contribution of Working Groups I, II and III to the Fifth Assessment Report of the IPCC, Core Writing Team, Pachauri, R.K. and Meyer, L.A., Geneva: Intergovernmental Panel on Climate Change, available at http://www.ipcc.ch/pdf/assessment-report/ar5/syr/AR5_SYR_FINAL_SPM.pdf (accessed February 2015).

Juncker, C. (1988) 'Writing (with) Cixous', *College English* 50: 424–436.

Kheel, M. (2008) *Nature Ethics: An Ecofeminist Perspective*, Lanham, MD: Rowman & Littlefield.

Kirby, V. (1999) 'Human nature', *Australian Feminist Studies* 14(29): 19–29.

Lahar, S. (1991) 'Ecofeminist theory and grassroots politics', *Hypatia* 6(1): 28–45.

Neimanis, A. and Walker, R.L. (2014) 'Weathering: climate change and the "thick time" of transcorporeality', *Hypatia* 29(3): 558–575.

Phillips, M. (2014) 'Re-writing corporate environmentalism: ecofeminism, corporeality and the language of feeling', *Gender, Work & Organization* 21(5): 443–458.

Plumwood, V. (1991) 'Nature, self and gender: feminism, environmental philosophy and the critique of rationalism', *Hypatia* 6(1): 3–27.

Plumwood, V. (1993) *Feminism and the Mastery of Nature*, London: Routledge.

Plumwood, V. (2007) 'Journey to the heart of stone', in *Culture, Creativity and Environment: New Environmentalist Criticism*, edited by Gifford, T. and Becket, F., New York: Rodopi, 17–36.

Richardson, S. (2010) *Where the Air is Rarefied*, Blaenau Ffestiniog: Cinnamon Press.

Sandilands, C. (1999) *The Good-Natured Feminist: Ecofeminism and the Quest for Democracy*, Minneapolis: University of Minnesota Press.

Shildrick, M. and Price, J. (1999) 'Openings on the body: a critical introduction', in *Feminist Theory and the Body: A Reader*, edited by Price, J. and Shildrick, M., Edinburgh: Edinburgh University Press, 1–14.

Shiva, V. (1989) *Staying Alive: Women, Ecology and Development*, London: Zed Books.

Sturgeon, N. (1997) *Ecofeminist Natures: Race, Gender, Feminist Theory and Political Action*, London: Routledge.

Taylor, C. (1995) *Philosophical Arguments*, Cambridge, MA: Harvard University Press.

Thompson, C. (2006) 'Back to nature? Resurrecting ecofeminism after poststructuralist and third-wave feminism', *Isis* 97(3): 505–512.

Twine, R.T. (2001) 'Ma(r)king essence: ecofeminism and embodiment', *Ethics and the Environment* 6(2): 31–58.

Twine, R.T. (n.d.) 'Masculinity, nature, ecofeminism', *Ecofem.org/journal*, available at http://richardtwine.com/ecofem/masc.pdf (accessed April 2012).

Warren, K. (2000) *Ecofeminist Philosophy: A Western Perspective on What It Is and Why It Matters*, Lanham, MD: Rowman & Littlefield.

Wittneben, B.F., Okereke, C., Banerjee, S.B. and Levy, D.L. (2012) 'Climate change and the emergence of new organizational landscapes', *Organization Studies* 33(11): 1431–1450.

Witz, A. (2000) 'Whose body matters? Feminist sociology and the corporeal turn in sociology and feminism', *Body & Society* 6(1): 1–24.

# 4 Regeneration in limbo

## Ecofeminist perspectives on the multiple crisis and social contract

*Adelheid Biesecker and Uta von Winterfeld*

> The non-monetary but regenerative activities of this hitherto nameless class are entirely necessary for the global economy to function.
>
> (Ariel Salleh 2009: 6)

### Introduction

That the capitalist world is experiencing a crisis has been made clear through recent tumultuous economic events which have resulted in it being conceptualized as a multiple crisis. The term highlights how the global economic or financial crisis is also an ecological crisis of climate, natural resources and carrying capacity; a social crisis involving the retreat of welfare states and social coherence or solidarity; and a political crisis of state management or governance (Demirović et al. 2011; Salleh 2009). From a feminist perspective, the notion of multiple crisis inevitably leads us to focus on the crisis of work – understood as integrating the 'productive' work included within the market and 'reproductive' work that takes place outside. The crisis of reproductive work is a central point in feminist analysis of the multiple crisis (see Wichterich 2011).

In Germany, a 'Social Contract for Sustainability' (WBGU et al. 2011) is proposed as a solution to the ecological crisis, and especially that relating to climate change. Hence the reaction to the multiple crisis is to construct a social contract. This is the starting point of our argument which sees the social contract as part of the crisis but, if re-cast, as potentially part of a sustainable solution. However, in opposition to the Wissenschaftlicher Beirat der Bundesregierung Globale Umweltveränderungen (WBGU; German Advisory Council on Global Change), we will discuss the ecological crisis as an integral part of the multiple crisis which, in our opinion, must be seen as a crisis of regeneration of nature and social reproduction. A new social contract therefore has to include a new concept of work as important to the process of social reproduction.

Our feminist analysis of the multiple crisis and the concept of a social contract is founded on a critique of domination based in three central principles:

- alienation and reification;
- dualism, separation and identification;
- instrumentalism and objectification.

In the background of our argument is the Marxian critique of capitalism where people are alienated from one another and from their human nature, and where social relations between them are transformed into relations of exchange of commodities, a process which Marx calls reification. The first feminist ingredient is Carole Pateman's critical deconstruction of the classical theory of social contract proposed by philosophers such as Thomas Hobbes and John Locke and set out in her book *The Sexual Contract* (1988). Though not necessarily ecofeminist, her analysis is helpful for understanding the problems associated with social contracts. According to her, classical theory tells only half the story because the implicit sexual contract is ignored in that women are excluded from the original contract *and* incorporated into the new contractual order. The defining quality of this social contract, then, is the *separating inclusion* of women. This *separating inclusion* is constituted through dualisms such as nature and society, private and public sphere (separating women from the latter), and productive and reproductive work. This produces a concept of the individual which is identified with a male central political actor and, at the same time, instrumentalizes and objectifies women's bodies and labour. Though all people are pictured as 'naturally free and equal', contract theorists insist that men's right to dominate women has a natural basis (Pateman 1988: 41).

Pateman's concept of the individual leads to our second feminist foundation: Val Plumwood's (1991, 2002) ecofeminist analysis of the human self within the classical theories. In her discussion of the relation between human and nature, she makes clear that the main problem lies in the concept of the human self as disconnected from nature. We also refer to Ariel Salleh and her concept of ecological debt as embodied debt.

And finally, the quotation from Salleh (2009) with which this chapter opens signals the basis of our analysis. This is a feminist perspective that locates the primary cause of the multiple crisis in the structural separation between 'productive' and 'reproductive' in economic, political and societal systems. This structural separation is also consolidated by the social contract (Biesecker and von Winterfeld 2014). From our perspective of domination, this dualistic structure of modern capitalist societies is multi-faceted. Here we refer to Nancy Fraser's new interpretation of Polanyi's concept of *double movement* (characterizing the relationship between market and society) in *The Great Transformation* (Fraser 2012), where she makes clear that this double movement has to be developed to include emancipation, and is thus a triple movement.

Based on the perspectives of these feminist scholars, we have formulated our main idea as follows: the core of the multiple crisis as social, ecological, economic, financial and political crisis is the crisis of the so-called reproductive – nature with its regenerative power and unpaid work outside the market. A social contract is not the solution to the multiple crisis, but part of the problem while it fails to overcome the structure of *separating inclusion* and ecological embodied debt and the concept of an autonomous individual or self – and thus cannot ensure gender equity.

To further clarify this main idea, we first develop our analysis of multiple crisis as a crisis of the reproductive. The economic structure of separation as well as the role of capital as a social power relation will be made visible. Based on Carole Pateman's work, we then discuss the basic structure of the modern social contract to point to its main weakness – the 'separating inclusion' of women. Here we also refer to Val Plumwood's critique of the separated self (1991) which is part of all classical conceptions of social contract. She proposes a relational account of the human being as a foundation for a new social contract for sustainability. We continue with ecofeminist approaches to political economy and political ecology to show how inclusive separation works as externalization (e.g. in the form of debts) and the solutions that are proposed. The relation between the transformation process and the social contract is discussed in the final section through the example of the WBGU's 'Social Contract for Sustainability'. Here we investigate the ideas of man, nature and work, of policy and economy as well as of emancipation, and present our conclusions.

## Multiple crisis as a crisis of the reproductive

The concept of multiple crisis elucidates the broad character of crisis but does not clarify its origins. Here we offer an explanation. Our point of departure is, as Nancy Fraser's, the structure of modern capitalist economies and democracies. We share her view that this structure is characterized by separation: economically distinguishing the *productive* and the *reproductive*; politically divorcing the public (democratic) and the private (domestic) sphere. Very narrow definitions of the economy as well as of the political sphere follow from this structural separation. The economy is identified only with self-regulating markets, and work only with paid work performed to produce commodities and services for and within the market. This work is embedded into a production system that transforms resources into waste – with growing speed. It is unsustainable work which demonstrates that a new social contract for a sustainable world needs a new, sustainable concept of work. Only paid work, with a value represented by a wage, is considered as gainful employment and as productive. But this is only half of the story. Work such as caring work to sustain human life, voluntary work for the benefit of society, or work to enhance individual or group political engagement is predominantly outside the market. This work is seen as unproductive, or at best as reproductive. Nature and the 'work' of nature is similarly regarded such that both are externalized from the economic sphere.

This externalization is an intrinsic characteristic of the capitalist economy such that we speak about 'externalization as principle'. It points to the invisible and unvalued 'shadow' of paid work. But markets, including job markets, could not exist without this shadow. They depend on this unvalued social and care work and the ecological 'resources' of nature. 'Externalization as principle' involves a hierarchy whereby the market stands above the non-market sphere and because unpaid care work is mostly done by women, it also entails hierarchal gender relations. The consequence of this 'externalization as principle' is the multiple crisis that we have described, and it now becomes clear that this crisis is, at its very core, a crisis of the 'reproductive'. Modern economies produce wealth and growth by systemically destroying the basic living productivities on which growth depends so that these economies, with their narrow concept of paid work, are not sustainable.

The same is true for the political sphere because only the public sphere is subject to democratic control and regulation. The capitalist character of the economy becomes apparent not only through the guiding principle of profit maximization, but also and foremost by the alienation of people and reification of their social relations. This is Marx's *commodity fetish*; workers sell their labour power as a commodity to capitalists who control working conditions and appropriate products and profits. Thus the workers are alienated from their products. All specific qualities of labour are converted into a quantitative equivalent, the value of commodities for exchange on the market. The qualitative variety of various forms of labour as well as the class relation between workers and capitalists are obscured. People are not related to each other as members of the human race and of civil society, but only as owners of commodities, only in exchange. That is the exclusive social relationship they have. The core of the commodity fetish is that the mutual relations of the producers 'take the form of a social relation between the products' (Marx 1867/1972: 86, own translation). Capital as a power relation seems to have disappeared.

Though production always needs the *reproductive* element, it has no value for actors in the market economy. No human production process can happen without the previous productive input of nature; and it cannot happen without previous processes of caring, mostly provided by women. Capitalist production is not possible without the exploitation of these externalized regenerative forces originating from the life-world. And the same is true for the political realm; the public sphere always needs the *private* as its foundation, but the private sphere has no voice. The consequence is the ongoing damage and destruction of the regenerative and the private sphere.

Rosa Luxemburg (1981/1925) discussed this dualistic structure of capitalism in detail. For her, the externalized forces are foundational conditions of vital importance for the capitalist system. She highlights that the relation between the two spheres – the 'productive' and the 'reproductive' – is a relation of domination, and she reveals the role of political power in altering and reforming the boundaries between the two spheres. In her words, political influence is only 'a vehicle of the economic process' (Luxemburg 1981/1913: 397–98, own translation). While Luxemburg sees the dualistic structure as capitalist versus non-capitalist, feminist theory has since built on this distinction to emphasize that the two sides of the dualism are integral parts of the capitalist system. From a feminist perspective, the process of the accumulation of capital can be seen as an ongoing process of changing the boundaries between these two spheres and of redefining what is considered as 'internal' and as 'external' (for an overview see Biesecker and von Winterfeld 2014).

By making explicit the definition of 'internal' (economic and political realms) and 'external' (reproductive and private spheres), the importance of 'identification' becomes apparent. At the same time, instrumentalism and objectification are taken into account by analysing the function of identification as inclusion and exclusion. By drawing on the rhetoric of public myths and prejudices, identification excludes and stigmatizes certain groups as *others* (Hirschman 1991). For example, cuts in welfare benefits are legitimized by stigmatizing some sections of the population as lazy parasites and as objects of anger (*scroungers* in the UK or *welfare moms* in the USA). The victim is blamed, rather than neoliberal social policies and politics being critiqued. However, such boundaries define the 'external'. The capitalist economic sphere therefore needs unvalued work and resources for new processes of evaluation, for creating value in the first place. They are appropriated in an instrumental way and as silent objects. Moreover, the political sphere is often reactive in trying to create a facilitating environment for capitalist economic activities and not for citizens. At its core, the multiple crisis is a crisis of the basic reproductive forces of the capitalist society and its economy. The phenomena which are associated with the ecological crisis (e.g. loss of natural productivity and of biodiversity, scarcity of food, resources and energy, climate change) are phenomena of the capitalist appropriation of nature. And the phenomena which are associated with the social crisis (e.g. lack of provision and care, welfare state crisis, the problem of overwork and low-paid, flexible and reproductive work, child poverty) are phenomena of the capitalist appropriation of reproductive work as well as of shaping politically public infrastructures.

Moreover, even the financial crisis can be seen as a *reproductive* crisis. Here the target of exploitation is the real economy. For instance, companies are destroyed when bought and then sliced up and sold for short-term profits by hedge funds and other financial speculators. Speculative behaviour like this caused the debt crisis. It leads to the installation of over-capacity and supply-side economics, and a weakening of the demand side which includes reallocation of production, wage dumping and a downgrading of the welfare state. The general conclusion to be drawn is that there is an indissoluble friction between the profit motive and regeneration.

As a result, modern capitalist economies produce wealth and growth by systemically destroying the basic natural and social productive resources for this growth. Systemically, those economies create products and processes which are not sustainable. Modern economic policies are focused on gaining or preserving power and deal only with a narrow time frame. They are concerned with supporting the globalization of national capital, often against the public will (as a recent example see the negotiations about the free-trade agreement [Transatlantic Trade and Investment Partnership, TTIP] between the EU and the USA). Expressions of the crisis of representation, a parliamentary crisis, are low voter turnouts, and loss of confidence and legitimacy. Consequences are nationalism, racism and the danger of a new authoritarian state, a Hobbesian 'Leviathan'. Systematically, economic practices and policies create societies which are not sustainable. Proposed solutions to these problems often tend to intensify the multiple crisis because they are based in the same rationality that caused the crisis in the first place. As examples we can point to the commercialization of nature to solve the biodiversity crisis, or the development of agrofuels which created a new crisis of food scarcity instead of solving gaps in energy supply and climate change. We also highlight the development of global care chains to solve the care crisis in the Global North, which shifts the care crisis to the bottom of the chain in the Global South.

Such global care chains are part of a restructuring of gender relations that is an element of the multiple crisis. According to Christa Wichterich, the multiple crisis can be seen as a reconfiguration of economic gender roles under neoliberal conditions, as a new gender-related international division of labour (Wichterich 2011). The erosion of the male breadwinner model is accompanied by a growing responsibility placed on women for a substantial contribution to the family wage. Despite these changes, the hierarchal structure of gender relations stays intact. Wichterich goes on to distinguish between two particular crises: the crisis of paid work and the crisis of the care economy. Here we observe that new boundaries and a new definition of *internal* and *external* are drawn. The crisis of paid work is characterized by a reduction of availability of normal employment and by a growth of informal and non-permanent labour contracts. Wichterich calls this the 'feminization of paid work' (Wichterich 2011: 133, own translation). Symptoms of this particular crisis include precarious work, vulnerable work (in which 52 per cent of women are engaged), and the growth of the working poor (60 per cent of whom are women) (ibid.: 132) – which can be seen as a form of outsourcing from paid to unpaid or underpaid work. This means that the increase in female labour force participation signifies not emancipation but integration under the ever-worsening conditions of the capitalist labour market. Here again we draw attention to Polanyi, who has categorically warned against this transformation of work and nature to commodities whereby the capabilities to regenerate are destroyed. For Polanyi this means the destruction of humanity and nature (Polanyi 1944, and see note 1 below).

The crisis of the care economy is based on a crisis of public debt, especially in the Global North. This leads to privatization with a consequential shift of public and paid care work towards more unpaid care work for women. In the global context, the crisis of care work finds its expression, as already mentioned, in global care chains. This leads to a global shift of care work from South to North and from East to West. This reinforces what Ariel Salleh calls 'the *embodied debt* owed North and South to unpaid reproductive workers who provide use values and regenerate the conditions of production, including the future labour force of capitalism' (Salleh 2009: 5).

## What's wrong with the social contract and what's wrong with the individual?

A society with an economic and a political system which leads systemically to non-sustainability must be founded on the wrong set of constitutional principles. In the history of political thought this general constitutional con-struction has been called the social contract (Reitzig 2005). Therefore, drawing on the critical approach taken by Carol Pateman, we ask what is wrong with this contract? As we will see, the various concepts of the social contract are based on very particular views of nature and man and the relation between them. The latter is the main focus of ecofeminist philosopher Val Plum-wood's academic work. Referring to her concept of the self-in-relationship (Plumwood 1991), we then discuss this specific approach to the individual combined with a variety of conceptions of social contract and with the prospect of a sustainable future.

### What's wrong with the social contract?

In the 1970s, the philosopher John Rawls formulated his influential theory of justice within the framework of political social contract theory (Rawls 1999/1971). In the 1980s, Carole Pateman presented her analysis of the social contract as a sexual contract (Pateman 1988). Recently, the WBGU has argued that sustainability and sustainable transformation *need* to be founded on a new social contract (WBGU et al. 2011). A broader view of the origins of the multiple crises and the present-day debate about a new social contract has to reflect on the structure of the social contract and to ask: what is a social contract? And, why do we need it?

The story of the social contract tells us how a new civil society and a new form of political rights and political order are created through an original constitutional agreement. This original contract is a fiction (contract *theory*). It is situated at the threshold from a 'state of nature' to a 'civil society'. Each theorist has a concept of the state of nature which corresponds to his idea of civil society, which includes a particular view of the human individual. For Thomas Hobbes, the *state of nature* is a state of war – each against the other – that calls for a strong state: the Leviathan. According to John Locke, the state of nature is a state of peace. Nature is God's gift and is common property. However, this state of nature is without progress so that if people want to live comfortably, they need private property. Today, contract theory is about justice (John Rawls) and about transformation: sustainable transformation *needs* a new social contract. But in criticizing their implicit domination perspective, Carole Pateman's analysis points to important problems of these contractarian positions. First, men's freedom and women's subjugation are both created by the original contract (Pateman 1988: 2). The contract establishes men's political rights over women and also sexual rights in the sense of establishing orderly access by men to women's bodies (ibid.). Second, patriarchal civil society is divided into two spheres, but the story is only about the creation of the public sphere and of civil freedom. The private sphere is not considered as politically relevant (ibid.: 3). Third, the subject of all contract theories is a specific kind of property and individuals are defined as owners of their personal traits (body, mind, talents etc.). However, only male beings are endowed with the attributes and capacities necessary to enter into contracts so only men are *individuals* (ibid.: 5, 6). For example, John Locke argues that every man has ownership of himself as a person. In these ways, the contract always generates political rights in the form of relations of domination and subordination (ibid.: 8). Moreover, the order of the *natural* (natural state) excludes the *civil* and vice versa (ibid.: 11) such that the principle of identification – of inclusion and exclusion – is again applied.

The story has further complications. Women are *excluded* from the original contract, but *incorporated* into the new order. Women have no active part in the original contract, but their alignment with the state of nature is required in order to give meaning to the public sphere. The private, womanly sphere (natural) and the masculine public sphere (civil) are opposed but derive their meaning from each other. This separating inclusion is necessary because the identity formation of what civil society and the new political order *is* needs the counterpart of what it *is not*. What it means to be an *individual*, a party to contracts and civilly free is constituted in contrast to the subjugation of women within the private sphere (ibid.: 11).

To understand the labour and marriage contracts as sexual contracts, it is necessary to see and analyse them as connected. Carole Pateman emphasizes in her examination of 'Wives, slaves and wage slaves':

> The father and his family wage, not the mother, provided the necessary subsistence to maintain children. The political economists were thus able to see the mother's labours as 'the raw material on which economic forces acted, the elements of nature with which human [i.e., civil] societies were built'. The father/breadwinner gained 'the status of value-creator'. Or, to make the point a different way, men as wage labourers share in the masculine capacity to create and nurture new political life.
>
> (Pateman 1988: 138)

The story of the social contract expresses a specifically masculine creative power; the capacity to generate and give birth to new forms of political life (ibid.: 220). At this point, we find yet another reason for the regenerative crisis because the masculine is understood as *Homo faber* or as a generating individual, in neglect of regeneration and in separation from the regenerative sphere.

Freedom as guaranteed by the social contract is enjoyed by all *individuals*. But a curious and ambivalent message is sent out to women, who represent everything the individual is *not*. The *individual* is constructed as a male body so that its identity is always masculine (ibid.: 221, 223). In this context, Carole Pateman criticizes the version of the state of nature within the theory of justice of John Rawls. Rawls constructs a 'veil of ignorance' to represent the state of nature such that nobody knows his own situation and position and so the contract has to take account of the situation and position of the weakest members of society. In this way, a social contract of justice emerges. But: 'In effect, as Rawls' version of the state of nature shows, there is only one individual, duplicated endlessly. How the duplication takes place is a mystery' (ibid.: 223); moreover, as a rational and disembodied entity, it is male. Therefore, as such a contract can only conceive of an individual as male, it is part of the sexual contract.

The meaning of the *individual* remains intact only as long as the dichotomies integral to civil society between natural and civil, private and public, women and individual, remain intact (ibid.: 225). If men's mastery is to be replaced by the mutual autonomy of women and men, individual freedom must be limited by the structure of social relations in which freedom inheres (ibid.: 232). When the repressed story of the political genesis of the social contract is brought to the surface, the political landscape can never look the same again (ibid.: 233). Carole Pateman's conclusion, therefore, is unequivocal: 'A free social order cannot be a contractual order' (ibid.: 232).

This would undermine all suggestions of a new social contract (for sustainability or for sustainable transformation) as unavoidably contaminated by domination so that the social contract appears to be part of the problem, and not a solution to the multiple crises. Three other arguments support this conclusion. The first additional flaw is that the men who agreed to the original contract are *white* men. Therefore their *fraternal* pact is a social contract, a sexual contract *and* a *slave contract* (legitimizing the rule of white over black) (ibid.: 222). The second of Pateman's arguments is based on a critique of Hegel's philosophy of right. Hegel criticizes Jean-Jacques Rousseau's social contract theory and Immanuel Kant's marriage contract. But Hegel also claims that women are naturally lacking 'in the capacity to submit to the demands of universality' (ibid.: 176). Starting from his *natural* difference principle, Pateman reconstructs Hegel's point of view: 'Women are what they are by nature; men must create themselves and public life, and they are endowed with the masculine capacity to do so' (ibid.). Finally, *nature* is not only represented by women but also, for example, by land, indigenous peoples, the descendants of the slaves and animals (ibid.: 226). Pateman's analysis is not just historical, revealing a phenomenon of the past. She argues that the simultaneous denial and affirmation of the freedom of women fostered by

contract theorists is continually reconstructed because freedom as autonomy
is still coupled with sexual domination (ibid.: 230).

Up to now we are not sure if we should accept Pateman's conclusion that
a free social order cannot be a contractual order. To further develop our
position, we want to formulate three questions to consider, to develop
contemporary approaches to concepts of a social contract.

- What about the idea of man and work – is it still an idea of *man*, an
  individual conceived as masculine and 'productive'?
- What about the idea of nature – is it inseparably linked to instrumentalism
  and objectification?
- What is the understanding of the economy and policy within new contractual approaches, and what is the relationship between the two
  spheres?

For answers to the third question we already have at our disposal some
material provided by Nancy Fraser and our own analysis of the capitalist
structure. As already mentioned, Fraser offers a new interpretation of Polanyi's
work. Polanyi analyses the development of capitalism as processes of 'dis-
embedding' markets from nature and society and of 'reembedding' them
politically, and of commodification averted by social protection (Fraser 2012).
Fraser places an emphasis on the structure of modern societies. Referring to
Hegel's statement that the sphere of contractual relations (the market sphere)
is based on non-contractual relations (the non-market sphere), she finds the
roots of the capitalist crisis in the ongoing 'fictitious commodification', as
Polanyi called it, of the non-market sphere by which capitalism undermines
and destroys its own basis.[1] For Fraser, it is necessary to connect 'a structural
critique of fictitious commodification to a critique of domination' (Fraser
2012: 12). She criticizes Polanyi for implicitly valuing embedded markets as
'good' and disembedded ones as 'bad' such that he does not see that the
political sphere as well as the economic sphere is a realm of domination. She
therefore argues that there are three targets for social movements: 'Not just
marketization and social protection, but also emancipation' (Fraser 2012: 9). In
an earlier paper, she makes clear that:

> Present day critical theorists must revise this framework. Avoiding both
> wholesale condemnation of disembedding and wholesale approbation of
> reembedding, we must open both marketization and social protection to
> critical scrutiny. Exposing the normative deficits of society, as well as
> those of economy, we must validate struggles against domination *wherever*
> it roots.
>
> (Fraser 2011: 144)

To think about a new social contract for sustainability therefore means to
rethink the role of 'struggles for emancipation' (ibid.); and to include a new

sexual contract as part of the new social contract especially means to take note of feminist struggles. However, the questions about the concept of the individual and its relation to nature, the first and second questions we posed above, still require a response.

### What's wrong with the individual and its relation to nature?

As we have seen, a lot is wrong with the social contract. And we shall add: a lot is also wrong with the concept of the individual that underpins the contractual order. This foundational concept for the classical theories of the social contract fits in with the structural dualism of capitalist societies. The individual with its defined attributes belongs to the market sphere and to the public sphere. It is characterized by masculinity, and it is disconnected from nature and from social relations. This individual is conceptualized as an autonomous self. Its economic form is *Homo œconomicus*: a solitary individual, related only to the world of commodities to satisfy its wants. It maximizes its own satisfaction. To pursue this single-minded goal, it acts rationally. It is dominated by the fetish character of commodities – alienated from its human nature, related to others only in a contractual manner as a buyer or seller of commodities.

The critique of this concept of the individual and the related concept of rationality is at the centre of Val Plumwood's work. For her, 'rationalism is the key to the connected oppression of women and nature in the West' (Plumwood 1991: 3). The particular and the emotional are seen as enemies of this kind of rationality. Plumwood regards 'the definition of the human self as separate from nature, the connection between this and the instrumental view of nature, and broader political aspects of the critique of instrumentalism' as the overall problem (ibid.: 10). This instrumental reason, she argues, perceives others only as *resources*. They are valued not for their own sake, but for their effects in producing gratification. In her last book (Plumwood 2002) she emphasizes again and again that this form of rationality is highly irrational. For her, the main cause for the destruction of the natural world must be seen in the incapability of those 'rational' individuals to accept nature as it is, and not only as an instrument for human life. And she develops her own improved concept of rationality, where rationality is not only a principle of acting and thinking, but a specific form of life, 'a matter of balance, harmony, and reconcilability among an organism's identities, faculties and ends, a harmony that has regard to the kind of being as it is' (Plumwood 2002: 67).

For Plumwood, the ethical foundation for such a notion of rationality is the ethic of care: 'The ethic of care and responsibility ... seems to extend much less problematically to the nonhuman world than do the impersonal concepts ... and it also seems capable of providing an excellent basis for the non-instrumental treatment of nature' (Plumwood 1991: 9). Based on these two philosophical concepts (rationality as a form of life and the ethic of care), Plumwood can formulate her alternative concept of the individual – a relational account: 'we must see human beings and their interests as *essentially* related and interdependent' (ibid.: 20). She regards nature not as an external element but as a part of our identity. 'On this relational account, respect for the other ... is an *expression* of self in relationship, not egoistic self as merged with the other but self as embedded in a network of essential relationships with distinct others' (ibid.). This self in relationship is no longer characterized by masculinity, but by qualities currently constructed as feminine. It is capable of caring for others – for other people today and in the future as well as for nature. Sustainability requires such a concept of human beings and their interests as essentially related and interdependent.

Sustainability also requires us to look at the 'costs of "othering" bodies and ecosystems' (Salleh 2009: ix). Salleh's notion of eco-sufficiency from the perspective of global and gender justice is the task not just of ecology-minded consumers, but of all economic, political and social actors. Eco-sufficiency means 'cancel the debt': namely the social debt (capitalistic exploitation of labour); the ecological debt (Northern exploitation of Southern 'natural means of production or livelihood of non-industrial peoples', Salleh 2009: 4, 5); and the embodied debt (exploitation of unpaid reproductive workers). Following Salleh and others, ecofeminism is an 'environmentalism of the poor' (ibid.: 291), recognizing that poverty, including an inability to save for contingencies, is the result of unvaluing regenerative labour. From this perspective, eco-sufficiency is not the duty to consume less, but the right to a surplus of the poorest who are struggling for survival. This concept of eco-sufficiency refers strongly to the regenerative labour of the global majority; that of 'indigenous, peasant and care-giving workers' (ibid.: 291) who Salleh calls meta-industrial workers: 'Meta-industrial provisioning is eco-sufficient because it does not externalize costs through debt' (ibid.: 303).

## Consequences for social–ecological transformation processes – a new social contract?

In our introduction, we mentioned a German approach that links the construction of a new social contract to the social–ecological transformation process. This proposal for a social contract for sustainability is a reaction to the multiple crisis, especially to climate change. The necessary reforms to meet this crisis are meant 'to go far beyond technological and technocratic reforms: the business of society must be founded on a new "business basis". *This is, in fact, all about a new global social contract for a low-carbon and sustainable global economic system*' (WBGU et al. 2011: 1, italics in original).

To further develop our position regarding the concept of a social contract and its possible role in the transformation process, we come back to Pateman's conclusion that a free social order cannot be a contractual order, and to our three questions for timely approaches to the social contract: the questions about the idea of man and work, the concept of nature, and the understanding of the economic and political system. We start with the idea of man and work as it is detailed in the flagship report of the German Advisory Council on Global Change (WBGU).

This idea corresponds to the main concern of the Advisory Council: a climate-compatible society. People are 'quite capable of reducing the degree of their own spontaneous first-tier desires (short-term preferences) in favour of second-tier desires' (WBGU et al. 2011: 80); in other words, they are capable of committing to cooperation and to develop a precautionary attitude. However, the Advisory Council's construction of 'man' is conflicted and ambiguous; at times an enlightened citizen, at others a pioneer or as an abstract concept that cannot be recognized as a human individual. Moreover, 'Homo œconomicus' is lurking when the council explains the gap between attitude and actual behaviour: 'long-term oriented decisions are accompanied by higher costs in the short-term than exclusively short-term oriented decisions' (ibid.: 78). But overall the flagship report does not tell us anything about actual human beings or concrete persons and it does not tell us anything about working people inside and outside the market. There are change agents, and there are many stories about engineers, urban planners and architects. These change agents could be part of a resistance movement like the Black Forest 'electricity rebels' from Schönau, or enterprises like Deutsche Bahn (the German national railway company) or the technical large-scale project DESERTEC. Human actors remain abstract and without contours. They are sexless transformation agents (mostly mentioned in a rhetoric of 'best practice'), but not real people and not individuals. These change agents are first and foremost designed in an instrumental and objectifying way – only insofar as they correspond to the transformation concerns of the Advisory Council. Detail is largely absent because the whole report is written on a very high level of abstraction. Real people in their daily life and engaged in social movements are not on the radar.

Our inference is that this kind of new social contract tends to reproduce old rationales (see also Biesecker and von Winterfeld 2013) and, because throughout the whole report nothing is said about working processes, we see the danger that the old concept of work with its hierarchical gender relations will be part of the new social contract. A notion of sustainability that includes this old concept of work is inherently unsustainable, as we have seen. To bring about change, we need instead to listen to the stories of daily life and social movements, told by and made up of real people, engaged in market and non-market activities. They are making small and concrete new social contracts. These stories and movements also make clear that sustainability means to overcome 'externalization as principle'. For the concept of work, it means to integrate the 'productive' and the 'reproductive' work as well as the capabilities of nature to regenerate. The principle of care, then, would replace the current hegemonic principle of profit-maximization.

Now we can return to and answer our three questions – the idea of man and work; the idea of nature; the understanding of the economy and policy. The *idea of man and work* has to be changed qualitatively if caring activities are central to a new concept of work. Caring means working in relationships to others and to nature, as Plumwood has made clear. It means a caring concern not only for the present but also for the future, which is understood as the present of next generations. It encompasses responsibility because participants are not co-present. This also means responsibility for the consequences of our actions. From this it follows that the concept of work in a sustainable society (understood, now, as 'reproductive' and 'productive' work) must take into account the long-term consequences for nature, and that products and processes must be designed that enhance natural and social regeneration. Such an understanding of work would also address the contradiction between 'work' and 'nature' such that workers are no longer played off against nature. In this concept of work, everybody can participate in all fields of work. No field is better than another. The experiences of every woman and man in all spheres of work are necessary for the further development of the reproductive process. This also means to surrender the model of the human being as manlike, as egoistic and autonomous. Sustainable work is based on the concept of self in relationship, and in this sense on equity between genders.

The *idea of nature* is currently linked to instrumentalism and objectification because nature is seen as a resource and as an object of human activities. The concept of nature, and therefore the basis for the new social contract in the report, is the anthropocene: 'the geological age in which the detrimental effects of human actions on the environment have reached a dimension that is comparable to natural influences' (WGBU et al. 2011: 62). This concept is important for emphasizing the responsibility of human beings. But it is still based on a strict separation of humans from nature. Human beings influence nature – and they do this in such a way that nature as nature disappears. There is no nature then, there are only effects of human influence and action, only raw materials, nutrient cycles, resources, pollutants, energy carriers and so on. Our analysis shows that the idea of the anthropocene and non-nature implies once again instrumental and objectifying attitudes. It fails with regard to an alternative human and social relationship to nature, a relationship where nature is not disconnected from human beings. In social movements for sustainability we find such nature-connected individuals. They struggle to establish a new human–nature relation where nature's capability of regeneration can be sustained. Again, we interpret these activities as an approach to small and concrete new social contracts.

The *understanding of the economy and policy* leads us back to the beginning of our chapter – to concepts of the economy and of the political realm. There we have made clear that, because of the structure of separation, the multiple crises are, at their very core, a crisis of the regenerative forces: namely nature's ability to regenerate, and caring activities outside the market. Based on Marx, we have shown that actors in the capitalist market sphere are dominated by alienation and reification. With the help of Fraser, who refers to Polanyi, we have criticized the tendency toward fictitious commodification and have highlighted the importance of struggles for emancipation and their relevance for the transformation process towards sustainability. Sustainability needs a different kind of rationality from the profit-oriented rationality of capitalism – a caring rationality with a long-term perspective.

Looking at the economic concept of the Advisory Council, we often find the expression 'precautionary principle' (e.g. WBGU et al. 2011: 5, 95, 102, 106, 107, 271, 328). This seems to refer to a long-term perspective, but neither the identification of the economy only with markets nor structural separation is challenged. The economy will be transformed into a climate-friendly system, but this will happen within the old behavioural model of profit-orientation. To encourage and accelerate investments into a low-carbon future (ibid.: 15–16), the Council asks for a stable framework for climate-friendly investments 'to raise the rate of return in investments ... and to minimise the risk' (ibid.: 15). Moreover, new business models will be encouraged. Instead of embedding or restricting markets, the fictitious commodification of nature is continued. But it was exactly this profit-oriented system that led to climate change being part of the multiple crises in the first place. The Advisory Council's approach to solving this crisis is based on the same rationality that caused it. Polanyi, to whom the Advisory Council also refers, has developed an alternative vision of a society where nature, labour and money are withdrawn from the market sphere. He speaks about 'the end of the market economy' (Polanyi 1944/1978: 339, own translation). His vision, therefore, is a new social contract with *a different kind of* economy.

Some social movements today have already begun to develop such an alternative kind of economy: for instance, the new commons movement, the movement for energy-autonomous regions, the movement for a joint economy and for other concepts of work. Here new economic rules are emerging, such as the common good instead of private property, cooperation instead of competition, caring for others and for nature instead of maximizing one's self-interested utility. Again, we interpret these movements as an approach to small and concrete new social contracts.

Part of these new contracts are new 'labour contracts' because time is needed for caring processes, for civil engagement, for cooperative processes with nature and its special temporal structure and rhythms. Barbara Adam has made clear that the quality of working time is up for discussion:

> In the context of working time and the challenge of work time reduction, sustainability takes on a particular meaning. It encompasses not just the quantity but also the quality of working time, not just the commodity but also the lived complexity. It involves combining into a coherent whole the incompatible time systems that currently stress and stretch our lives beyond endurance ... Working time understood in its economic, social and environmental complexity would therefore be the starting point from which we could begin to take account of the temporal needs

at all these levels and address current inequalities embedded therein. As such it would be an essential first step on the long path to sustainable work.

(Adam 2013: 38–39)

Here, organizations as actors in the transformation process towards sustainability come into sight. Small new social contracts about the change in the quality and quantity of working time are contracts between single workers or trade unions on one hand and organizations on the other. Sustainable organizations have to care for the social reproduction of their labour force as well as regeneration of the resources from nature that they use. New and complex time structures are central means to reach these targets.

Looking at the relationship between the political and the economic spheres, the Advisory Council admits that the whole social order is subject to economic principles such as cost–benefit analysis (ibid.: 67, 68). The Advisory Council concludes that the 'Great Transformation' needs a strong, organizing and 'Proactive State with Extended Opportunities for Participation' (ibid.: 203 f.). This sounds almost Polanyian – but there are some problematic unquestioned assumptions. First, some signs of crisis of 'democracy' are admitted, but democratization is regarded as an evolutionary process with a general trend worldwide towards it still in place (ibid.: 51, 52). This evolutionary perspective influences the idea of the state as both 'promoting and demanding'; for example, promoting the capabilities and potential of the jobless while demanding their willingness to work. Second, the concept of a proactive state includes an agenda 'from welfare to workfare' based on 'repressive inclusion', as we have called it. This proactive and therefore more interventionist state is a 'new statehood' ideal of the Advisory Council which:

> must be offset by 'more' citizen involvement in the form of a new social contract ... The key aspect of this (virtual) contract is that it confers rights and obligations to government and civil society actors by giving them responsibility for the ecological future with a view to common welfare goals and global collective goods.

(ibid.: 204)

We deduce that if the separating inclusion of women and the sexual contract are still at work, and furthermore completed by a repressive inclusion of the new proactive state, there is no chance for real participation or for a genuinely new social contract.

## Conclusion

Here we want to re-emphasize our three domination principles: alienation and reification; dualism, separation and identification; instrumentalism and objectification. From the perspective of *alienation and reification* we have to add that the critique of the egoistic self at the core of liberal individualism, as well as the critique of instrumental reason formulated by Val Plumwood, highlights the fundamental human alienation from nature. This alienation affects women as well as men. In addition, Carol Pateman has clarified another dimension of alienation for women in that they are alienated from *and* familiar with the new political order of the social contract because of the mechanism of separating inclusion. They are alienated from themselves by their economic and also by their political role. Equality gains do not solve this problem. If women want to take part, they have to participate in the new market order which is an implicit part of the political order, as we can show based on Thomas Hobbes. Within his state of nature as a state of war, individuals are fighting against each other because they compete for scarce goods. Hobbes' *Leviathan* does not undermine competition but guarantees suitable conditions (such as safety) for the emerging market society. Within this Hobbesian society, people are socially dispossessed: insular individuals with no social capabilities. They are reduced to an instrumental manner, and *Homo oeconomicus* is always looking for objects to satisfy his selfish wants and to enlarge his benefits and the other's disadvantages.

The economic order follows the principle and pattern of *dualism, separation and identification* as the economy is identified only with *separated* markets and human actors only as owners of commodities. The expansion of such an economy is causing the political order to take up a defensive position where states and politics are reacting to economic principles rather than forming policy on political principles. The state is intentionally shrinking the public sphere and growing the private sphere, and both empirically and with the advent of neoliberalism this is evident in the shrinking of public goods and growing private goods since the 1980s. The framework of identification, the differentiation between self and other, 'good' and 'bad', is strengthened in the current rationale for the existence of the state. It can be seen in the weakening of social policy and the welfare state and in the distinctions made between 'legitimate' and 'failed' states that are the focus of foreign and security policies. This is also the shadowing of the other.

Ariel Salleh (2009) demonstrates that an alternative concept of eco-sufficiency is necessary for overcoming or at least modifying the domination principle of *instrumentalism and objectification*. Within the practice of social, ecological and embodied debt, the instrumental and objectifying use of work and nature as means for others cannot be changed by ceasing to purchase, but only by ceasing to contract debts. This calls for a change in perspective from that of the market, of the abstract rational individual, of those who have power. The new perspective is the perspective of life-world, of women and men in contexts, of diversity. It is the perspective of the heretofore 'invisible' which is then made visible (O'Hara 2009: 184 ff.), especially by new methodological principles of valuation. In the old perspective, valuation means to use 'objective' measures such as GDP. But this objectification ignores the non-measurable aspects of the economics of daily life outside the market.

'Instead, the acceptance of context is a vote for detailed empirical observation, historical awareness ... This implies ... the often invisible expertise of locals ... the effective representation of situated agents' (ibid.: 189). 'Methods reflect power structure', writes Sabine O'Hara (ibid.: 187), and objectivity strengthens the structure of separation.

Relating our three domination principles to our questions regarding the social contract, we therefore want to mention another criterion of domination: a high level of abstraction and the absence of concrete individuals in the context of their daily lives. Our analysis of the WGBU report indicates that high levels of abstraction, and the absence of concrete individuals who are striving to find alternatives through participation in social movements, support these principles of domination. Rendering such alternatives invisible serves to keep them off the agenda and ignored. However, if their stories are told, then their struggles for emancipation and for new, more sustainable ways of living can be used to inspire others to follow their lead.

And here we are back in synch with Nancy Fraser's and Val Plumwood's conclusions: the transformation towards a sustainable future needs the power of social movements against domination, and it needs people who act in relation to concrete others and who feel essentially related to nature. We do not know whether a new social contract will emerge, but if it does surface then it has to be based on multiple small contracts that enable people to create their own sustainable relationships.

## Note

1 Polanyi called this commodification 'fictitious' to make clear that those fundamental bases of social life such as labour, land and money cannot be commodities (which are produced for the market) and would be damaged and destroyed if they were treated as such (Polanyi 1944, ch. 6).

## References

Adam, B. (2013) 'Clock time: tyrannies and alternatives', in *Time on our Side: Why we all Need a Shorter Working Week*, edited by Coot, A. and Franklin, J., London: New Economics Foundation, 31–39.

Biesecker, A. and von Winterfeld, U. (2013) 'Alte Rationalitätsmuster und neue Beharrlichkeiten: Impulse zu blinden Flecken der Transformationsdebatte' [Old rationales and new persistences: impulses concerning blind spots in the debate about transformation], *GAIA – Ecological Perspectives for Science and Society* 22(3): 160–165.

Biesecker, A. and von Winterfeld, U. (2014) *Extern? Weshalb und inwiefern moderne Gesellschaften Externalisierung brauchen und erzeugen*, Working Paper 2/2014, Jena: DFG-Kollegforscher Innengruppe Postwachstumsgesellschaften.

Demirović, A., Dück, J., Becker, F. and Bader, P. (2011) 'VielfachKrise', in *Im Finanzmarktdominierten Kapitalismus*, Hamburg: VSA-Verlag.

Fraser, N. (2011) 'Marketization, social protection, emancipation: toward a neo-Polanyian concept of capitalist crisis', in *Business as Usual: The Roots of the Global*

*Financial Meltdown* (Vol. 1), edited by Calhoun, C.J. and Derluguian, G.M., New York: New York University Press, 137–158.

Fraser, N. (2012) *Can Society be Commodities All the Way Down? Polanyian Reflections on Capitalist Crisis*, Working Paper 18, Paris: Fondation Maison des sciences de l'homme, available online: https://halshs.archives-ouvertes.fr/halshs-00725060/document.

Hirschman, A.O. (1991) *The Rhetoric of Reaction*, Cambridge, MA: Harvard University Press.

Luxemburg, R. (1981/1913) 'Die Akkumulation des Kapitals', in *Gesammelte Werke Bd. 5* (Ökonomische Schriften), Berlin: Dietz.

Luxemburg, R. (1981/1925) 'Einführung in die Nationalökonomie', in *Gesammelte Werke Bd. 5* (Ökonomische Schriften), Berlin: Dietz.

Marx, K. (1867/1972) *Das Kapital Bd. 1*, Berlin: Dietz-Verlag.

O'Hara, S. (2009) 'Feminist ecological economics in theory and practice', in *Eco-Sufficiency and Global Justice: Women Write Political Ecology*, edited by Salleh, A., London/New York: Pluto Press, 180–196.

Pateman, C. (1988) *The Sexual Contract*, Stanford, CA: Stanford University Press.

Plumwood, V. (1991) 'Nature, self, and gender: feminism, environmental philosophy, and the critique of rationalism', *Hypatia* 6(1): 3–27.

Plumwood, V. (2002) *Environmental Culture: The Ecological Crisis of Reason*, London: Routledge.

Polanyi, K. (1944/1978) *The Great Transformation: Politische und ökonomische Ursprünge von Gesellschaften und Wirtschaftssystemen*, Frankfurt am Main: Suhrkamp.

Rawls, J. (1999/1971) *A Theory of Justice*, Cambridge, MA: Belknap Press.

Reitzig, J. (2005) *Gesellschaftsvertrag, Gerechtigkeit, Arbeit. Eine hegemonietheoretische Analyse zur Debatte um einen 'Neuen Gesellschaftsvertrag' im postfordistischen Kapitalismus*, Münster: Westfälisches Dampfboot.

Salleh, A. (ed.) (2009) *Eco-Sufficiency and Global Justice: Women Write Political Ecology*, London/New York: Pluto Press

WBGU, Schellnhuber, H.J., Messner, D., Leggewie, C., Leinfelder, R., Nakicenovic, N., Rahmstorf, S., Schlacke, S., Schmid, J. and Schubert, R. (2011) *World in Transition: A Social Contract for Sustainability*, Flagship Report, Berlin: Wissenschaftlicher Beirat der Bundesregierung Globale Umweltveränderungen (WBGU, German Advisory Council on Global Change).

Wichterich, C. (2011) 'Krise der Ernährermännlichkeit und neoliberale Gleichstellung durch die Krise', in *Im Finanzmarktdominierten Kapitalismus*, edited by Demirović, A. et al., Hamburg: VSA-Verlag, 129–145.

# 5   Where rivers meet

## Exploring the confluence of ecofeminism, covenantal ethics and action research

*Mary Brydon-Miller and Anne Inga Hilsen*

## Introduction

The Ohio River is born at the confluence of the Allegheny and Monongahela Rivers in Pittsburgh, Pennsylvania, USA. It flows nearly 1,000 miles until it meets with the Mississippi River in Cairo, Illinois, with over 20 other rivers and streams joining it along the way. From there the river flows another 1,000 miles on down to New Orleans, where it finally empties into the Gulf of Mexico.

Ecologically the confluence of rivers is an important phenomenon because it is a dramatic and fragile point at which systems intermingle with the potential to nourish life both within and along the water. The systems created by this coming together of rivers have also supported the growth and development of human communities throughout time. Along the Ohio many Native American communities flourished in the centuries before European settlement and it later served as a major transportation route with cities growing up along its banks. Politically rivers can also serve as important pathways and boundaries. The Ohio River was the starting point for the Lewis and Clark expedition to explore and claim lands west of the Mississippi, and also separated the South from the North before the American Civil War, making its crossing a critical point for slaves escaping along the route of the Underground Railroad.

The confluence of rivers can also create serious environmental threats, as is the case when pollution or other hazards enter the water system at one point, only to be carried along, perhaps many hundreds of miles, affecting the health of the river, the plants and animals living there, and the people, many of whom depend on these systems for drinking water and to support agriculture.

This notion of a confluence where rivers or streams join and where the living systems of each mingle and merge provides an apt metaphor both for ecofeminism and for the various approaches to research ethics which inform the theory and practice of action research as described in this chapter. We examine here the intersections among these concepts with a view toward extending the commitment action researchers make to work for positive social change to include recognition of our responsibility to promote environmental justice and to acknowledge the inextricable relationship between ourselves and nature. And so we invite you to take a journey with us along the Ohio and Mississippi Rivers as we explore this confluence of ecofeminism, ethics and action research.

## First stop – Charleston, West Virginia

*Our journey starts along the banks of the Elk River, upstream from Charleston, West Virginia on 9 January 2014 when a chemical leak was discovered in which an estimated 10,000 gallons of 4-methylcyclohexane methanol seeped into the river and into the public water supply. Some 300,000 residents of the area were advised not to drink, cook with, bathe in, or wash with the water which was marked by an odd licorice-tinged odor. Meanwhile communities downstream along the Kanawha River and on downstream to the Ohio waited to hear if their water would be affected as well. Because of a lack of research on this particular chemical compound, little is known about possible health effects for persons or the environment, but public health officials at the Centers for Disease Control, in a report dated 5 February, noted: 'Due to limited availability of data, and out of an abundance of caution, pregnant women may wish to consider an alternative drinking water source until the chemical is at non-detectable levels in the water distribution system.'*

Ecofeminism provides a useful framework for understanding the ways in which women and other marginalized groups are often more seriously affected by such environmental disasters, and action research offers strategies for enabling a shift toward greater engagement and leadership among members of these groups to address these inequalities. There are many ways of defining ecofeminism, but one way to understand it is as 'the position that there are important connections between how one treats women, people of colour, and the underclass on one hand, and how one treats the nonhuman natural environment on the other' (Warren 1997: xi). Ecofeminism is in itself a confluence of ideas from different disciplines and approaches to science and the natural world (Warren 2000), but at its core it aims at exposing the underlying mentality of exploitation that is directed against women and nature within the patriarchal world.

Warren (2000) uses the metaphor of quilting to describe the many influences that make up the pattern of ecofeminist philosophy. Quilting is a metaphor that captures both the diversity and the overall inclusive or exclusive principles of what belongs/cannot belong to ecofeminism. As she defines it, 'nothing that is knowingly, intentionally, or consciously naturist, sexist, racist, or classist – which reinforces or maintains "isms of domination" – belongs on the quilt'. What is required to be included is for the contribution to 'express some aspect of that quilter's perspectives on women–other human Others–nature interconnections' (2000: 67). In this way the quilt of ecofeminism has some guiding principles as to what the theme of the quilt expresses, while at the same time allowing diversity and different perspectives within this theme.

Interestingly, the same metaphor of the quilt was used in organizing the conference on feminism and action research that led to the publication of *Traveling Companions: Feminism, Teaching, and Action Research* (Brydon-Miller et al. 2004). In an effort to escape the confines of traditional academic conferences, participants were asked to bring a piece of cloth that somehow represented their contribution to our work together.

> The stories the participants told about themselves via their pieces of fabric focused on a host of experiences, identities, and events. We spoke about being mothers and grandmothers; about celebrating traditions and honoring memories; about friendships and the deep personal relationships we have developed with a variety of communities and within our birth families. We also talked about the long years many of us have been working together for change and how our life experiences underscore our commitments to democratic practice and social justice.
>
> (ibid.: xvii)

The quilt which was created from these pieces of cloth has hung in the Action Research Center at the University of Cincinnati for many years.

So while we see this as a powerful image, our metaphor of confluence is intended to capture something different, as it both serves to describe the process of coming together and allows the contributions ('rivers joining') to come from even distant sources or headwaters as long as, in the end, they join in the bigger whole of the river. Also it allows the examination of contributions to the river whether they are predefined as 'acceptable' or not. In this chapter we want to build an argument for the mutual usefulness of contrasting and combining the knowledge-making process of action research with ecofeminism, and to explore the ethical sources of these systems.

Given its own multiple disciplinary histories and current theoretical foundations, action research can be defined in many ways. Reason and Bradbury define it thus:

> Action research is a participatory, democratic process concerned with developing practical knowing in the pursuit of worthwhile human purposes, grounded in a participatory worldview.
>
> (Reason and Bradbury 2001: 1)

It might be most accurate to say that what actually links all the various forms of action research is a shared values stance.

> A respect for people and for the knowledge and experience they bring to the research process, a belief in the ability of democratic processes to achieve positive social change, and a commitment to action.
>
> (Brydon-Miller et al. 2003: 15)

In this chapter we emphasize the commitment action researchers make to work for positive social change to include recognition of our responsibility to promote environmental justice and to acknowledge the inextricable relationship between ourselves and nature.

In fact, this recognition of our responsibility to engage environmental issues has always been a part of action research. In the first *Handbook of Action Research*, Reason and Bradbury noted that the goal of action research is to contribute to

> the increased well-being – economic, political, psychological, spiritual – of human persons and communities, *and to a more equitable and sustainable relationship with the wider ecology of the planet of which we are an intrinsic part.*
>
> (Reason and Bradbury 2001: 2; italics added)

Reading about the chemical spill described above reminded us of an action research project conducted many years ago by members of the Yellow Creek Concerned Communities organization in the state of Kentucky and researchers and students from Vanderbilt University in Nashville, Tennessee, reported on by Juliet Merrifield (1993). In this example of what was sometimes termed 'housewife epidemiology', community residents conducted a health risk assessment of households affected by chemicals from a local tannery, tracking higher levels of kidney ailments, gastrointestinal problems, and a significantly higher rate of miscarriages following the introduction of the use of toxic chemicals at the facility. Studies such as this, Merrifield suggests, might inform the development of a 'new science', based on the development of 'cooperative relationships between scientists and citizens, with a view to research that meets people's needs' (ibid.: 76). In addition to the actual research results that emerged, Merrifield also notes that the project 'broadened and strengthened the leadership within the group' in part due to the role of women 'who became better informed and more vocal and confident through their work with the survey' (ibid.: 78).

This explicit commitment to environmental justice links action research to the basic values put forth by ecofeminists (Gaard 2011). Central both to ecofeminism as understood by Warren (1997, 2000) and to our definition is the concept of 'othering'. Othering is the basic principle behind 'domination, exploitation, and colonization of certain groups ("Others") who have subordinate status in institutions and relationships of domination and subordination' (Warren 2000: xiv).

For the domination of 'Others', whether they be women, other human 'Others' (such as indigenous people, the poor, children, the old, etc.), or nature ('Earth Others'), to be seen as justified demands more than sheer power; it requires that this control be defined as a part of the 'natural order of things'. Mary Douglas (1986), quoting Needham (1973), argues for the grounding of conventions (in her case the conventions surrounding *division of labor*) in analogies to the natural world by which 'the complementarity of the right and left hand and the complementarity of gender provide a great rhetorical resource' (Douglas 1986: 49). Appealing to the natural world, such complementarities seem given instead of socially constructed. Building complementarities such as 'female is to male' as 'left is to right' as 'people are to king', she opens perspectives on domination based in this 'taken-for-granted' understanding of natural order. 'Ultimately, the whole system is grounded in nature, on the pre-eminence of the right hand over the left' (ibid.: 49). Douglas critiques this naturalization of such complementarities which in each case define one component of the duality as dominant to the other, whether it is *the right hand to the left* or *man to woman*. Dominations rationalized as natural phenomena are more difficult to challenge. Although Douglas does not define herself as an ecofeminist, her discussion is valuable to understand the continued support of models of domination and othering, so important to ecofeminism.

Also central to the epistemological foundations of both ecofeminism and action research are challenges to assumptions grounded in a positivist view of knowledge, which are part of this patriarchal system of control.

> Ecofeminists interested in epistemology challenge some trademark Western views about knowledge; for example, that knowledge is objective; that the 'knower' is an objective, detached, independent, and rational observer.
>
> (Warren 2000: 33)

In contrast to such a positivist position, both ecofeminism and action research can be said to be based on a more critical understanding of knowledge generation with an ethical foundation of democratic engagement, the right of participation, recognition of power inequalities, and an emphasis on the importance of local dialogue as a means of building and sustaining relationships. In action research the local participants in the research field are seen as collaborators in developing knowledge and learning in the projects, not as objects of research (Greenwood and Levin 1998).

Warren claims that 'all ecofeminists agree that there are important connections between the unjustified domination of women and nature' (2000: 21), but there is less unity regarding why and how this came about. Some ecofeminists support their argument with historical or archaeological evidence of a pre-dominant culture that supposedly was then overrun by competing cultures. Riane Eisler describes such a set of competing human relationships – partnership and domination – in her book *The Chalice and the Blade* (1988). The Chalice describes a peaceful, egalitarian partnership society, exemplified by early agrarian societies, which were overrun by nomadic tribes from Eurasia around the sixth to the third millennium BCE. The Blade then became the dominant cultural mode which still typifies most of Western culture. Whether this 'historical description' is based on evidence or rather on wishful thinking, as some critics, such as Janet Biehl (1991), have claimed is not relevant to our discussion in this chapter. More importantly, Eisler's theory of culture presents two modes of human interaction; one based on domination, the other on partnership. By doing so she also challenges how these modes influence our ways of thinking and doing research. In an interview with Hilary Bradbury (2004), Eisler discusses the relevance of these ideas to action research. Action research sets up an alternative to the dominant mode of objectifying research where the researcher is in charge of the process of knowledge generation and the research subjects are objects for study. In contrast, 'action research offers the possibility of a partnership orientation to doing research' (2004: 212), where the relationship between researcher and local participants is that of equals in the process of cogeneration of knowledge.

## Next stop – Paducah, Kentucky

*Moving downriver to Paducah, Kentucky, just east of the confluence of the Ohio and Mississippi Rivers, you encounter the Paducah Gaseous Diffusion Plant that produced enriched uranium from 1952 to 2013 for use in the US nuclear arms industry. In a recent article from the Louisville* Courier-Journal, *some of the problems associated with the plant were made clear:*

> The Energy Department, in an effort to prop up a troubled uranium enrichment company, arranged for uranium transfers that failed to comply with laws about fair pricing, national security determinations and limits to prevent the department from flooding the domestic uranium market, the Government Accountability Office said in a report released to the public Monday.
>
> (*Courier-Journal*, 9 June 2014)

*The plant is also located in a region near the New Madrid Fault, making it prone to earthquakes and an area that experiences severe weather and occasional tornadoes, as occurred on 17 November 2013, causing damage to the plant but no reported release of hazardous of radioactive materials. There are many competing interests involved here, including local economic impacts related to potential job losses, federal government interests in maintaining domestic sources for enriched uranium, and health and environmental activists who share concerns about the apparent lack of care being taken in decommissioning the plant. In a moving presentation by whistle-blower Joe Carson, licensed Professional Engineer, and a facility representative and safety inspector from the US Department of Energy (DOE), in Oak Ridge, Tennessee to sick workers from the Paducah plant, the speaker said, 'If DOE gets away with it, it's legal. If it's legal, it's ethical. The only right you have as a DOE employee is the right to seek employment elsewhere.' He then adds, 'My profession let you down'.*[1]

This complex, one might say convoluted, case and Carson's testimony point to the important role that professional ethics have to play in guiding practice – and the challenges sometimes faced by those who seek to live by these principles in the face of institutional and even governmental opposition. In our experience, being grounded in a set of ethical principles can help those faced with such challenges, whether they are professionals or researchers, to act in ways that are consistent with the values they would seek to uphold.

The main tributary of our work in research ethics has been covenantal ethics, but this stream is fed by feminist, environmental, and communitarian ethics as well. In an article focused on ethics and politics in action research, Hilsen (2006) defines covenantal ethics as 'the unconditional responsibility and the ethical demand to act in the best interest of our fellow human beings'. Covenantal ethics is 'responsive and reciprocal in character. It acknowledges a two-way process of giving and receiving' (May 1980: 367). Based on the concept from the Bible of a *covenant* between God and humankind, it describes a relationship of exchange of gifts (such as *life*) given and received. The ethical responsibility is one of gratitude and care for this gift. Whether one believes in God or not – and one can equally as well understand the covenant to be one between ourselves and the natural world – the concept of receiving a gift so valuable it can never be earned or paid back places the recipients in a situation of caring for the gift as well as possible. The gift of life can be compared to the gift of nature. Nature is there as a gift to humankind, beyond our ability to create ourselves, and therefore places on us the responsibility to care for and respect nature in gratitude.

By incorporating the perspective of ecofeminism and the stated commitment of action research to environmentalism in our work together since then, we have added to this the responsibility to act in the best interests of the environment, acknowledging the interconnectedness of the human and non-human components of the biosphere.

The core values of covenantal ethics have been described as the acknowledgement of human interdependency, the cogeneration of knowledge, and the development of fairer power relations (Hilsen 2006). As argued above, covenantal ethics can be extended to encompass the relationship between humans and nature. By integrating the values of ecofeminism, we understand this interdependency to include not only our fellow human beings, but a recognition of the fundamental interdependency of humans as part of the natural world. And the notion of fairer power relations suggests that we focus not on achieving ever more disastrous levels of environmental domination, but rather on nurturing a deeper respect and reverence for nature.

The rejection of seeing the local participants of research as 'others' and the understanding of the importance of the cogeneration of knowledge is one area in which action research and covenantal ethics can make the most important contribution to ecofeminism. Ecofeminism will be effective only when communities are brought into the process of critically examining and addressing local environmental issues as equal partners. The local knowledge of the participants is necessary to this process. Rather than searching for universal truths that can only be found by objective researchers on the outside, cogeneration of knowledge presupposes a joint process where the situated knowledge of the participants is central. The concept of local theory is crucial to action research. As Elden (1983) argues, the local knowledge of the people living and working in a setting will always be richer than outsiders can achieve. Their stories will be more robust in the sense that they have specific knowledge about how to do the work they do, achieved through their daily practice. Outsiders (such as researchers) see the local context from a more distant perspective, and their explanations will therefore lack the complex and detailed knowledge of the local participants. Instead of the researchers coming in from the outside to diagnose a situation, the local participants are seen as experts of their own situation, and their knowledge as invaluable to any action plan for changing practice (Elden 1983; Pålshaugen 1998). This position echoes Donna Haraway's 'argument for situated and embodied knowledges and an argument against various forms of unlocated, and so irresponsible, knowledge claims' (Haraway 1988: 583).

Feminist ethicists have begun to echo this same recognition of the unity and interdependency of our world and, while we do not necessarily support the claim that some feminist environmental ethicists might make that women have a deeper natural connection to nature and a clearer moral vision of environmental ethics, we do believe that the focus on caring and the nurturing of relationships reflected in much feminist thought resonates with the fundamental principles of covenantal ethics (Brabeck and Ting 2000; Noddings 1984/2003).

A similar list of ethical principles from an ecofeminist perspective has recently been articulated by Stephens (2013):

- be gender sensitive;
- value voices from the margins;
- center nature;
- select appropriate methodologies;
- undertake research towards social change.

Likewise, environmental ethics (Bannon 2013) and communitarian ethics, with their grounding in the same understanding that humans are interdependent and socially defined (Tam 2011), reflect these same basic principles. Denzin and Giardina (2007) capture this notion of the confluence of ethical systems especially well in their description of a 'performative, indigenous, feminist, communitarian ethic', which they describe as a 'sacred epistemology' that 'stresses the values of empowerment, shared governance, care, solidarity, love, community, covenant, morally involved observers, and civic transformation' (ibid.: 29).

The challenge then for ethicists, whatever their persuasion, is to develop a system for operationalizing the basic principles to which they ascribe in practice. In working to operationalize the values of covenantal ethics in the context of action research, we have developed a process of structured ethical reflection (SER) in which researchers and their community partners are invited to reflect upon the shared values that inform their inquiry and to consider how these are translated into practice (Brydon-Miller 2012; Brydon-Miller et al.

2015). This process begins with the identification of a set of values upon which the researchers and their partners wish to base their collaboration. Looking across the sets of ethical principles discussed above, we might suggest the following as a starting point for this process:

• reverence for nature and humans as a part of the natural world;
• recognition of our interdependency with one another and with nature;
• respect for people's knowledge and experience;
• belief in democratic participation;
• responsibility to contribute to positive change.

Once a set of shared ethical principles has been agreed upon, researchers and their community partners can then consider the ways in which they enact these principles at each stage of the research process, from the initial development of partnerships through to the implementation of findings to promote social change and the dissemination of the knowledge created in order to inform the actions of other researchers and activists. This process can be traced through the use of the structured ethical reflection grid (Figure 5.1) by developing a set of key questions or statements designed to inform our actions at each stage of the research process.

## Final stop – New Orleans, Louisiana

*To examine the question of how we might put these values into practice, let us finish our journey with a visit to New Orleans in the aftermath of Hurricane Katrina. In their book,* Hurricane Katrina: America's Unnatural Disaster, *Levitt and Whitaker describe what happened on 29 August 2005.*

The storm surge caused catastrophic destruction along the Gulf Coast. In Louisiana, the flood protection system in New Orleans failed in fifty-three different places. Nearly every levee in metro New Orleans breached as Hurricane Katrina's 140-mile-an-hour gale force winds, torrential rain, and thunderous floodwaters rolled eastward through the city, flooding 80 per cent of the city and many areas of neighboring parishes for weeks.

(Levitt and Whitaker 2009: 2)

| Basic values | Developing research partnerships | Constructing research questions | Seeking funding | Identifying sources of data | Gathering data | Analyzing data | Taking action | Disseminating knowledge | Moving on |
|---|---|---|---|---|---|---|---|---|---|
| | | | | | | | | | |
| | | | | | | | | | |
| | | | | | | | | | |

*Figure 5.1* Structured ethical reflection grid

*But the unnatural part of the disaster as they describe it, the huge loss of life and property meted out most heavily on the African American community and other low-income residents of the city, was due to failures of local, state, and federal government to provide adequate protection and emergency services both during and for months following the disaster.*

Scheib and Lykes pick up the story of post-Katrina New Orleans in 2007 in their description of a participatory action research project carried out by a group of African American and Latina community health workers together with their university-based partners. Specifically,

> through participatory and collaborative efforts, the project coresearchers sought to enhance participants' well-being, visualize the critical but often unseen or undervalued knowledge of women community-based health promoters, and consolidate an emerging model of cross-community women's leadership as one resource for responding to post-disaster contexts.
>
> (Scheib and Lykes 2013: 1070)

The aftermath of Hurricane Katrina saw a significant influx of Latin Americans to the New Orleans area, attracted in large part due to increased opportunities in building trades as the city sought to rebuild following the disaster. This put new demands upon local community health workers charged with providing outreach to these recently arrived residents, all of whom were new to the community and many of whom were not native English speakers. In responding to these concerns, African American community health workers, known in the community as Walker Talkers, and Latina Promotoras came together to improve service provision throughout the community. In this project, these two groups of community health workers examined the challenges to addressing community health issues in post-Katrina New Orleans. Using a variation of the photovoice process, they recorded and discussed ongoing impediments to improving local health outcomes. Photovoice is an action research methodology in which participants take photographic images around themes relevant to the research topic, which are then discussed with a view toward both creating a shared understanding of the issue and developing materials to publicize the image more broadly within the community (Lykes 2001; Wang and Burris 1997).

> The community-based health workers documented and critically analyzed structural inequalities due to impoverishment and racism. As significantly, they recognized class-based similarities despite ethnic, racial, and linguistic differences among themselves and in their communities, forging solidarity within a city that all too frequently evidences fractures and conflict along these lines.
>
> (Scheib and Lykes 2013: 1082)

Using this study as a model, we can examine the ways in which an action research project can be seen to reflect the values of ecofeminist and covenantal ethics throughout the research process. By focusing specifically on the experiences of women, the project reflected sensitivity to gender and provided the participants an opportunity to explore shared understandings of the experience of being women community health workers in the city. The project's focus on bringing together African American and Latina participants reflected the principle of 'valuing voices from the margins'. At the same time the project acknowledged the impact of the deterioration of the natural environment on the lives of the most vulnerable members of the community. These values were apparent from the outset in the way in which the original organizational partnerships were established through the final stages of organizing opportunities for the participants to present their findings to a broader public audience. The selection of methodologies reflected the researchers' commitment to valuing the experiences and understandings of their collaborators, and by providing training and support they made it possible for the women to gain confidence in their abilities as researchers. And finally, while the project itself was relatively modest in scope, the long-term impact of bringing these two groups of community workers together and offering them opportunities to come to understand one another's cultures and to see the commonalities of their experience are an important starting point for any effort to address the larger structural inequalities that the project participants identified.

Another ongoing project growing out of local response to Hurricane Katrina is the work being done to challenge environmental racism by the Vietnamese American Young Leaders Association of New Orleans (VAYLA-NO).[2] The aftermath of Hurricane Katrina created tons of waste from devastated homes and businesses, waste which local officials originally planned to place in a dump site in East New Orleans close to where most of the members of the local Vietnamese community lived and near the Bayou Sauvage National Wildlife Refuge, the largest urban wildlife refuge in the USA. As the VAYLA-NO website describes the situation,

> When the mayor of New Orleans made it publicly known that he was considering placing a landfill in New Orleans East, community members spoke out against the proposal. Before Hurricane Katrina, the elders of the community were the leaders who made all the decisions without much input from younger generation. The crisis of the landfill galvanized the entire community and created an opportunity for the youth to play a lead role. Language barriers prevented the elders from effectively organizing against the local power structure.[3]

In an effort similar to the Yellow Creek Concerned Communities project described above, local residents – in this case the youth of the community in particular – were galvanized to become politically involved by a potential environmental threat to their community and to their way of life. Since its founding, VAYLA has reached out to other local minority youth and extended their mission to include programs focused on educational and health equity. But they define their strategy as

> to amplify the voices of the youth, which demand an end to environmental oppression, and seek to envision a solution to toxic dumping that is ecologically sound and contributes to the health of our residents.[4]

## Conclusion

So what lessons do we take from this trip of nearly 2,000 miles from Pittsburgh to New Orleans? First, a renewed appreciation for the beauty and fragility of the natural world and the myriad ways in which human action (and inaction) can affect the health of ecosystems not just close by but many hundreds of miles away. And with this renewed appreciation, a recommitment to taking responsibility for insuring the health of this natural world – and by extension the health of all of those, both human and non-human, who are dependent upon it.

Covenantal ethics sees this an 'unconditional responsibility' (Hilsen 2006: 28) to take action to promote greater social and environmental justice which demands that our research focus on working together with local partners to find practical solutions to pressing environmental issues, with a view toward generating knowledge that can support change on a global scale. From the perspective of the ecofeminist action researcher, this means articulating a set of ethical principles that align with this responsibility and seeking out ways to conduct our research that best embody these principles – with care, compassion, and commitment.

The studies described here illustrate how powerful these principles can be, in addressing current environmental challenges, and perhaps more importantly in fostering relationships of trust and mutual respect that allow local communities to continue their efforts to work together to address critical social, economic, political, and environmental problems.

## Notes

1  http://ecowatch.com/2013/06/04/stiffed-usec-sues-feds-in-nuclear-slugfest
2  Our thanks to Dr. Allison Padilla-Goodman, action researcher and New Orleans native, for her insight and guidance in learning about the extraordinary work of this organization.
3  http://vayla-no.org/about/history/
4  https://sites.google.com/a/vayla-no.org/home/campaigns

## References

Bannon, B.E. (2013) 'From intrinsic value to compassion: a place-based ethic', *Environmental Ethics* 35(3): 259–278.

Biehl, J. (1991) *Rethinking Ecofeminist Politics*, Boston: South End Press.
Brabeck, M. and Ting, K. (2000) 'Introduction', in *Practicing Feminist Ethics in Psychology*, edited by Brabeck, M., Washington, DC: American Psychological Association, 3–16.
Bradbury, H. (2004) 'Doing work that matters despite the obstacles', *Action Research* 2(2): 209–227.
Brydon-Miller, M. (2012) 'Addressing the ethical challenges of community-based research', *Teaching Ethics* 12(2): 157–162.
Brydon-Miller, M., Greenwood, D. and Maguire, P. (2003) 'Why action research?', *Action Research* 1(1): 9–28.
Brydon-Miller, M., Maguire, P. and McIntyre, A. (eds) (2004) *Traveling Companions: Feminism, Teaching, and Action Research*, Westport, CT: Praeger.
Brydon-Miller, M., Rector-Aranda, A. and Stevens, D. (2015) 'Widening the circle: research ethics education and institutional change', in *Sage Handbook of Action Research*, 3rd edn, edited by Bradbury, H., London: Sage.
Denzin, N.K. and Giardina, M.D. (2007) 'Introduction', in *Ethical Futures in Qualitative Research: Decolonizing the Politics of Knowledge*, edited by Denzin, N.K. and Giardina, M.D., Walnut Creek, CA: Left Coast Press.
Douglas, M. (1986) *How Institutions Think*, Syracuse, NY: Syracuse University Press.
Eisler, R. (1988) *The Chalice and the Blade: Our History, Our Future*, San Francisco, CA: Harper.
Elden, M. (1983) 'Democratization and participative research in developing local theory', *Journal of Occupational Behaviour* 4: 21–34.
Gaard, G. (2011) 'Ecofeminism revisited: rejecting essentialism and re-placing species in a material feminist environmentalism', *Feminist Formations* 23(2): 26–53.
Greenwood, D. and Levin, M. (1998) *Introduction to Action Research: Social Research for Social Change*, Thousand Oaks, CA: Sage.
Haraway, D. (1988) 'Situated knowledge: the science question in feminism and the privilege of partial perspective', *Feminist Studies* 14(3): 575–599.
Hilsen, A.I. (2006) 'And they shall be known by their deeds: ethics and politics in action research', *Action Research* 4(1): 23–36.
Levitt, J.I. and Whitaker, M.C. (2009) *Hurricane Katrina: America's Unnatural Disaster*, Lincoln, NE: University of Nebraska Press.
Lykes, M.B. (2001) 'Creative arts and photography in participatory action research in Guatemala', in *Handbook of Action Research*, edited by Reason, P. and Bradbury, H., Thousand Oaks, CA: Sage.
May, W. (1980) 'Doing ethics: the bearing of ethical theories on fieldwork', *Social Problems* (27)3: 358–370.
Merrifield, J. (1993) 'Putting scientists in their place: participatory research in environmental and occupational health', in *Voices of Change: Participatory Research in the United States and Canada*, edited by Park, P., Brydon-Miller, M., Hall, B. and Jackson, E., Westport, CT: Bergin and Garvey, 65–84.
Needham, R. (1973) *Right and Left, Essays on Dual Classification*, Chicago: University of Chicago Press.
Noddings, N. (1984/2003) *Caring: A Feminine Approach to Ethics and Moral Education*, Berkeley, CA: University of California Press.
Pålshaugen, Ø. (1998) *The End of Organization Theory?* Amsterdam, PA: John Benjamins.
Reason, P. and Bradbury, H. (eds) (2001) *Handbook of Action Research: Participative Inquiry and Practice*, London: Sage.

Scheib, H.S. and Lykes, M.B. (2013) 'African American and Latina community health workers engage photoPAR as a resource in a post-disaster context: Katrina at 5 years', *Journal of Health Psychology* 18(8): 1069–1084.

Stephens, A. (2013) *Ecofeminism and Systems Thinking*, New York: Routledge.

Tam, H. (2011) 'Rejuvenating democracy: lessons from a communitarian experiment', *Forum* 53(3): 407–420.

Wang, C. and Burris, M.A. (1997) 'Photovoice: concept, methodology, and use for participatory needs assessment', *Health Education and Behavior* 24(3): 369–387.

Warren, K.J. (ed.) (1997) *Ecofeminism: Women, Culture, Nature*, Bloomington, IN: Indiana University Press.

Warren, K.J. (2000) *Ecofeminist Philosophy*, Lanham, MD: Rowman & Littlefield.

# Part II

# Practice

# 6 Climate adaptation in the Global South

## Funding women's farming[1]

*Trish Glazebrook*

## Introduction

This chapter provides an ecofeminist argument for implementation of the United Nations Climate Adaptation Funds to support the needs of women subsistence farmers in the Global South. I begin with neo-Marxist arguments that most pressing in feminism are the needs of women in the Global South. I explain climate change (CC) and assess its impacts using the Fifth Assessment Report of the Intergovernmental Panel on CC. I outline growing crises in agriculture and food security in Africa, followed by a case study presenting my research on women's farming in Ghana, which uncovers inadequacies of current policy approaches, especially science-based approaches, to address women's needs. I next make recommendations concerning how the Adaptation Fund and the Green Climate Fund established by the United Nations Framework Convention on Climate Change (UNFCCC) might ensure they meet the needs of women farmers in the Global South. I conclude that women subsistence agriculturalists practice logics of care irreducible to the logic of domination of global capital, and suggest that UNFCCC implementation of Adaptation Funds has the potential to realign global economics from capital to care by internalizing the difference between cash cropping and subsistence farming. Yes, I'm a dreamer; but I'm not the only one.

## From feminism to ecofeminism

An argument that feminists attend to the needs of women in the Global South is not a call to support the merely victimized. These women are strong, resilient and capable of doing things I could not, like live on less than a dollar a day, or grow my family's food. In a double breach of distributive justice, these women suffer the worst consequences of CC, while reaping the least benefit from its drivers. Rather than help or pity, they need global capital to stop rendering their lives untenable through indifferent marginalization, disruption of their ecosystem management practices, and destruction of their resource base.

Gender difference is a complex issue. Simone de Beauvoir's argument that 'One is not born, but rather becomes, a woman' (de Beauvoir 1952: 267) was a crucial insight for women who wanted equality in the public sphere but were constrained by essentialist assumptions relegating them to childcare, domestic work and servicing men. Two inadequacies emerged, however, in the nature/nurture debate.

First, women's experience is not determined by nature *or* nurture, but both. There is no access to biology independent of social construction; and such construction takes its prompt from biological realities. For example, the experience of menstruation varies greatly across socio-cultural contexts, yet each experience is constructed around the bodily event. Accordingly, woman's body, both natured and nurtured, is a political site (Glazebrook 2010a: 250–51). The political economy of women's bodies is evident in rape as a military tactic, women's treatment as political prisoners (cf. Panjabi 1997), abortion debates, and each society's foundational marriage arrangements that determine who gets access to women's bodies under what conditions and toward what ends. Salleh's (1997) 'embodied materialism' expresses beautifully that woman is not just her biology, but nor is gender purely cultural.

Secondly, second-wave feminism fails to include perspectives beyond a small demographic, i.e. white, middle-class, college-educated women in the Global North. hooks (1984) argues that non-inclusive feminisms are one-dimensional. Walker described herself as womanist, which she said 'is to feminist as purple is to lavender' (Walker 1983: xi). Lugones and Spelman (1983) use cross-cultural dialogue to examine and model inclusivist practices. Johnson-Odim argues that feminism in the Global North 'narrowly confines itself to a struggle against gender discrimination' (Johnson-Odim 1991: 315), but women's struggle against racism and economic exploitation in the Global South is also shared by men. Her insight as a 'third-world' feminist applies globally: women's oppression is constituted along several interconnected axes, of which sexism is but one.

Feminists thus recognize the value of empirical data (Warren 1997; cf. Fonow and Cook 1991; Plumwood 1991; Baylis et al. 1998; Sherwin 1998; Warren 2000; Jaggar 2008). Understanding women's lived experience is crucial for addressing women's complex oppressions. Feminists thus also re-conceive epistemic authority in terms of narrative voice (Moulton 1983; Allen 1988; Sherwin 1988; Whitbeck 1984; Garry and Pearsall 1989; Warren 1990). I use narrative voice in my research by conducting semi-structured interviews and focus groups that generate qualitative data. The evidence-based assessments I also draw from are largely quantitative. All the data sets I generate or have examined converge on the urgent crisis of CC. What makes me an *ecofeminist* is my assumption of a widely recognized connection between the feminization of poverty and environmental degradation. Climate change is the largest environmental degrader at present on the planet, and affects most of the women throughout the globe by exacerbating the difficult conditions in which they feed their family. It threatens both capital economies and subsistence livelihoods. Ecofeminism is accordingly for me not just another feminism. Rather, because ecofeminism values women's subsistence practices, it is a paradigm-shifting de-centering of neoliberal egalitarianism that focuses on women's shared oppression under the logic of domination of global capital. Ecofeminist analysis shows how conceptual frameworks support logics of domination, how such logics are the culmination of the intellectual history of the West in modernity, and what a different logic might look like.

Warren (1990) argued that oppressive conceptual frameworks function as logics of domination by starting with a dualism, e.g. man/woman or man/nature, ordering them into a hierarchy, and then using the hierarchical structure to justify exploitation of the lower by the higher, i.e. man's domination of woman and nature. Ecofeminists argue that the logic of domination underwriting modern science privileges men in the contemporary epistemological and ontological paradigm (Merchant 1980; Shiva 1989; Plumwood 1991; Plumwood 1993). This paradigm aligns man/woman with reason/emotion, and denigrates emotion as feminine and women as irrational (cf. Finn 1982). The scientific ideology of objectivity moreover precludes contextualization and prizes disinterested impartiality.

I have traced the history of nature's subjection to human needs from the collapse of Aristotle's distinction between nature and artifact to contemporary technoscience that recognizes only instrumental value (Glazebrook 2000). Technoscience thus overruns the globe in systems of global capital (Glazebrook and Olusanya 2011) that reduce nature and peoples to their exploitable value (Glazebrook 2015). Beyond devaluing long-standing knowledge traditions unvalidated by systems such as peer review, the logic of capital provides no basis for ethical behavior or accountability because its foundation in an ontology of objective reckonability is compounded by neoliberal principles of market, competition, individualism and profit. Human fulfillment appears therein as the individual accumulation of private wealth.

In contrast, logics of care depend on relational values of cooperation, dependency and flourishing (Glazebrook and Olusanya 2011). Rejection of nature/nurture dualism does not found logics of care in some innately female capacity. Neo-Marxist, materialist logics of care are not informed by an ontology of objectivity, but gynocentrically by the economics (literally, household laws) of women's work. Such logics do not dispose of technoscience or capital, which would be impossible (Glazebrook 2005), but work embedded in and around systems of capital to evolve its logic toward care. Neo-Marxist care-logics are predicated on women's labor, and recognize contemporary exploitation of the Global South by the North as a new kind of class war. The crisis of CC is pivotal in this class struggle. It is where care-logics are needed most.

## Climate change (CC)

Some of the sun's rays reflect off the Earth back into space, taking heat. Climate change happens when greenhouse gases (GHGs), especially carbon dioxide ($CO_2$) and methane, trap the sun's heat in the atmosphere. Retained heat increases the global temperature, much as sunshine heats a room through a window. The planet is not a room, however: escaping GHGs would take the atmosphere with them. Moreover, the planet is a complex system throughout which a mean temperature increase is not evenly distributed (IPCC 2014: 12). The temperate and tropical regions mediate the temperature difference between the equatorial and polar regions. Equatorial regions heat more quickly than poles, so the temperature difference between poles and the equator increases with CC. Mediating winds drive weather systems, so increased temperature differential means more severe, less predictable winds and weather. The current global crisis is not so much climate *change* as climate *chaos*.

The Fifth Assessment Report (AR5) of the Intergovernmental Panel on Climate Change (IPCC) affirms that anthropogenic influence is causing CC beyond seasonal changes and geologic cycle. AR5's three Working Groups (WGs) assess the science; impacts, adaptations and vulnerability; and mitigation. Material discussed here focuses on discussions of water, crop production and food security in Africa from WGII's Summary for Policymakers. AR5 qualifies its predictions from 'exceptionally unlikely' to 'virtually certain'; its confidence in its conclusions from 'very low' to 'very high'; its evidence base as 'limited', 'medium' or 'robust'; and the strength of WGII members' agreement as 'low', 'medium' or 'high'. Throughout discussion of Africa, the message is clear: CC is having a massive impact on food security.

Impacts are already documented in all continents and oceans, including melting of polar ice-caps and rising sea-levels; ocean acidification affecting fish stocks and coral that supports underwater ecosystems; retreat of glaciers, whose run-off in the Himalayas, for example, supports 20 per cent of the world's people and drives the South Asian monsoon; rainfall decrease and unpredictability affecting crops and food security; increase of food-, water- and vector-borne diseases; biodiversity loss; extreme climate events; and population impacts such as displacement and conflict.

Concerning agriculture, key risks identified include food insecurity, breakdown of food systems and loss of livelihoods due to reduced production. These risks are especially challenging in semi-arid regions of least developed countries with limited ability to cope (IPCC 2014: 13). Approximately 10 per cent of published scientific research predicts crop losses of about 25 per cent (against twentieth-century yields) by 2050, coupled with rapidly rising demand (IPCC 2014: 18). All aspects of food security, including production, access, utilization and price, are potentially affected (IPCC 2014: 18).

Vulnerability to CC impacts varies with multidimensional and intersecting inequalities, including discrimination on the basis of gender, class, ethnicity, age and disability that affect socio-economic status and increase exposure to risks and harms, such as heat waves, droughts and floods that disrupt food production and water supply (IPCC 2014: 6). WGII notes that the 'socially, economically, culturally, politically, institutionally, or otherwise marginalized are especially vulnerable', and CC hazards exacerbate other livelihood stressors for people living in poverty, especially decreasing crop yield (IPCC 2014: 6–8).

Most GHGs are generated in the Global North. Modernity theory suggests that 'development' means following the Global North's development path by industrializing. At the UNFCCC annual climate negotiations, the current stalemate began as reluctance on the part of the Global North to make the economic and political sacrifices that would decrease emissions, if development simply meant massive increases in emissions from the Global South. As the Deputy Minister of Environment from India stated explicitly at a meeting in Doha, however, 'the only development pathway is green and sustainable; low emissions are not contradictory to development but are the only way'. Yet representatives from the Global North continue to block progress toward a climate accord. I have argued elsewhere that, given massive humanitarian CC crises already under way in the Global South, continued refusal to reach functional agreement (with good faith implementation on both mitigation and adaptation) constitutes negligent genocide (Glazebrook 2010b).

## Food security in Africa

Food security in the face of CC has been a documented concern globally for some time (Longhurst 1986; Bohle et al. 1994; Al-Hassan et al. 1997; Okai 1997), but there has been no scientific basis for linking CC to specific food threats. By 1991, researchers knew that drought was increasing in sub-Saharan Africa, but were unable to determine why (Pearce 1991). Ethiopia's 2011 drought was the first extreme weather event to be linked conclusively to CC (Lott et al. 2013). Approximately 11 per cent of both the world's population and the world's arable land is found in Africa (World Bank 2008), where 80 per cent of farmers are subsistence agriculturalists who use only hoes and cutlasses (Scialabba 2007). African food security depends on these subsistence farmers, about 50 per cent of whom are women (World Bank 2014).

Focus on global hunger in 2008 generated a wealth of data. The number of undernourished people in sub-Saharan Africa rose from 169 million in 1990–92 to 212 million in 2003–05 (Biavaschi 2008). The proportion of the world's hungry living in Africa rose from 1/5 to 1/4 (FAO 2008). Of 36 countries in the world facing food insecurity in 2008, 21 were in Africa (Kabasa and Sage 2009), where modern inputs to increase agricultural yield were lagging (World Bank 2008: 52), growth in GDP per agricultural population was globally the lowest (World Bank 2008: 53), and yield gaps were widening compared with other regions (World Bank 2008: 28, 51). The UN Food and Agriculture Organization (FAO) identified four African countries in 'acute food crisis', i.e. 'an exceptional shortfall in aggregate food production/supplies as result of crop failure, natural disasters, interruption of imports, disruption of distribution, excessive post-harvest losses or other supply bottlenecks' (FAO 2008: 1). Four others experienced widespread lack of access to food; 13 had localized issues because of population displacement or combinations of deep poverty and crop failure; and four more expected shortfalls in current production. Some 235 million sub-Saharan Africans were 'chronically hungry' (Kabasa and Sage 2009). Today, sub-Saharan Africa still has the highest prevalence of hunger: every fourth person is undernourished (WFP 2014).

By 2050, a 10–20 per cent increase in the number of people at risk of hunger in Africa is predicted, including a 21 per cent increase (to 24 million) amongst children along with a 26 per cent increase (to 10 million) of malnourished children. Long-term health consequences of poor nutrition, such as brain, bone and organ maldevelopment and disease vulnerability, mean that Africa's children are being born into a growing breach of intergenerational justice. By 2080, 75 per cent of the human population at risk of hunger are anticipated to be living in Africa. In 2012, 24 per cent of the world's undernourished were in Africa, but by 2080, 40–50 per cent will be. A massive humanitarian crisis of starvation is under way in Africa, and is set to accelerate.

The factor most affecting African food security is CC. The UNFCCC assessed Africa as 'already a continent under pressure from climate stresses' and 'highly vulnerable to the impacts of CC' (UNFCCC 2007: 18) such as longer, hotter dry periods, decreased rainfall, unpredictable rainfall patterns, increased temperature, desertification, loss of coastal land to sea-level rise, and severe weather events such as heat waves, drought and floods. A third of Africans live in drought-prone areas: 220 million are exposed to drought every year, and 250 million are predicted to experience water stress (Kabasa and Sage 2009). Changing weather patterns are especially threatening to farmers who rely on the rainy season. Only 3.7 per cent of Africa is irrigated (FAO 2004). Longer, hotter dry periods shorten the growing season and, in combination with unpredictable rainfall, make it hard to know when best to plant, cultivate and harvest (Jennings and Magrath 2009). Decreased yield has been directly correlated to CC. Rice, for example, undergoes 10 per cent decline for each 1°C rise (Baker et al. 1990). AR5 assesses impacts of increases up to 4°C, and models anticipate that sub-Saharan Africa is likely to experience catastrophic declines in yield of 20–30 per cent by 2080, rising as high as 50 per cent in Sudan and Senegal (Cline 2007). Sixty per cent of sub-Saharan Africans depend on livestock, but CC impacts mean less forage and feed crops, and less water for animals.

Farmers throughout the world typically use fertilizers to increase yield. Africans use only about 1 per cent of the world's fertilizer, the lowest consumption globally. Average use in developing countries is 109 kilograms per hectare of arable land (kg/ha); Africa uses only 12.6 kg/ha (FAO 2004). Many farmers fertilize only through collection of animal dung (Glazebrook 2011).

When a crop fails, the farmer might fall back on community support; when crops fail regionally, farmers might look to their government for support. In developing countries, governments often cannot support programs to provide a social safety net. Aid and development resources are aimed at structural adjustment and specific development projects that aim to improve GDP and GNP and other traditional economic indices, rather than ameliorating ground-level subsistence crises. The farmer's only practical alternative, especially given the immediacy of the situation, is to buy food. By 2008 200 million people in sub-Saharan Africa were living on less than $1 a day (World Bank 2008: 3). AR5 recommends insurance programs, social protection measures and disaster risk management to enhance livelihood resilience (IPCC 2014: 20). Given projections of decreasing crops and increasing demand, and the many development crises facing federal governments in many African countries, as well as long-standing conflicts and widespread corruption in some, how realistic are these recommendations? A case study conducted in Ghana – a peaceful, stable, relatively well developed country in West Africa – uncovers limitations in international approaches to CC adaptation in Africa.

## Gender and agriculture in Ghana: a 2007–14 case study

Ghana lies in West Africa, where AR5 anticipates major impacts on crop production (IPCC 2014: 7). Women and children are extremely vulnerable to the incremental impacts of CC on food and agriculture, though they have the least amount of political, economic and social resources to recover (Peacock et al. 1997; Morrow 1999). In 2007, Ghana's Director of Environment noted that 'women are particularly vulnerable to the impacts of climate change, both socially and economically' (Kuuzegh 2007, n.p.), and in 2009 that 'land degradation, desertification and soil erosion hit hardest at the local level and those most affected are the poor, especially women who depend on natural resources for their survival' (Kuuzegh 2009, n.p.). Ghana provides a case study to situate the data provided above on CC and African food security in the context of women's lived experience in order to assess limitations of IPCC adaptation recommendations. Since 2007, I have been working with groups of women outside Bolgatanga in Ghana's Upper Eastern Region to document their experiences of CC, identify their adaptation strategies, and bring their situation and expertise to academic and policy contexts.

Just before I arrived in 2007, Ghana's Upper Regions were swept by a devastating flood. In the Region where I work, 31 people were killed and 100,000 left homeless (GhanaWeb 2007). Of the approximately 150 women with whom I conducted research over the next six months, all had lost most if not all their crop (Glazebrook 2011). They had on average six dependants, but supported as many as 17. Since the system for rebuilding traditional mud houses destroyed in the flood involved the men of the village going from house to house as a group, households headed by single women were the last to have their hut rebuilt, if it was rebuilt at all. This case study is not about the threat of climate change, but its actuality, impacts and consequences.

Though 70 per cent of the world's farmers are women (Women for Women International 2010), in parts of Africa women contribute 80 per cent of food production. In 2003, Ghanaian women were growing 70 per cent of food crops; Ghana's first Poverty Reduction Strategy recognized that nearly half the female population was working in agriculture, but said that too little was known about their situations to develop useful policy (GPRS I 2003–05). The Ghana Social Watch Coalition reported that Ghana would be unable to meet Millennium Development Goals precisely because of women's marginalization, and requested the Poverty Reduction Strategy to incorporate gender. The second Poverty Reduction Strategy (GPRS II 2006–09) did give attention to gender, but strategies were directed at mechanization and emphasized industrial farming. Development models in agriculture, including participatory ones, mostly aim at capital-intensive, large-scale, industrial farming. Little assessment exists of the adequacy and effectiveness of such approaches for meeting women's needs as farmers, but these approaches are obviously not readily compatible with women's subsistence farming, which is typically small-scale and low-tech with minimal capital input. Nonetheless, by 2010 Ghanaian women were growing an impressive 87 per cent of food crops (Social Watch Coalition 2010). Ghana's food security has thus been left in the hands of women who have been left almost entirely to their own devices.

Ghana suffers the well documented 'gender gap' in development (Dwivedi 1980; Shiva 1989; Bakker 1994; Nesmith and Wright 1995; Venkateswaran 1995; Dwivedi et al. 2001), compounded by persistent social inequalities. Only 19 per cent of women in Ghana complete formal education, compared with 37 per cent of men (Social Watch Coalition 2010), and only 42 per cent are literate, compared with 66 per cent of men (GPRS II 2006–09). Women have a 15–20 per cent longer workday than men (Haddad 1991; Lloyd and Gage-Brandon 1993). Their work includes primary medical care for the family, so CC-related increase in disease adds to their workload at the same time as it may be affecting their health and capacity to cope.

Waring (1988, 1999) showed clearly that women's labor is largely invisible in the Global South because their participation in alternative and subsistence economies falls under the radar of traditional economic reckoning that tracks only market exchange. Leghorn and Parker (1991: 14) note that 'women are one-third of the world's formal labor force and do four-fifths of all informal work, but receive only ten percent of the world's income'. Their agricultural labor is thus largely overlooked by policy-makers because traditional economic indices cannot account for subsistence livelihoods. The Genuine Progress Index (GPI) provides an alternative economic reckoning consistent with the lived experience of poverty rather than tracking of business-based factors of production and profit. Yet the GPI does not account for the crucial contribution women make to the national food baskets, without which governments in Africa could not function. I have documented the dependency in Ghana of government-employed family members, whose salary is inadequate to meet daily living expenses, on the food grown by their mother (Glazebrook 2011). So Ghana is increasingly dependent on women's subsistence farming, though their situation is precarious.

Land tenure is a problem for women globally – women own less than 1 per cent of the world's property (Leghorn and Parker 1991: 14) – and is especially challenging in Ghana where women have weak land tenure rights

(Awanyo 2003; Whitehead and Tsikata 2003). Declines in Africa's agricultural production have been attributed to large-scale land acquisitions that displace locals from the land on which they depend for food and livelihood (Cotula et al. 2009). In Ghana, women have little to defend themselves from land-grabbing. I interviewed two women in 2008 whose brothers-in-law came after the death of the husband to claim the land the women had farmed for decades. Both women appealed to their local chief under the traditional justice system; in both cases the chief decided that the woman had the right to farm the land until her natural death. Corporate land-grabbers are not, however, likely to recognize this adjudication system. Women subsistence farmers cannot afford representation in the postcolonial, official legal system to resist land appropriation, and their livelihood is destroyed as growing and planting seasons pass while waiting for an outcome. Well intentioned development programs can simply fail to recognize women's interests because of their economic invisibility. Land-grabbing also happens through bribery and corruption, so compromise of community trust compounds gender injustices of land displacement, loss of livelihood, food insecurity, environmental degradation through poor soil practices and chemical inputs, and poverty exacerbation.

Government aid is often inaccessible to women because of their political and economic marginalization. The women I work with describe visits every few years from government officials who recommend that they participate in government loan and grant programs to buy fertilizers. To access the programs, they require a bank account into which the money can be deposited. The bank will not open an account without a deposit. They cannot get the loan without the account, or the account without the loan. Another official arrives some time later, and the cycle of frustration begins again. Increased cooperation by the bank or more realistic program implementation seem obvious solutions; yet women's needs are marginalized in both contexts, and neither the bank manager nor the program officer steps up to break the cycle. So Ghana is increasingly dependent on women's subsistence farming, yet government support cannot encompass their needs.

Women cannot simply move elsewhere when they lose their land. They head 30 per cent of households in Ghana (Lloyd and Gage-Brandon 1993), but are unlikely to have the resources to relocate, and may be constrained by other barriers. For example, a woman heading a Fra Fra family in a small village is almost certain to speak only Fra Fra, so language is a huge barrier to relocation. Moreover, where would she go? Given impacts of CC exacerbating long-standing problems in urban development, and employment barriers of education and literacy, moving to an urban area is unlikely to improve her or her family's situation. Other rural areas face the same challenges as hers, and AR5 documents the CC impact of population displacement as a source of conflict.

Nor can they relocate when growing conditions deteriorate. The IPCC expects major rural impacts in the near term concerning water availability, food security and agricultural incomes, including shifts in production areas. Expectation is also that the rural poor, such as female-headed households and those with limited access to land, agricultural inputs, infrastructure and education, will be affected disproportionately (IPCC 2014: 19). AR5 suggests that policy takes into account rural decision-making contexts, and uses trade reform and investment to improve market access for small-scale farms (IPCC 2014: 19). The report also states that 'the agricultural self-employed could benefit' from CC (IPCC 2014: 20). The women I interview all report that the rains are less, and are increasingly unpredictable. Assessment of women subsistence farmers' situation in Ghana makes it hard to see how they might benefit from CC, or how market access helps the subsistence farmer. Crops grown by women subsistence farmers in Ghana are declining because of CC, and are at increasing risk.

The 2014 statement by the International Monetary Fund's Executive Director for Ghana indicates that short-term vulnerabilities have risen in Ghana (IMF 2014). Ghana exceeded the 2013 fiscal deficit target of 9 per cent GDP by hitting 10.9 per cent, and by late August the 2014 deficit was projected at 10.25 per cent. The international reserve position was weakened alongside mounting public debt. High interest and depreciating currency were undermining the private sector, and growth had slowed from 5.5 per cent in 2013 to 4.75 per cent in 2014, with inflation rapidly up from 13.5 per cent at the end of 2013 to 14.5 per cent by March. These factors put at risk Ghana's transformation agenda of economic diversification, shared growth, job creation and macroeconomic stability. Given the IMF report, crisis prevention in the financial sector will likely receive more attention and resources at the national level than long-standing issues that have never anyway been central to the development agenda.

So Ghana is increasingly dependent on women farmers whose already precarious situation is being exacerbated by CC, whose needs have long been marginalized, and whose government is struggling to make ends meet. Can international funding sources respond to Africa's growing humanitarian food crisis?

## IPCC and policy

Key CC risks in Africa affect water and crops (IPCC 2014: 21). At 2°C warming, strong adaptations may keep both risks down to medium; no adaptation attempts keeps water risk high and crop risk very high. At 4°C, strong adaptation reduces water risk to high, but very high crop risk is irreducible. In comparison, European water risks can be kept to medium, and food security is not an indicated risk for Europe, Australia or North America. Asia's crop risk can be kept to medium. Central and South America bear the overall highest water and crop risks, but adaptation can limit crop risk to medium.

Particular challenges keep Africa's crop risk very high. Though most national governments are initiating adaptation governance, efforts are isolated. Risks evolve as socio-economic trends interact with CC (IPCC 2014: 8), and vary substantially across development pathways, sectors, regions and time periods (IPCC 2014: 11). Understanding vulnerability is challenging because interacting social, economic and cultural factors (wealth distribution, demographics, migration, access to technology and information, employment patterns, the quality of adaptive resources, societal values, governance structures, and institutions to resolve conflicts) are under-researched (IPCC 2014: 11).

Several factors identified – access to technology and information, the quality of adaptive resources, and societal values – especially affect women's vulnerability because of their limited access to credit, machinery, labor, fertilizer and agricultural extension services (University of Sussex 1994). Women's poverty precludes access, for example, to genetically modified seeds. Literacy and language issues limit employment potential and information access. Women I interviewed in 2007 learned about CC from local-language radio broadcasts and community meetings organized by local chiefs. By 2012, however, women attributed CC to 'the gods' will'. This indicates that discussions of the 2007 flood paid little attention to other climate impacts – women had local access to 'crisis information' but no sustained analysis. Taken together, these vulnerability factors indicate that women are substantially affected by persistent social inequalities, but assessments track symptoms of their vulnerability without making explicit this root cause. The 'elephant in the room' is gender vulnerability itself.

Gender is addressed in several boxes and graphics in AR5 (specifically chs 9, 11–13 and the Technical Summary). Yet the 'Summary for Policy-Makers' that explicitly intends to support adaptation planning does not mainstream gender in understanding vulnerability. This 'gender gap' can be attributed to failure to understand the depth of women's economic invisibility and the extent to which their agriculture supports national economies. The IPCC consists of experts collaborating to summarize the state of climate research. AR4 noted insufficient research to down-scale predictions to regional levels; AR5 notes that social, economic and cultural factors are under-studied. Explicitly noting the inadequacy of gender-based research might prompt attention to women's urgent needs concerning food security.

For example, drought figures throughout AR5, but for women interviewed in 2014, unpredictability is more pressing: 'I rise in the morning, see cloud; but afternoon, no rain come.' This makes it harder to know when to plant. Moreover, traditional crops are risky when the rainy season wavers unpredictably. Millet, a primary food crop, needs regular rain. Likewise, if groundnuts, also a local staple, do not get regular rain, leaves grow above ground but the nuts below do not; resources are wasted and harvests are inadequate to last until the next growing season. The women adapt by diversifying crop selection to include rice. Rice grows with sporadic rainfall; but rice does not contain the protein of groundnut and millet, or millet's calcium which is especially important for children and pregnant or lactating women. The women are accordingly obliged to sacrifice the nutritional base to put at least something in the belly until the next growing season.

Overlooking gender may account for the fact that 23 per cent of Ghana's children under five years showed stunted growth in 2011, despite Ghana having met its 2015 Millennium Development Goal with respect to hunger by 2002 and having less than 5 per cent of its population undernourished in 2011–13 (FAO et al. 2013: 31–32). The latter UN report on food insecurity does not identify transition to rice as a factor explaining this stunting – impacts of women's crop selection adaptations remain below the radar of the experts on whom governments and international governance institutions like the UN rely for policy guidance. The report does note that poverty is highest in the Upper Regions in Ghana, and recommends accessing the Livelihood Empowerment Against Poverty program; but, as noted above, such conditional cash transfer programs are short-sighted concerning women's situation.

Regarding water, the IPCC suggests strengthening demand management, integrating waste-water planning, and integrating land and water governance. Since the Ghanaian women have no access to water for irrigation and use well-water in the home, planning and governance have little to offer. Assuring women's land tenure rights would increase their visibility and decrease vulnerability to land-grabbing, but integrating land and water governance seems largely irrelevant, and benefits to male cash croppers may reduce local water tables.

IPCC crop adaptation suggestions include strengthening institutions to support gender-oriented policy, and also technological adaptations such as stress-tolerant crop varieties and irrigation; enhancing smallholder access to credit and production resources; diversifying livelihoods; strengthening institutions and regional supports; and agronomic responses including agro-forestry and conservation agriculture (IPCC 2014: 21). Diversifying livelihood would help women buy food when crops fail or are inadequate. Other suggestions are likely to improve conditions for those already able to access technology and credit, and who practice agroforestry from which women are traditionally excluded. Strengthening institutions to support gender-oriented policy is a helpful suggestion, but treats gender as a single factor among many and as a kind of add-on to the recommendation to strengthen institutions to support agriculture that does not distinguish cash cropping from subsistence. As has been seen so often in UNFCCC finalized reports from annual Conferences of Parties (COPs), the gender add-on is easily dropped when space is limited. Gender is rather a cross-cutting issue that warrants specific attention if food security in the Global South is not to be devastated by CC.

The World Bank's 2008 report on agriculture for development indeed neglected gender. The Bank's President failed to mention gender in his Foreword (World Bank 2008: xiii). 'Gender' appears in no titles, figures, tables, maps or boxes, and 'women' appears only in comparison of women's participation in agriculture against men's (ibid.: 80), and when a women's cooperative in India provides an example (ibid.: 211). The World Bank strongly recommends modernization, mechanization and extension technologies. These approaches are (as discussed above) inadequate to meet women's needs. Also, they commonly displace women subsistence farmers from land in favor of male-owned, capital- and technology-intensive cash cropping, in which women's function is reduced to waged labor. Since profit is the surplus value provided by her labor, capital necessitates she earn less than crops sell for – she may do the same work on the same land, but no longer be able to afford for her family to eat what she grows. Gender indifference in international governance is thus not indifferent at all from women's perspective: practically, it generates harms. Unless development programs make gender central, they risk bulldozing women's livelihoods. They also render invisible the CC adaptations women have already adopted.

## Funding adaptation

The UNFCCC has established two funds to implement adaptation: the Climate Adaptation Fund (AF) and the Green Climate Fund (GCF). The AF was established in 2001 and launched in 2007 to finance concrete adaptation projects in developing countries. By the end of 2013, the AF had allocated about US$200 million to projects in 29 countries. The GCF was established at COP 16 at Cancun in 2010 to support CC projects, programs and policies in developing countries, with initial resource mobilization planned for COP 20 at Lima in December 2014.

A project proposal in Ghana for over US$8 million funding was submitted to the AF in April 2013: 'Increased resilience to climate change in Northern Ghana through the management of water resources and diversification of livelihoods'. Confluence between the UNFCCC and the IPCC is a healthy sign of integration of the current states of knowledge and policy. Water management and livelihood diversification are among the IPCC's suggested adaptations. Certainly, irrigation would be a boon to women of the Upper Eastern Region simply by decreasing rain dependence. Yet irrigation ultimately depends too on rainfall. I have already undertaken livelihood diversification with three groups of women by establishing a small basket production, import and distribution system to fund their microcredit collective. But the project proposed to the AF provides no indication that it addresses gender. The AF has the potential better to connect international policy with women's lived experience by drawing a clear distinction between cash cropping and subsistence agriculture. This distinction recognizes that gender is central and not just an add-on.

A Decision was taken at the UNFCCC's Seventh COP to increase women's participation as delegates in negotiating teams. COP 13 included a further Decision to advance gender balance and women's empowerment in international climate policy. Yet at COP 18, Decision 23/CP.18, 'Promoting gender balance and improving the participation of women in UNFCCC negotiations …' (UNFCCC 2013), that I will simply call 'the Gender Decision', notes women's under-representation. This Decision, adopted under the leadership of Christiana Figueres and strongly facilitated by Mary Robinson, former President of Ireland, recognizes the need for gender representation in delegations 'to inform gender-responsive climate policy' (UNFCCC 2013: 47). It asks the UNFCCC Secretariat to make gender a standing agenda item at COPs, and to provide budgets to track gender composition of delegations and organize workshops at COP 19 on gender balance, gender sensitivity, and capacity-building (ibid.: 48). It acknowledges women's leadership in vital contributions to sustainable development and notes the UN's emphasis on substantial increase in the number of women in leadership roles (ibid.: 47). This Decision, beyond calling for women's inclusion in climate policy, is a reminder to the UNFCCC of the UN's commitment to women's participation and empowerment in governance.

Since both the AF and GCF are under the UNFCCC umbrella, they are obliged to follow the Gender Decision. Specific strategies for gender-responsive approaches include requiring gender budgets that fund women's initiatives, gender vulnerability assessments, and gender impact assessments in proposal submissions. Post-award reporting mechanisms could also ask for detailed follow-up assessments of gender impacts and outcomes. These strategies standardize gender inclusivity and sensitivity across projects, and function educationally to increase awareness of policy-makers and implementers concerning the relevance, significance and necessity of addressing gender in order for adaptation investments effectively to strengthen food security and alleviate poverty.

Gender has been mainstreamed throughout much development policy and activity, but is not yet successfully thematized in international climate negotiations, despite Decisions at COP 7 and COP 13. If the COP 18 Gender Decision is likewise futile, climate policy will continue to work with a deficient theoretical paradigm and inadequate praxis. Hope for a binding, international CC agreement, now that the ineffective Kyoto Protocol has expired, is strongly pinned on COP 21 at Paris in 2015, for which the Lima COP of 2014 is being considered preparatory. Many challenges need to be addressed in this agreement. Gender is a cross-cutting factor warranting attention throughout, though I focus here on agricultural adaptations that impact food security.

The truth is, any policy that sustains the almost two-decades-long failure to make focal women's needs and expertise is working against its own adaptation targets. Women's on-the-ground efforts play a central role in filling national food baskets throughout much of the globe, especially in the Global South, where poverty and hunger are most pressing, and women have specialized experience and knowledge concerning both impacts and adaptations in agriculture. Implementing the Gender Decision through the AF and GCF is a way of putting the money where the mouths are – both the negotiating mouths of national delegations that decide and answer for how these Funds are used, and the mouths of the many whose survival depends on women's capacity to grow food.

## Conclusion

My ecofeminist analysis of CC impacts and adaptations shows the necessity for gender inclusion to address global food security. Women farmers have specialized agricultural expertise, and urgent need to adapt to CC. Because their labor reproduces the material conditions of daily living for their family, their ongoing adaptation strategies function in logics of care embedded in, but irreducible to, the logic of domination of global capital. Care arises not from ontological essentialism, but from the material conditions of women's labor. Asked whether they ever sell any of their crop, all of the Ghanaian women interviewed who said yes explained, 'small, small', to pay for school books, uniforms or school fees. Thus capital, i.e. monetary exchange systems, can function in alternative logics that, in this example, enact intergenerational justice by using money as a means rather than an end in itself. These women care for their children, their land, their animals and their family members who cannot support themselves because of disability, health issues and/or a national economy being strangled by the global logic of capital. Their care picks up where global, national and local systems of capital fail. Indifference to their needs (and their expertise) contravenes recognition justice by rendering them and their knowledge systems invisible; gender justice by devaluing their labor and excluding them from leadership and governance; and distributive justice by increasing their workload, destroying their resource base, and leaving them to bear the costs of CC disproportionately despite their negligible contribution. Their care practices include subsistence agriculture which is embedded in, and moreover supports, capital systems.

Subsistence logics of care aim at supporting life rather than the individual accumulation of private wealth that drives the logic of domination of global capital. Women farmers in the Global South are not waiting for the UNFCCC to meet their needs, but organizing into groups that voice their perspectives throughout side-events at COPs. Mainstreaming gender in AF and GCF implementation means not just trying to mechanize women's farming and up its capital- and technology-intensity. It means recognizing how women's subsistence agriculture is inherently different in its very logic, that is to say, its economics, from male-dominated practices of corporate agriculture. Thus these Funds can institutionalize women's praxical logics of care, and respect distributive, recognition and intergenerational justices precluded by the logic of capital by supporting women's adaptations to conditions they have not created, acknowledging their labor and economic contribution, and helping them feed their children. In doing so, they re-orient global economics, both ontologically (the value of women's labor) and epistemologically (the value of women's knowledge), through management of CC that is arguably the most influential economic issue in the contemporary epoch.

Based on IPCC predictions, the situation for women farmers in Africa seems especially hopeless. Yet as Sartre put it, 'one need not hope in order to undertake one's work' (Sartre 1989). It has always been women's work to feed the children of Africa. These women are strong, and know how to grow food. Since women's farming in the Global South aims virtually entirely at subsistence, not profit, their work models logics of care, rather than embodying destructive logics of capital. Gender is not an add-on but a cross-cutting issue, without attention to which food security in the Global South faces impending collapse. If the AF and the GCF make gender their starting point and purpose, CC adaptation has the potential to reveal what the IPCC, the IMF, the World Bank and other governance institutions driven by the logic of capital are blind to: gender is a game-changer, like Descartes' Archimedean fulcrum, with the potential to shift economic logics from profit-exploiting systems of injustice to functional praxes of life-affirming care for ecosystems, human others, and planetary co-habitants. Sounds absurd, I know. And yet ... I would rather be wrong and work for such a vision than be right and do nothing at all. And I have the privilege of choosing how I work.

## Note

1 Thank you for your help and support in conducting this research to the women of Kantia and Zuarongu who participated in the study; to Franciska, Mary Margaret and Beatrice Issaka of the Center for Sustainable Development Initiatives in Bolga-tanga, Stella and the women of the Single Mothers' Association in Zuarongu, and the Kantia Alternative Development Association; and to Christiana Figueres and Mary Robinson, without whom all my work is wasted breath. This research was supported by the Social Sciences and Humanities Council of Canada, Dalhousie University, the University of North Texas, and Gender CC: Women for Climate Justice.

## References

Al-Hassan, R., Famiyeh, J.A. and de Jager, A. (1997) 'Farm household strategies for food security in northern Ghana: a comparative study of high and low population farming systems', in *Sustainable Food Security in West Africa*, edited by Asenso-Okyere, W.K., Benneh, G. and Tims, W., Dordrecht: Kluwer, 129–152.

Allen, J. (1988) 'Women who beget women must thwart major sophisms', *Philosophy and Social Criticism* 13(4): 315–326.

Awanyo, L. (2003) 'Land tenure and agricultural development in Ghana: the inter-section of class, culture and gender', in *Critical Perspectives on Politics and Socio-Economic Development in Ghana*, edited by Puplampu, K., Tettey, W. and Berman, B., Boston: Brill Academic Publishers, 273–304.

Baker, J.T., Allen Jr, L.H. and Boote, K.J. (1990) 'Growth and yield responses of rice to carbon dioxide concentration', *Journal of Agricultural Science* 115: 313–320.

Bakker, I. (1994) *The Strategic Silence: Gender and Economic Policy*, London: Zed Books.

Baylis, F., Downie, J. and Sherwin, S. (1998) 'Reframing research involving humans', in *The Politics of Women's Health*, edited by Sherwin, S., Philadelphia: Temple University Press, 234–260.

de Beauvoir, S. (1952) *The Second Sex*, translated by Parshley, H.M., New York: Vintage Books.

Biavaschi, E. (2008) 'Women and food-security in sub-Saharan Africa', in *PHE 510: Public Health and Social Justice*, available at http://www.phsj.org/women-and-food-security-in-sub-saharan-africa-paper-biaschivi-2008.doc (accessed 20 December 2010).

Bohle, H.G., Downing, T.E. and Watts, M.C. (1994) 'Climate change and social vulnerability: toward a sociology and geography of food insecurity', *Global Environmental Change* 4(1): 37–48.

Cline, W. (2007) *Global Warming and Agriculture: Impact Estimates by Country*, Washington, DC: Center for Global Development/Peterson Institute for International Economics.

Cotula, L., Vermeulen, S., Leonard, R. and Keeley, J. (2009) *Land Grab or Development Opportunity? Agricultural Investment and International Land Deals in Africa*, London/Rome: IIED/FAO/IFAD.

Dwivedi, O.P. (1980) *Resources and the Environment: Policy Perspectives for Canada*, Toronto: McClelland & Stewart.

Dwivedi, O.P., Kyba, J.P., Stoett, P. and Tiessen, R. (2001) *Sustainable Development and Canada: National and International Perspectives*, Peterborough, ON: Broadview Press.

FAO (2004) 'Fertilizer development in support of the comprehensive Africa agriculture development programme (CAADP)', in *Proceedings of the 23rd Regional Conference for Africa*, Johannesburg, South Africa, 1–5 March, Rome: UN Food and Agriculture Organization, available at http://www.fao.org/docrep/meeting/008/J1662e.htm (accessed 12 September 2014).

FAO (2008) 'Countries in crisis requiring external assistance', *Crop Prospects and Food Situation*, No. 2, Rome: UN Food and Agriculture Organization, Economic and Social Development Department, available at http://www.fao.org/docrep/010/ai465e/ai465e02.htm (accessed 28 July 2014).

FAO, IFAD and WFP (2013) *The State of Food Insecurity in the World 2013: The Multiple Dimensions of Food Security*, Rome: UN Food and Agriculture Organization, available at http://www.fao.org/docrep/018/i3434e/i3434e00.htm (accessed 30 July 2014).

Finn, G. (1982) 'On the oppression of women in philosophy – Or, whatever happened to objectivity?', in *Feminism in Canada: From Pressure to Politics*, edited by Miles, A. and Finn, G., Montreal: Black Rose Books, 145–173.

Fonow, M.M. and Cook, J.A. (eds) (1991) *Beyond Methodology: Feminist Scholarship as Lived Research*, Bloomington: Indiana University Press.

Garry, A. and Pearsall, M. (eds) (1989) *Women, Knowledge and Reality*, Boston: Unwin Hyman.

GhanaWeb (2007) '56 deaths reported in flood disaster', 28 September, available at http://www.ghanaweb.com/GhanaHomePage/NewsArchive/artikel.php?ID=131481 (accessed 29 September 2007).

Glazebrook, T. (2000) 'From physis to nature, technê to technology: Heidegger on Aristotle, Galileo and Newton', *Southern Journal of Philosophy* 38(1): 95–118.

Glazebrook, T. (2005) 'Gynocentric eco-logics', *Ethics and the Environment* 10(2): 75–99.

Glazebrook, T. (2010a) 'What women want: an (eco)feminist in dialogue with John D. Caputo', in *Cross and Khôra: Deconstruction and Christianity in the Work of John D. Caputo*, edited by Zlomislić, M. and Deroo, N., Eugene, OR: Pickwick Publications, Wipf and Stock, ch. 9.

Glazebrook, T. (2010b) 'Gender and climate change: an environmental justice perspective', in *Heidegger and Climate Change*, edited by Irwin, R., London: Continuum.

Glazebrook, T. (2011) 'Women and climate change: a case study from northeast Ghana', *Hypatia* 26(4): 762–782.

Glazebrook, T. (2015) 'Ecofeminism without borders: the power of method', in *Environmental Ethics for Canadians*, 2nd edn, edited by Williston, B., Oxford: Oxford University Press, forthcoming.

Glazebrook, T. and Olusanya, A.K. (2011) 'Justice, conflict, capital, and care: oil in the Niger Delta', *Environmental Ethics* 33(2): 163–184.

GPRS I (2003–05) *Ghana Poverty Reduction Strategy: 2003–2005*, available at https://www.imf.org/external/pubs/ft/scr/2003/cr0356.pdf (accessed 24 June 2013).

GPRS II (2006–09) *Ghana Poverty Reduction Strategy: 2006–2009*, available at http://www.imf.org/external/pubs/ft/scr/2006/cr06225.pdf (accessed 30 July 2014).

Haddad, L. (1991) 'Gender and poverty in Ghana: a descriptive analysis of selected outcomes and processes', *IDS Bulletin* 22(1): 5–16.

hooks, bell (1984) 'Black women: shaping feminist theory', in *Feminist Theory: From Margin to Center*, Cambridge, MA: South End Press.

IMF (2014) *Ghana: 2014 Article IV Consultation–Staff Report; Press Release; and Statement by the Executive Director for Ghana*, Washington, DC: International Monetary Fund, available at http://www.imf.org/external/pubs/cat/longres.aspx?sk=41574.0 (accessed 30 July 2014).

IPCC (2014) 'Summary for policymakers', in *Climate Change 2014: Impacts, Adaptation, and Vulnerability. Part A: Global and Sectoral Aspects*, Contribution of Working Group II to the Fifth Assessment Report of the Intergovernmental Panel on Climate Change, edited by Field, C.B. et al., Cambridge, UK: Cambridge University Press.

Jaggar, A. (ed.) (2008) *Just Methods: An Interdisciplinary Feminist Reader*, Boulder, CO: Paradigm Publishers.

Jennings, J. and Magrath, J. (2009) *What Happened to the Seasons*, Oxford: Oxfam, available at http://publications.oxfam.org.uk/display.asp?k=002R0193 (accessed 15 January 2011).

Johnson-Odim, C. (1991) 'Common themes, different contexts: third world women and feminism', in *Third World Women and the Politics of Feminism*, edited by Mohanty, C., Russo, A. and Torres, L., Bloomington: Indiana University Press, 314–327.

Kabasa, J.D. and Sage, I. (2009) 'Climate change and food security in Africa', in *Climate Change in Africa: Adaptation, Mitigation and Governance Challenges*, CIGI Special Report, edited by Besada, H. and Sewankambo, N.K., Waterloo, Canada: Centre for International Governance Innovation.

Kuuzegh, R.S. (2007) 'Comments by Mr. Rudolph S. Kuuzegh, Director of Environment of Ghana, during the session on policy option and possible action on climate change for sustainable development', available at http://www.un.org/esa/sustdev/csd/csd15/statements/ghana_1may_cc.pdf (accessed 20 July 2014).

Kuuzegh, R.S. (2009) 'Remarks by Mr. Rudolph S. Kuuzegh, Director, Ministry of Environment, Science and Technology at the Intergovernmental Preparatory Meeting of CSD-17, New York, 23–27 February 2009', available at https://sustainabledevelopment.un.org/content/documents/2639Ghana.pdf (accessed 20 June 2014).

Leghorn, L. and Parker, K. (1991) *Women's Worth: Sexual Economics and the World of Women*, Boston, MA: Routledge.

Lloyd, C.B. and Gage-Brandon, A.J. (1993) 'Women's role in maintaining households: family welfare and sexual inequality in Ghana', *Population Studies* 47(1): 115–131.

Longhurst, R. (1986) 'Household food strategies in response to seasonality and famine', *IDS Bulletin* 17(3): 27–35.

Lott, F.C., Christidis, N. and Stott, P.A. (2013) 'Can the 2011 East African drought be attributed to human-induced climate change?', *Geophysical Research Letters* 40(6): 1177–1181.

Lugones, M. and Spelman, E. (1983) 'Have we got a theory for you! Feminist theory, cultural imperialism and the demand for "the women's voice"', *Women's Studies International Forum* 6(6): 573–581.

Merchant, C. (1980) *The Death of Nature: Women, Ecology and the Scientific Revolution*, San Francisco: Harper.

Morrow, B.H. (1999) 'Identifying and mapping community vulnerability', *Disasters* 23(1): 1–18.

Moulton, J. (1983) 'A paradigm of philosophy: the adversary method', in *Discovering Reality*, edited by Harding, S. and Hintikka, M.B., Dordrecht: Reidel.

Nesmith, C. and Wright, P. (1995) 'Gender, resources and environmental management', in *Resource and Environmental Management in Canada: Addressing Conflict and Uncertainty*, edited by Mitchell, B., Toronto: Oxford University Press, 80–98.

Okai, M. (1997) 'Agricultural production, food security and poverty in West Africa', in *Sustainable Food Security in West Africa*, edited by Asenso-Okyere, W.K., Benneh, G. and Tims, W., Dordrecht: Kluwer, 14–34.

Panjabi, K. (1997) 'Probing "morality" and state violence: feminist values and communicative interaction in prison testimonios in India and Argentina', in *Feminist Genealogies, Colonial Legacies, Democratic Futures*, edited by Alexander, M.J. and Mohanty, C.T., New York: Routledge, 151–169.

Peacock, W.G., Morrow, B.H. and Gladwin, H. (1997) *Hurricane Andrew: Ethnicity, Gender and the Sociology of Disaster*, New York: Routledge.

Pearce, F. (1991) 'A sea change in the Sahel', *New Scientist* 1754: 22–24.

Plumwood, V. (1991) 'Nature, self and gender: feminism, environmental philosophy and the critique of rationalism', *Hypatia* 6(1): 3–27.

Plumwood, V. (1993) *Feminism and the Mastery of Nature*, New York: Routledge.

Salleh, A. (1997) *Ecofeminism as Politics: Nature, Marx and the Postmodern*, London: Zed Books.

Sartre, J.P. (1989) 'Existentialism is a Humanism', in *Existentialism from Dostoyevsky to Sartre*, edited by Kaufman, W., Santa Barbara, CA: Meridian.

Scialabba, N.E. (2007) 'Organic agriculture and food security in Africa', in *Can Africa Feed Itself?*, edited by Naerstad, E., Oslo: AiR AS e-dit.

Sherwin, S. (1988) 'Philosophical methodology and feminist methodology: are they compatible?', in *Feminist Perspectives: Philosophical Essays on Method and Morals*, edited by Code, L., Overall, C. and Mullet, S., Toronto: University of Toronto Press, 13–28.

Sherwin, S. (1998) 'Introduction', in *The Politics of Women's Health*, edited by Sherwin, S., Philadelphia: Temple University Press, 1–18.

Shiva, V. (1989) *Staying Alive: Women, Ecology, and Development*, London: Zed Books.

Social Watch Coalition (2010) 'MDGs remain elusive', Ghana Social Watch Coalition Report 2004, Social Watch: Poverty Eradication and Gender Justice, available at http://www.socialwatch.org/node/12082 (accessed 17 December 2010).

UNFCCC (2007) *Climate Change: Impacts, Vulnerabilities and Adaptation in Developing Countries*, Bonn: United Nations Framework Convention on Climate Change, available at unfccc.int/resource/docs/publications/impacts.pdf (accessed 20 January 2015).

UNFCCC (2013) 'Addendum: Part Two: Action taken by the Conference of the Parties at its eighteenth session', in *Report of the Conference of the Parties on its Eighteenth Session, held in Doha from 26 November to 8 December 2012*, Decision 23/CP.18, Bonn: United Nations Framework Convention on Climate Change, available at http://unfccc.int/resource/docs/2012/cop18/eng/08a03.pdf#page=47 (accessed 31 July 2014).

University of Sussex (1994) *Background Paper on Gender Issues in Ghana*, Brighton, UK: Institute of Development Studies.

Venkateswaran, S. (1995) *Environment, Development and the Gender Gap*, New Delhi: Sage.

Walker, A. (1983) *In Search of Our Mother's Garden*, New York: Harcourt, Brace, Jovanovich.

Waring, M. (1988) *If Women Counted: A New Feminist Economics*, New York: Harper & Row.

Waring, M. (1999) *Counting for Nothing: What Men Value and What Women are Worth*, Toronto: University of Toronto Press.

Warren, K. (1990) 'The power and promise of ecofeminism', *Environmental Ethics* 12(3): 125–146.

Warren, K. (1997) 'Taking empirical data seriously: an ecofeminist philosophical perspective', in *Ecofeminism: Women, Culture, Nature*, edited by Warren, K., Bloomington, IN: Indiana University Press, 3–20.

Warren, K. (2000) *Ecofeminist Philosophy: A Western Perspective on What It Is and Why It Matters*, Oxford: Rowman & Littlefield.

WFP (2014) World Food Program: Hunger Statistics, available at http://www.wfp.org/hunger/stats (accessed 6 October 2014).

Whitbeck, C. (1984) 'A different reality: feminist ontology', in *Beyond Domination: New Perspectives on Women and Philosophy*, edited by Gould, C., Totowa, NJ: Rowman & Allanheld, 64–88.

Whitehead, A. and Tsikata, D. (2003) 'Policy discourses on women's land rights in sub-Saharan Africa: the implications of the return to the customary', *Journal of Agrarian Change* 3(1/2): 67–112.

Women for Women International (2010) 'Women in agriculture and food security', available at http://www.womenforwomen.org/news-women-for-women/agriculture-food-security.php (accessed 30 January 2011).

World Bank (2008) *World Development Report 2008: Agriculture for Development*, Washington, DC: World Bank, available at https://openknowledge.worldbank.org/handle/10986/5990 (accessed 30 July 2014).

World Bank (2014) 'Levelling the field: improving opportunities for women farmers in Africa', available at http://www.worldbank.org/en/region/afr/publication/levelling-the-field-improving-opportunities-for-women-farmers-in-africa (accessed 6 October 2014).

# 7 Hidden lives, invisible vocation?

## Giving voice to game rangers' wives in KwaZulu-Natal, South Africa

*Ida Sabelis, Tamarisk van Vliet and Harry Wels*

## Introduction

Until the 1980s, the impact of women's support for men's work in developing the wilderness areas of KwaZulu-Natal (KZN), South Africa was neither recognized nor problematized. This rendered a large part of women's work invisible, or at least forgotten from a present perspective, behind the public and professional status, the payment and the identity related to the men's professions. It was only in the 1980s that some (feminist) writers started problematizing the role and position of the invisible work of women in general, wondering what it means to be generally referred to as 'the wife of …' (Hochschild 1983; Daniels 1987; Tancred 1995). Combining the notion of 'giving voice' to women involved in their men's work, and our access to game rangers' wives in KZN, we wondered why women chose this life. And, more importantly, how they made sense of their lives in the context of a men's world of rifles, shooting 'problem animals', chasing poachers and telling adventure stories around the campfire. This latter world, or rather its construction in terms of adventure and action, became familiar to us through the many memoirs of male game rangers over the years; from classics like James Stevenson Hamilton (1993/1937) and Harry Wolhuter (1948) to current-day memoirs of Bruce Bryden (2005), Graham Root (n.d.), Keith Thomas (2008), Mario Cesare (2009) and Ron Selley (2009). In their memoirs they sometimes refer to their wives and family, but in an ephemeral manner such that women are barely apparent. The lives of the 'wives of …' remain hidden, together with ways in which they contributed to and actually enabled much of the conservation work of their husbands. Kobie Krüger, Daphne Sheldrick and Lynne Tinley are the few women we know of who came out of the shadows of their husbands' work as game rangers and con-servationists to write about their lives with husband and family in the wild (Tinley 1979; Krüger 1994, 1996; Sheldrick 2012[1]). No matter that many of these memoirs paint a rather romantic picture of life in the wilderness. One of the bush wives told us in a private conversation that there was 'nothing romantic about it, it was a hard life'. This implies not only that there might be some interesting stories hidden from public knowledge, but also that the overall image of 'the wilderness experience' is one-sided. We are not suggesting that the women's voices are so much different from the men's, but their experiences and the ways in which their opinions, thoughts and views developed are simply not included in both historical and present 'authentic' presentations of why there should be wildlife conservation in its present form.

This chapter therefore focuses on the role of those *bush wives*, the women who followed their spouses into the wilderness of the game reserves and national parks during the late 1950s until the 1990s.[2] In the course of our life history-inspired research, we focused on questions such as: what did you do, how, at what cost, and with what type of ideas about wilderness and conservation? We recount parts of their life stories as gathered during fieldwork in 2010 in KwaZulu-Natal, South Africa by Tamarisk van Vliet (2011) and Ida Sabelis (from 2012), subsequently analysed with Harry Wels. This venture marks the beginning of a special branch of back-stage research in nature conservation about the women behind (beside) the masculine front-stage of nature conservation in (South and southern) Africa. These women were, and are, living what is now theoretically termed 'post-human intersectionality' (Twine 2010: 401). This is a specific type of situatedness where humans are vulnerable to nature and (other) animals and, in this context, where the raw relationship between human and animal means that humans are confronted with their own positionality with animals and with each other. They were also expected to control and 'manage' family and work. They lived in remote areas, surrounded by, coping with and being cautious of 'wild' animals; and therefore had an opportunity to problematize their situation and develop an understanding of nature available to few other people.[3] In their accounts of being *bush wives*, they bring to the fore emotions and opinions related to 'being part of' nature, and of living with animals, illustrating the notion of a relational, companion understanding of human–animal–nature. Of course, we look at their stories with a contemporary gaze, knowing that 'nature' as they experienced it no longer exists due to commodification and the growth of interdependencies between nature conservation, tourist industry and political developments (Zwarenstein 2012; Snijders 2015). Also we acknowledge that it was never their intention to convey postmodern feminism. However, something emerges from their stories that makes them all the more interesting from a contemporary view: the way their relation to nature mirrors some of the contemporary issues in human–animal–nature relationships. This generates insights into specific types of sense-making seemingly helpful in current debates over nature conservation. Ultimately, the opinions and stories reveal aspects of what we now call 'ecofeminist' (Twine 2001; Phillips 2014) and 'utopian' stories (Sargisson 2001; Schönpflug 2008), the latter understood as necessary counterpoint to a merely economic view on our relations to nature, including conservation.

The position of the bush wives was not only at the side of their men, anchoring their families' position in the bigger structure of a growing organization of natural parks (the Natal Parks Board, NPB). In addition, their experiences apart from their men, as 'lonely women who did not take part in the entertainment'[4] (quoting conservationist Ian Player) are worth studying, as they did develop a life of their own that in turn influenced nature conservation via their husbands and the overarching organization. Ultimately, we question and try to recast images of 'saving nature' because the women's voices were never included when these were debated. Before we set out on this quest, we need to picture the context of these women's lives. Therefore we first introduce the stories of 14 women who are (or were) married to a game ranger or a section ranger,[5] covering their experiences from the 1960s to the 1990s. We started gathering their stories more or less coincidentally: Harry composed a biography of Nick Steele from working notes and archives in the home of his widow, Nola Steele. Obviously, we thus heard her stories, and those of her mother Thurl Perkins. Although we couldn't imagine that nobody had entered the women's realm before, it turned out nobody had. Thus Tamarisk wrote the first explorative story based on a three-month field work period (2010) in which she visited 14 women in the Durban–Howick area. Ida then followed up by sharing time with Nola and Thurl (three periods of some weeks from 2012 to the present), and building a network in which she met more and more people from the NPB community from that particular period. Harry and Ida are currently working on the theoretical impact of narratives emerging from the field notes, transcribed interviews, family album pictures and – most of all – the ongoing narratives that reach us from the network of former 'rhino-saving' families. Together with a growing interest to combine the life-story approach to nature conservation with notions of feminist–ecologist theory (or sustainability from ecofeminist perspectives), we seem to have stumbled upon a source of rich images from the past that are useful for our present day and future.

The time covered by the bush wives' stories is a crucial period in conservation history. It refers to the transition from the romantic ideal of 'nature conservation' of the nineteenth century to the contemporary phase of ecotourism, game farming and unsuccessful sustainability policies,[6] highlighting how the women and their families were living through a period of liminality between wilderness-as-endangered and wilderness-as-commodity.

## Everyday life

> You meet authentic people and you learn what is really important in life, and how to respect nature.
>
> (Camilla, April 2010)

This was an answer to the question: what is the most significant aspect about your life in a game reserve that you would like to share? There is consensus among the women about belonging to and living in the wilderness. Meeting 'authentic people' means that they met people from different places who shared a similar interest and passion for nature and wildlife conservation.[7] 'Authentic' is a term frequently used by the women when referring to people in their network and those who shared the same ideas. It serves as a marker between 'us', living close to nature and wilderness, and 'them', the people who live outside the game reserve. As Jenny states:

> [Wilderness life] has influenced me in getting a love of being alone, a sense of being in the wilderness. It is not that we didn't like other people, but we are different from most of the people around us [city people]. We enjoyed company, but it is like having a separate identity to people around you. I don't want to sound arrogant, but there are just a few of us [other wives and game rangers] out there.
>
> (Jenny, March 2010)

This identity-marking process vis-à-vis people from outside the game reserve (the 'others', 'them') also suggests similarity with people 'like her', those who live or lived in game reserves.

> I enjoy the peace of the section. I enjoy the fact that the people we mostly meet in the park are a far outcry from the 'modern town' people, where status and the latest model car/phone/house etc. is so important to them.
>
> (Kerrin, May 2010)

The perception of people inside as opposed to outside the game reserve is framed by what they believe is important in life. Both quotes suggest a sense of belonging to something bigger than everyday life, because they have not met a lot of people living the life they did in the game reserve.

> It makes you focused on individual things, when things flower, the butterflies come out. Here [city] you take control of it, of time, there [bush] it is fascinating to get to grips with it, the things, time. I loved the bush! It cleans the mind of shops and traffic and you concentrate on what you want and where you are and the perception of time is different! People don't live by the clock; when you want to watch the sunset, you do that.
>
> (Susan, April 2010)

This quote suggests that on the 'outside' people are more controlled by time in comparison with people in the wilderness. The latter are supposed to be more controlled by their natural surroundings instead of by 'the clock', as Susan suggests. The women frequently answered like this when asked to describe their daily routines: starting at first daylight and ending with nightfall, mainly because their husbands start working at daybreak, temperatures increase quickly as the sun rises, and because of the lack of electricity at night. Furthermore, the rules of the NPB (now Ezemvelo KZN Wildlife) stipulated that all lights must be switched off at 9 pm because of the animals.

So, instead of living by the clock, these women lived 'by nature', just like their husbands.

Living outside clock times also relates to the dictum that 'flexibility is everything in the bush'. As there are frequent incidents in the bush that can keep them busy for hours, such as fires or animals breaking into their garden, they must relate flexibly to any planning that they might have for the day. The women from the game reserves all share this understanding of flexibility. Moreover, because they understand each other, it unites them and again marks them off against outsiders ('them') who 'do not understand what it is like to live in a remote area and what kind of planning goes in a visit to town or even a meal' (Kerrin, May 2010).

Typically, the women describe and label their mutual understanding or connection most often as 'authentic' (i.e. giving special meaning to people who share their vision of conserving wilderness and wildlife). Furthermore, the term 'authentic' seems to suggest a sense of self as well as something 'pure'. It runs parallel with a discourse on wilderness landscape as 'untouched' by human interference. Similarly they are people 'not influenced' and 'unspoiled' – with the latter's important connotations of hygiene, cleanliness and purity (cf. Ten Bos and Kaulingfreks 2001) – by modern industrialization. The women ascribe authenticity to people who appreciate this and to places that capture the same sense of 'aesthetic' appreciation of wilderness that they adhere to. The overall sense is that the so-called 'city-slickers' [people who live in cities] (Camilla, April 2010) do not share the same interest in and appreciation of nature. Furthermore, the wilderness in which they lived is preferred to today's game reserves, and for that matter to everything outside the game reserve, especially 'the city'.

Despite the nostalgia and longing, the women state that it was not by any means an idyllic and romantic life, because they experienced particular social hardship too. For example, one of the wives talked about how she noticed competition among the wives regarding who had the best garden (as pure and indigenous, with 'alien species' thoroughly eliminated), parallel to 'whose baby behaved best'. This complex and layered relationship is all part of the passion they felt for conserving 'their' places in order to keep the landscape as it was or, for some, as it should be. That is, as a 'pure wilderness' untouched by humans, a place of solitude without waste, roads or buildings and one that needs to be conserved for the future.

'Conservation has a religious flavour to it', one of the women said when describing what conservation meant to her husband as well as to other game rangers. What has changed is the landscape of the game reserves which, according to them, has lost its 'authentic character' of wilderness and now includes fences, houses, tar roads, underpinning the presence of humans and human intervention. Again, this is what the game rangers and the NPB strived for: to reconstruct and intensely conserve wilderness landscapes and wildlife, to which they would dedicate their entire lives, including those of their wives and families. Nature conservation was their life.

## Nature conservation

> You live it, conservation.
>
> (Margareth B, April 2010)

This quote suggests that conservation is embedded in every element of Margareth's life. For her, conservation required full commitment and was not a half-hearted effort. The next quote also emphasizes the all-embracing nature of conservation:

> Conservation is my husband's life. It is all-encompassing. A very necessary part of the soul.
>
> (Alison, May 2010)

Alison lived in the bush for 35 years and her statement reflects the overall impression the majority of the women had about their life as game rangers' family. For these women, their life primarily consists of complying with that of their husband. 'Conservation came first' sums up the encompassing significance that conserving the landscape had, and still has, for their husbands. Conservation was an important part of their husband's job as a game ranger, but when a job encompasses not only work but also social events, family life and personal wellbeing, it is much more than just a job, because it is, as another woman put it:

> more a way of life. It must be because it consumes a lot of time. They [husbands] are very passionate about it. It is a lifestyle that we are in, not a job, which seeps into all areas of our life.
>
> (Kerrin, May 2010)

Being a game ranger went beyond having a job. It became a way of life because of its impact on every part of life, not just for the husband but also for the wife and their family. There are no boundaries between work and family life where conservation is concerned. Their private life together living in the game reserve is completely dependent on the job. From the moment they wake up, when and what they eat, to when they go to bed, it is all connected to living the life of a game ranger's family. It is primarily their husband's life that these women joined, and to which they had to adapt in order to be able to continue to live in a game reserve.

> Most of the Game Rangers were very passionate about conservation. It had a religious flavour to it. This is why you had different opinions, for example, between rangers and researchers/scientists. As a wife, you would stick with your husband's point of view.
>
> (Jenny, March 2010)

Their stories show that there was hardly any room for different viewpoints. This affected the women too because they necessarily supported their husband's perspective, as the context was 'his job, constituent for *our* life'. As one woman put it: 'you didn't want to endanger his career' (Heather, April 2010). For most women, this meant they were cautious about expressing their own opinions, but remained hidden and invisible.

This 'religious flavour' also seems a strategy for legitimizing the recurrent absence of their husband. After all, a husband who is completely devoted to a noble cause is more acceptable than somebody who is 'just away' all the time. The women not only had to accept and adapt to this way of life, but also seemed to share and feed the devotion their game ranger husbands expressed for conservation.

> Conservation isn't done for the right reasons now. We had no money. X [husband] was there for the animals. There is no respect for nature any more. It is a romantic job, I suppose, but now people start at 7 and are off at 4 and poachers know that (...) It is so upsetting! The ethos has shifted.
>
> (Trelda, March 2010)

This complaint, apart from critiquing the differences in the organization of work, illustrates the all-encompassing feeling that game rangers and their wives had about conservation, and which they use as a marker to denounce contemporary habits. It includes, among other things, the notion that the job was more of a calling than anything else, as it was done not for money, but out of respect and love for nature and animals. Thus it feeds into the holistic image, suggested via a sense of spirituality and also, on a more mundane level, into a growing awareness of sustainability at a time when this was not so common.

Living in a game reserve with a game ranger husband resulted in these women gaining knowledge about how the reserve's flora and fauna is conserved and managed as part of their husband's job, which in turn played a significant role in their passion for conservation.

> At St. Lucia I also set up a nursery because I was gardening a lot and others [employees NPB, inhabitants of St. Lucia] noticed this; setting up this nursery meant that others could buy the plants for very little cost and I could keep gardening.
>
> (Elsa, May 2010)

All women had a great interest and respect for nature and wildlife, for the indigenous plants and trees, and for the animals their husbands were most concerned with such as rhinos, elephants and lions. Furthermore, they were very proud of this interest in and knowledge about conserving indigenous plants and trees. Gardening is an important element in their lives. For example, one woman showed us her garden, also 'completely indigenous', and immediately started naming all the plants and trees growing in her garden. Another woman stated:

> having a nice garden was quite important. You would see other wives',
> for example the chief's wife would have a beautiful garden, and it felt
> not really as a competition but similar. It was also nice to be creative
> during the day. You could make your garden into your own little oasis.
> The gardens of our houses were always very green and taken care of.
>
> (Jenny, March 2010)

It seems as if their husbands' passion for conserving indigenous nature in the game reserve influenced their own interest in indigenous vegetation and their passion for preserving nature on a smaller scale. In a way, the women who did the gardening were copying their husband's job, yet on a smaller scale, fitting and matching their 'hidden lives' and 'invisible work' behind the backs of their husbands. The women appreciated nature enough to strive for a garden of their own, as a result of which they gained more knowledge about their surroundings as well as their husband's efforts to conserve nature. This brings up another aspect of life on the reserves, namely the roles these women constructed between work, family and their own desires and ambitions, and how this influenced conservation work.

## Women's invisible work

> I did help my husband after I stopped working and I didn't get paid for
> that. I did his typing and most of the wives worked and helped their
> husbands, some worked part-time and got paid a minimum salary. You
> just helped out to smooth things along. You did what you had to do, it
> was part of life.
>
> (Heather, April 2010)

Heather helped her husband with his job by doing a lot of different tasks to 'smooth things along', as did all of the women interviewed. The ways in which they assisted their husband varied from being his secretary and doing administrative tasks, to occasionally helping in the field to fight fires, catch baby rhinos or troubled elephants, or to count animals. This was 'part of life' to which these women adapted. It also made their life easier, as helping out would take some pressure off their husband and it was a way to spend more time with him in the bush. If a wife could help out her husband with his job in order to 'smooth things along' for him, it benefited their private life as well. Another significant point from the previous quote was the topic of payment. Most women did not receive any payment, some very little. This makes us wonder if the NPB knew, or wanted to know, that these women were assisting their husbands, thus contributing to their game reserve, or not. In either case, what does this tell us about the NPB as an organization?

The NPB is a semi-military organization with minimal interest in wives: one clothes cupboard in the bedroom ... but who nevertheless relied heavily on the wives for help, but would not acknowledge them. All correspondence was done through the husbands – 'tell your wife that ...' and any pathetic payment also sent to the husbands to pass on ... maybe ...

(Alison, May 2010)

This suggests that not only were the wives ignored by the organization in terms of work-related aspects, such as acknowledging their contribution to the NPB organization by way of payment or personal recognition, but they were ignored as providers and maintainers of family life, which made it easier for the husband to spend all his time doing his job, indirectly benefiting the NPB yet again. Not adding another wardrobe is just one example of the NPB's highly gendered perspective: not even acknowledging the presence of a woman, a wife or a mother. One of the other interviewees expands on this:

I have to say that there was no support from the authorities [NPB] and I think husbands were sometimes placed in uncomfortable situations. It was a harsh working environment for the men and it had quite militaristic lines. If your wife wasn't happy, it was their [the husband's] problem. I remember we had 48 hours to pack up our belongings and move to another location and I had two little children to take care of! But you didn't want to make a fuss because you didn't want to endanger your husband's career.

(Heather, April 2010)

This quote shows the non-existent, or at least permeable barrier between working life and private life, as practised by the NPB organization. It also shows that by ordering the family with two small children to move within 48 hours' notice, these women were not afforded any of the understanding they should have received from the NPB. As Heather explains, she did not want to jeopardize her husband's career because there were many devoted and ambitious game rangers competing for scarce career opportunities. As a wife, you did not want to endanger your husband's future within the organization, which added to the hardship of isolation. Both formal and informal positioning required skill and patience to cope with those challenges: keeping quiet and simultaneously developing not just a garden, but internal arguments to convince themselves that they could bear the hardships which could be turned into less tangible forms of wealth. This provided a basis for developing spirituality, religious feelings, or near transcendental endurance in accepting that the NPB had a near complete control over their husband's life, and at the same time escaping from the sometimes harsh regime for daily life:

Well when we just married, for only a week my husband left on a 10-day patrol! I think they [NPB] could have done it before we got married ... but anyway I didn't really like that. I didn't meet any of the other wives just yet so I was all alone and I did feel a little bit of a loss and isolated.

(Margareth B, April 2010)

Margareth was shocked to be left alone after just a week of marriage, which as a result of the NPB's inconsiderate planning meant she only had a week of getting used to living in a remote area before being left on her own. Another bush wife commented:

This is a very lonely life and thank goodness I am self-sufficient, can entertain myself and am happy within myself. My first Christmas was spent alone with a pineapple sandwich for Christmas fare as X [husband] was away in the bush. Traumatic experience.

(Alison, May 2010)

This last quote captures the essence of another attribute of the women, self-sufficiency, or being able to entertain oneself and being happy with that. These abilities are very important, because there were no other diversions such as television, bars or shops. Bush wives had to create their own happiness and entertain themselves by using and incorporating the surrounding nature. Another example of the intertwined relationship between work, social life and safety created by the conservation life is recounted by Margareth, who went away on a wilderness patrol with another wife and their respective husbands. During the patrol, the men suddenly had to leave because of a poacher alert. The women ended up waiting because they could not, and were not allowed to, go along:

We couldn't keep up with them. It started to get dark, so we had to make a decision: poachers or lions. Should we start a fire? Yes: because it keeps away lions and other animals; no: because poachers will see it ... but we can't do nothing, it is getting dark.

(Margareth, May 2010)

So they went up a tree on the banks of the Zambezi river and waited for the men. She continues:

There you have two ladies up a tree feeling really sorry for themselves [laughs]. Luckily the men did come back a while later.

For these women, serenity and spiritual experiences resulted from the sense of natural peace and security they felt in the game reserve – but mixed with a down-to-earth sense of humour.

## Wilderness as spiritual

> Nature is everything: beautiful, cruel, enlightening, awesome, fragile, powerful, education ... A spiritual journey; just between you and God.
>
> (Alison, May 2010)

A sense of spirituality experienced through living in the wilderness is shared by all the women we talked to. In one sense it parallels the European Romantic landscape discourse about wilderness that at some point set in motion the movement that led to the establishment of 'national parks' (Beinart and Coates 1995; Hofmeister 2009). With hindsight, we can now assume that where cities and industries grew, simultaneously the desire to protect certain areas from that type of interference grew as well. Being away from the noise, the smell and the restless mechanical speed of cities (Hall 1983; Lefèbvre 2004) is a romantic longing for the opportunity to experience silence, one's own pace, and a vast and flowing horizon, very much in the spirit of the American transcendentalist Henry David Thoreau's *Walden; or, Life in the Woods*, published in 1854. At the same time, in the women's accounts this spirituality of nature and wilderness is beautifully connected and contrasted with the mundane:

> It is nice to come back after a day of shopping and just sit at the rock [outlook in the garden] and relax. It does calm you down. I can't wait to come back from town.
>
> (Kerrin, May 2010)

and

> I don't know how people can say there is no God when there is so much beauty in nature! Nature is spiritual because it is like being in church, with the big trees, the birds singing – it looks like a cathedral. I even feel closer to God there than in church and it is such a calm feeling. The wilderness is very spiritual, it charges my batteries.
>
> (Trelda, March 2010)

Trelda highlights the connection to a landscape in which human tradition, culture and spirituality are reflected (cf. Schama 1996). For her, Christianity is important in life and not being able to attend church every Sunday was hard for her until she decided that God is even closer to her in nature than in church. That is how she legitimated and found peace in her choices in life.

> The bush is indeed very spiritual, definitely, 100 per cent, when you look at it in this sense: where did Jesus go when he had problems? To the wilderness! So I agree with that. Everyone is different in spirituality too: Christians, non-Christians, atheists, in their own way spiritual. It is their personal situation it occurs in.
>
> (Andrea, May 2010)

This quote expresses a direct connection between wilderness and religion but not exclusively in Christian terms. Spirituality is not considered the exclusive domain of Christians. In a way, what people experience is what makes wilderness spiritual to them:

> It is spiritual for me at least. I went on many wilderness trails before I got married and met the most interesting people, ... walking through the bush, you feel that you are walking in their [the animals'] territory, the rhino, the buffalos ... you realize that you are not that important.
>
> (Camilla, April 2010)

The realization of sharing the animals' territory, of being included in a nature's realm, and rendering one's own position relative makes Camilla aware of wo/man's position in nature. Her sense of self in this particular quote is connected to a sense of place, the animals' territory. But there were also other territorial meanings embedded in the landscape: who is living in whose land and, more importantly, how can that experience be framed in terms of responsibility, future thinking and 'care'?

Feelings of belonging along with assigning spiritual qualities to an area of the bush emerged as significant elements for the majority of the women, very much as an illustration of how emotions work via the quality of being embodied and experienced via body and soul (Twine 2010). For one woman, her space in the game reserve was so precious and corporeal, and so emotionally laden, that she could not make herself go back there for 10 years after she had to leave. One reason for this was the element of change. Most of the women were disturbed by the more commercial changes that have taken place in the years after they have left. They regretted the way 'their space' is being *managed* in terms of wilderness and nature conservation, very often through the ecotourism industry. The appearance of the place triggers nostalgia and contrasts with the hope expressed through a discourse of 'building a new nation' (which is future-oriented and *postalgic*, cf. Ybema 2004). It simultaneously symbolizes their view on (loss of) wilderness and (hope for) conservation through new ways of managing game and parks.

> We left in 1974, so after that things did change. They started to put up fences: what a terrible idea!
>
> (Elsa, May 2010)

This quote highlights a perspective on landscape and scenery shared by most of the women. The connection to an 'unspoiled' Romantic wilderness landscape discourse is made via the dislike of fences, as they are considered artificial and shattering the unspoiled nature of the landscape. This reveals notions of aesthetics, and a strong normativity over wilderness landscapes; wilderness landscapes as they ought to be (cf. Wolmer 2007; Hofmeister 2009) and as they should be 'imposed' (cf. Neumann 1998). The fences clearly ruin women's image of the 'untouched wilderness' they once left behind. Obviously, wilderness should be something eternal, a landscape that defies and resists change (cf. Whiston Spirn 1998; Wels 2003).

The mental picture of the time they lived in the wilderness turns out to be nostalgic: the place no longer exists, but the feelings remain and spur a deep loathing for the changes that have occurred. Or, in reverse perspective, the degree to which the women expressed loss and framed the changes reflects their sense of being embodied in and emotionally connected to the spaces of their wilderness experience, their situatedness in a practical and historically liminal relation between nature and their very individual existence. This underlines a connection to Romanticism, while at the same time it reflects the genuine depth of natural experience for these women. The changes in the landscape contrast with their memories of a vast wilderness, where now the employees' houses represent human interference with the landscape.

> In 1996, I went back to the reserve. Before, we could see outside the reserve, see grass huts and no other people around. Now there is another structure, better tar roads: that's not isolation! The aesthetic feeling of nature is gone. It is the best life to live: in nature, the birds. Even now me and my husband live on a little reserve created by ourselves to take us as far back to the bush as possible. My husband and I would sit in our little reserve and he would say: I would never get enough of just looking at the trees ...
>
> (Jenny, March 2010)

Jenny and her husband reconstructed, as it were, a fraction of their past life in the game reserve by creating a (small) wilderness area to live in at their present home. She uses the term 'aesthetic', like many of the women, reconstructing their experience of how the wilderness was while they were living there. This reconfirms the notion of aesthetic wilderness as used in Romantic landscape discourse (cf. Whiston Spirn 1998; Hofmeister 2009) and which resonates with the discourse on conservation. At the same time, the focus on 'past times' marks the liminality of their experience and the beginning of the unintended consequences of their work: natural parks, fenced in and only viable via relentless economic exploitation (Zwarenstein 2012; Snijders 2015). The past represents a 'better' aesthetic image of wilderness compared with the changes that have taken place since.

## Conclusion

> Because they were women, because they were being good women, restructuring extended their workload to or beyond their coping capacities, shutting down their ability to fight back, endangering their health and the health of the farm and the community they were working for, and undermining their sense of themselves as having agency and power.
>
> (Heather et al. 2005: 89)

Originally, while embarking on the bush wives' project, we were just curious about their lives and what they would tell us that differs from the well known men's stories. Gradually, however, we came to realize that we could find a lot more than 'their stories'. Alison Forrest's (2000) 'cook book' with the ambiguous title *A Double Scoop* points at undercurrents in the understanding of bush life from a female, or rather a family perspective that goes beyond the work context. But, while unravelling the underlying patterns of the women's stories, we came to realize that there are other dimensions that need to be uncovered to contribute to the wider field of ecofeminism and the debates within ecofeminism about deeper revisions of human–animal–nature relationships (Plumwood 2000). Going beyond dualisms between these women and 'their men', and abandoning the idea of strict separation between the life-worlds of couples who were so dependent on each other, despite sometimes huge distances in space and time on a daily basis, we discovered trivialities coupled with subtle understanding, and perhaps re-construction of meaning in those life stories. We departed from assumptions based on the insight that *bush wives* had their own hardships, keeping afloat a household in the wilderness and often raising a family, including taking care of children's schooling (Ann Player and Nola Steele, private talks, 2014). We found that these women did develop, in interaction with their men, the plans, projects and practices of nature conservation: unacknowledged and unpaid for by the NPB, these women co-constructed the conservation practices of those days.

Our analysis shows that, from a structural and professional perspective, they invested much invisible labour that enabled their game ranger husbands to do the work they did. Indeed, we suggest that the women basically secured their husband's position by contributing to their reporting to the NPB headquarters. As the game reserves were very isolated, the NPB headquarters almost necessarily had to rely to a large extent on the reports coming in from their game rangers: the reports were windows into the work of the game rangers. To push this metaphor further, the women kept those windows clean.

Thus we might tentatively suggest that women played a more important role in conservation history than often assumed because they took care of the administrative 'hygiene' and visibility of their husbands, while at the same time co-constructing the image of wilderness 'purity'. Moreover, the women provided rest, rhythm and regularity, the foundations for their men's work. This consisted of planning the household, overseeing supplies, taking care of children, their schooling and animals, and providing continuity in the background, in sum linking all areas of life – but also actively maintaining a 'utopian' image of how human–nature relationships 'should be'. Their contribution to the overall achievements in nature conservation in KZN has to be read between the lines. Their stories convey experiences of being 'between the lines' in the liminal spaces between city and wilderness; between the NPB and their husband; between formal politics and their (black) neighbours' wishes and needs; between peace and quiet and being overwhelmed; between their gardens and the surrounding wilderness (the men's 'garden'); between different levels of dependency and autonomy and the balancing act between their families and conservation. Also, as suggested in the introduction, between wilderness protection and wilderness exploitation. Through their 'cleaning' and 'supporting' work, they added value and meaning to notions and values attached to conservation that were beginning to develop. Although this idea needs far more in-depth exploration in further research, we can state that what the women now term 'spirituality', and 'retreat', and 'being included in the animals' realm' anticipates the 'utopian' stories (cf. Sargisson 2001; Schönpflug 2008) presently promoted in an attempt to refute industrial conservation. In any case, the spiritual as utopian[8] points to a far deeper level of understanding and reconstruction of meaning than is apparent at first sight. These insights are not about agency and independence, but about reflexively 'being part of nature', not in an essentialist sense, but adding to the more formal, rational notions of 'conservation' as promulgated by the masculine images the men had to (and were sometimes eagerly willing to) live out.

However, from an ecofeminist point of view, we might wonder if it is fair to reduce the role of women in conservation to a 'pervading influence', which seems to reproduce the lack of recognition for these women's contribution emphasized in this study. Those contributions are important if not crucial, but in official conservation history the women remain invisible and their contribution neglected. Learning from their experiences might offer counter-arguments in terms of exposing the masculine dominance that led to exploitation of game and parks all the way into an ecotourist economy. In the context of emancipation, feminism and claiming rightful positions, it is time for game rangers' wives, and other excluded voices such as those of indigenous peoples, to demand, claim and appropriate their place in conservation history in KZN and South Africa in general.

Social sciences can play a facilitating role in this respect by conducting research on the issue, but also, and even more importantly, by conceptually interpreting and framing processes in nature conversation in terms of caring, inclusion and transforming conflict into new forms of situatedness (Twine 2010), rather than in terms of confrontation, 'warfare' and (economic) urgency. The masculine approach is considered more potent and worthy of scientific (rational) attention than more inclusive accounts focused on care,[9] for nature and people alike. Although one has to be careful with a bias deriving from gender dichotomy, ecofeminist perspectives seem more or less successful in offering wider perspectives than those which are merely economic, especially in promoting a more *ecocentric* (versus anthropocentric) engagement of nature (Phillips 2014). It is through surfacing and listening to counter-voices, or hitherto silenced voices, contemporary as well as from the past, that we can be inspired to find alternatives to rationalist exploitations of nature. Bush wives' voices help, as they contain the building blocks that make eco-inclusive approaches more than wishful thinking.

## Notes

1 Daphne Sheldrick wrote about life in Kenya (with some reference to South Africa), which is a different context in terms of both gender and conservation.
2 As it seems important to protect the women's privacy, but at the same time 'make their voices heard', we decided not to anonymize them, but only to use quotes they have specifically allowed us to use; and we only mention their first names. Exceptions are made for Nola Steele whose details cannot be hidden – and for Alison Forrest who published her own (cook) book *A Double Scoop* (2000) and coined the term 'bush wives'.
3 Of course, worldwide, millions of people live in 'remote' areas and 'cope with nature'. Here we take the perspective of the women involved: mainly white, educated, Western, and usually brought up in cities. We contend that their position 'in-between' two worlds is worth exploring, also as they were very much concerned about 'local' people as their first neighbours, and often reported that in terms of racism they also had to 'bridge' worlds, depending on the politically different positioning of 'nature conservation'. The latter is the theme of another article (in development).
4 Literally: … 'women had less of the, how shall I put it, entertainment is not the right word, but …' – private conversation Ian Player with Ida Sabelis, April 2014.
5 With the exception of one woman [Iona] who is married to a researcher and has lived in the wilderness of game reserves for many years; she experienced a similar life to that of the bush rangers' wives.
6 For a more complete historical–critical interpretation, see Draper 1998; Snijders 2015; Wels 2015 (forthcoming).
7 Contrary to what one might expect, 'authentic' hardly ever refers to local/black or Zulu people.
8 Which is also shared by many of the men after their retirement – with thanks to John Tinley for raising this point.
9 Compare for instance the way that Richard Leakey describes his life in nature conservation in his biographical book (Leakey and Morell 2001) and how, maybe except for Dian Fossey, Carole Jahme (2000) describes the various women in primate research and conservation.

## References

Beinart, W. and Coates, P. (1995) *Environment and History: The Taming of Nature in the USA and South Africa*, London: Routledge.

Bryden, B. (2005) *A Game Ranger Remembers*, Johannesburg/Cape Town: Jonathan Ball.

Cesare, M. (2009) *Man-Eaters, Mambas and Marula Madness: A Game Ranger's Life in the Lowveld*, Johannesburg/Cape Town: Jonathan Ball.

Daniels, A.K. (1987) 'Invisible work', *Social Problems* 34(5): 403–415.

Draper, M. (1998) 'Zen and the art of garden province maintenance: the soft intimacy of hard men in the wilderness of KwaZulu-Natal, South Africa, 1952–1997', *Journal of Southern African Studies* 24(4): 801–828, Special Issue on Masculinities in Southern Africa.

Forrest, A. (2000) *A Double Scoop: A Collection of Bush Wives Tales and Recipes*, Durban, SA: INTEC.

Hall, E.T. (1983) *The Dance of Life: The Other Dimension of Time*, New York: Doubleday.

Heather, B., Skillen, L., Young, J. and Vladicka, T. (2005) 'Women's gendered identities and the restructuring of rural Alberta', *Sociologia Ruralis* 45(1/2): 86–97.

Hochschild, A.R. (1983) *The Managed Heart*, Berkeley: University of California Press.

Hofmeister, S. (2009) 'Natures running wild: a social-ecological perspective on wilderness', *Nature and Culture* 4(3): 293–315.

Jahme, C. (2000) *Beauty and the Beasts: Woman, Ape and Evolution*, New York: Soho Press.

Krüger, K. (1994) *Mahlangeni: Stories of a Game Ranger's Family*, London: Penguin Books.

Krüger, K. (1996) *All Things Wild and Wonderful*, London: Penguin Books.

Leakey, R. and Morell, V. (2001) *Wildlife Wars: My Fight to Save Africa's Treasures*, New York: St Martin's Press.

Lefèbvre, H. (2004) *Rhythmanalysis: Space, Time and Everyday Life*, London: Continuum [1992, *Éléments de Rhythmanalyse*, Paris: Éditions Syllepse].

Neumann, R.P. (1998) *Imposing Wilderness: Struggles Over Livelihood and Nature Preservation in Africa*, Berkeley: University of California Press.

Phillips, M. (2014) 'Re-writing corporate environmentalism: ecofeminism, corporeality and the language of feeling', *Gender, Work & Organization* 21(5): 443–458.

Plumwood, V. (2000) 'Integrating ethical frameworks for animals, humans, and nature: a critical feminist eco-socialist analysis', *Ethics and the Environment* 5(2): 285–322.

Root, G. (n.d.) *Roots of a Game Ranger*, Vryheid: The Roots.

Sargisson, L. (2001) 'What's wrong with ecofeminism?', *Environmental Politics* 10(1): 52–64.

Schama, S. (1996) *Landscape and Memory*, New York: Vintage Books.

Schönpflug, K. (2008) *Feminism, Economics and Utopia: Time Travelling through Paradigms*, London: Routledge.

Selley, R. (2009) *West of the Moon: Early Zululand and a Game Ranger at War in Rhodesia*, Johannesburg: 30° South.

Sheldrick, D. (2012) *An African Love Story: Love, Life and Elephants*, London: Viking/ Penguin Books.

Snijders, D. (2015) 'Shifting species. Wildlife policy, rural consequences', dissertation, Amsterdam: Vrijes University.

Stevenson Hamilton, J. (1993/1937) *South African Eden: The Kruger National Park*, Cape Town: Struik.

Tancred, P. (1995) 'Women's work: a challenge to the sociology of work', *Gender, Work & Organization* 2(1): 11–20.

Ten Bos, R. and Kaulingfreks, R. (2001) *De hygiene machine. Kantekeningen bij de reinheidscultus in cultuur, organisaties en management*, Kampen: Agora.

Thomas, K. (2008) *Shadows in an African Twilight: Game Ranger, Soldier, Hunter*, Cape Town: uThekwane Press.

Thoreau, H.D. (1995/1854) *Walden; or, Life in the Woods*, Mineola, NY: Dover Publications.

Tinley, L. (1979) *Drawn from the Plains: Life in the Wilds of Southern Africa*, London: Collins & Sons.

Twine, R. (2001) 'Ecofeminisms in process', *ecofem.org/journal*, available at http://richa rdtwine.com/ecofem/ecofem2001.pdf.

Twine, R. (2010) 'Intersectional disgust? Animals and (eco) feminism', *Feminism and Psychology* 20(3): 397–406.

van Vliet, T. (2011) 'A woman's wilderness. When ignored contributions, nature conservation, and romantic landscape notions collide in the context of game reserves in KwaZulu-Natal, South Africa', dissertation, Amsterdam: Vrijes University.

Wels, H. (2003) *Private Wildlife Conservation in Zimbabwe: Joint Ventures and Reciprocity*, Leiden: Brill.

Wels, H. (2015) *Securing Wilderness Landscapes in South Africa: Nick Steele, Private Wildlife Conservancies and Saving Rhinos*, Leiden: Brill.

Whiston Spirn, A. (1998) *The Language of Landscape*, New Haven, CT: Yale University Press.

Wolhuter, H. (1948/1961) *Memories of a Game Ranger*, Johannesburg: Wild Life Protection Society of South Africa.

Wolmer, W. (2007) *From Wilderness Vision to Farm Invasions: Conservation and Development in Zimbabwe's South-east Lowveld*, Oxford: James Currey.

Ybema, S. (2004) 'Managerial postalgia: projecting a golden future', *Journal of Managerial Psychology* 19(8): 825–841.

Zwarenstein, C. (2012) 'Survival in the globalized commercial tourism industry: the case of "adventures with elephants"', dissertation, Amsterdam: Vrijes University.

# 8  The township gaze

## A postcolonial ecofeminist theory for touring the new South Africa

*Laura Wright*

In this chapter I examine the performative nature of the South African township tour in the construction of a specific tourist mythology with regard to landscape, gender politics and racially defined social mobility in the so-called 'new' South Africa. As a counter to the tourism industry's potentially reductive representations not only of the South African landscape (as at once uninhabited by people but populated by 'exotic' animals), but also of township spaces and residents, I posit that an informed postcolonial ecofeminism informed by the South African philosophy of *ubuntu* can serve to help tourists more fully historicize the various social, political and cultural realities that have displaced South Africans from specific spatial environments, more egalitarian and mutually beneficial gender roles, and mutually constitutive relationships with the land and animals. To this end, I offer an interconnected discussion of Sindiwe Magona's 1998 novel *Mother to Mother*, Stacy Vorster's reading of Clive van der Berg's 2007 sculpture *Eland*, and Zef group Die Antwoord's video for their 2012 song 'Fatty Boom Boom' as counter-narratives that speak back to a South African history that supports the slaughter of animals, constructs Africans as animals, and displaces indigenous peoples by placing them in townships, spatial environments that alienate them from the land and from one another.

Ecofeminist praxis recognizes that animals, women and nature (as well as children and colonized 'others') are placed on the same side of the binary divide as oppositional to humans, men and culture. In her foundational 'Living interconnections with animals and nature', Greta Gaard defines ecofeminism as follows:

> Drawing on the insights of ecology, feminism, and socialism, ecofeminism's basic premise is that the ideology that authorizes oppressions such as those based on race, class, gender, sexuality, physical abilities, and species is the same ideology that sanctions the oppression of nature.
>
> (Gaard 1993: 1)

Yet in a later essay, Gaard notes a tension that existed between ecofeminist views, which 'initially foregrounded gender, species, and sexuality', and environmental justice, which 'initially foregrounded race and class' (Gaard 2010: 5). In the context of a postcolonial country like South Africa, therefore, an ecofeminist position must take into account the ways that indigenous social hierarchies with regard to species and gender are further complicated by the imposition of colonial institutions that disrupt and displace indigenous politics, institutions and peoples. While the way women and nature have been conceptualized in the West has devalued women, nature, animals and emotion, and simultaneously elevated reason, humans, culture and the mind (Ashcroft et al. 1998: 26), ecofeminist theorizing in the context of South Africa must be informed by an understanding of the double-bind that marks black South African women as both female and colonized. As a result of these combined forces, Huey-Li Li claims, 'the woman–nature affinity' that is perceived as 'true of Western cultures, is not a cross cultural phenomenon' (Li 1993: 288).

If one of the goals of ecofeminism is to recognize that oppressions are linked and that in order to end one, all must be addressed, then the post-colonial condition offers a historical paradigm – with a 'before' and 'after' period – in which to actively examine the way that such oppressions are constructed and perpetuated. According to Al-Yasha Ilhaam, the effects of Westernization and colonization 'in Africa include rapid urbanization, the redistribution of natural resources towards export, and the promotion of industries such as oil and lumber whose products and management practices have far-reaching ecological consequences' (Ilhaam 2009: 141). The shift from 'traditional' to Westernized cultures impacts women in significant ways as well, exacerbating and complicating existing traditional (and patriarchal) gender relations; African feminisms, therefore, must address 'the complexities of traditional culture[s] and the changing roles of women in the postcolonial state' (ibid.: 142). Ecofeminist praxis in such a context may have a tendency, as Barbara Boswell notes, to look to precolonial history: 'for African eco-feminists, precolonial Africa offers a reference point for achieving … harmonious relationships between human beings themselves and human beings and the planet' (Boswell 2011: 34). I caution against the idea that there can be a return to any authentic precolonial moment, however, as such a tendency relies upon a conception of an imagined more egalitarian past. Nonetheless, precolonial history and memory necessarily haunt the contemporary South African present, and as 'the degradation of the earth is strongly linked to the abuse and exploitation of the majority of its black impoverished citizens, and … environmental abuse and social injustice have gone hand in hand' (ibid.: 34), the precolonial past – imagined and 'real' – necessarily informs an ecofeminist intrusion into the present moment.

A way of connecting ecofeminism – a Western concept – to a South African reality is to view ecofeminism as linked to *ubuntu*, a Zulu and Xhosa term that means, essentially, humanity towards others; *ubuntu* functions as a philosophy which recognizes that 'I am who I am, because of who we all are' (Rich 2012). It is a philosophy rooted in a communal, not individualistic, culture wherein members view themselves as parts of a greater whole, an interconnected and interdependent species with an inherent responsibility to treat one another humanely and carefully. Because *ubuntu* became popular during the Africanization period of the 1980s and 1990s, it is necessarily concerned with disrupting the 'us/them' Western binary thinking responsible for the colonial project – and these same dualisms divide nature from culture, women from men, and animals from humans. The falseness of these dualisms and the interconnectedness and interdependence of communities are what both ecofeminism and *ubuntu* seek to address. According to Anias Mutekwa and Terrence Musanga, because *ubuntu* is not premised on binarisms, it

> enables the existence of a worldview not premised on humanity's mastery of nature. *ubuntu* cosmology is holistic, as it integrates the social, the economic, the religious, and the environmental. In essence, *ubuntu* as an environmental philosophy fits under the rubric of what has been referred to as 'deep ecology', as it negates, and is an alternative to, the dominant ideology through which humanity's domination and exploitation of nature is mediated. So, *ubuntu* and ecofeminism have some shared commonalities and the two complement each other in furthering a deep ecological perspective.
>
> (Mutekwa and Musanga 2013: 254–55)

In the space of the South African township, it is immediately clear that colonization and apartheid have wreaked havoc on a lived ethic of *ubuntu*. An ecofeminist framework can provide a means for understanding how and why.

## The township gaze

Because of recent increased visibility of South Africa in Western media – as a result of the 2010 World Cup, the 2014 murder trial of high-profile South African athlete (the 'blade runner') Oscar Pistorius, and the media's fixation on Nelson Mandela's health and death in December 2013 – in many ways South Africa has come to signify as the visual and textual representation of the homogeneous 'Africa' of twenty-first century Western imagination. In the rhetoric of tourism, Africa is depicted as a monolithic entity and as an item for Western consumption; Stacy Vorster notes that 'the performance of culture is especially potent in Africa, where there is a deep history of anthropological constructions that misrepresent, idealize and primitivize cultural practice and aesthetics' (2013: 151). The constructions of which Vorster speaks focus primarily on landscape as uninhabited space, and secondarily, according to Scarlett Cornelissen, tourist conceptions of the African continent also include 'sexuality (either subordinate or feminine, or warrior ...), primevalism and exoticism' (2005: 679). Such understandings of place are posited through what John Urry calls the 'tourist gaze' (1990), a highly structured and choreographed view of place, people and animals determined by both tacit and overt rules established by the media, tour guides and tour companies. Since the end of apartheid in South Africa, the township tour has appealed to international tourists sensitive to, and invested in, the discontinuation of South Africa's racist apartheid legacy.

In South Africa, townships were mandated by the 1923 Urban Areas Act, which controlled the presence of black South Africans in urban areas. Essentially, the only reason why black South Africans were allowed in urban areas prior to and during apartheid was in order to work for white employers. According to Reni Eddo-Lodge, townships:

> were created to segregate and economically disadvantage black lives in every way. Defining features are their small, crowded living spaces. Their location on the edge of urban areas often mean longer commutes for black workers, who under apartheid, once they reached their places of work, had to carry passport-like documents in order to move around freely.
>
> (Eddo-Lodge 2013: n.p.)

In the 1990s, after apartheid ended, townships became sites of tourist inquiry, and a thriving tourism industry dedicated to taking curious outsiders into township spaces has developed. During a 2007 trip to South Africa, I took a township tour into Langa township just outside of Cape Town; the tour was run by a company called Cape Capers, the social responsibility preamble of which maintains that:

> We are committed to continue the struggle against inherited poverty and deprivation left behind by the apartheid Policies of the past, by spreading the benefits of Tourism to previously disadvantaged communities in the Townships and on the Cape Flats.
>
> We will share our skills and knowledge, by connecting communities with opportunities, funding, facilitation and volunteers.
>
> We will build itineraries to include local enterprises in craft, food and hospitality. As well as Social-Support projects and Environmental Resources Centers.
>
> (Cape Capers 2006a: n.p.)

My experience as a postcolonial scholar made the decision to take this tour complicated; I am very aware of the politics that such tours represent, primarily the reality that, as Bianca Freire-Medeiros notes, 'at the turn of the millennium, capitalism has framed the *experience of poverty* as a product for consumption through tourism' (2012: 1). Furthermore, township tourists are

> often generalized as 'white Europeans', while it is acknowledged that white South Africans do not 'tour' townships. Both perceptions contribute to critiques of tourism as a form of neo-colonial encounter.
>
> (Freire-Medeiros 2012: 32).

Pair these problematic realities with such tours' promise of the tourist's experience of the 'real' Africa or the 'real' Langa (Siwiwe Tours 2010), and the potential tourist is faced with various ethical conundrums with regard to the politics of the gaze (who stages what is seen, who is seen, and who sees and interprets what is seen); consumption of various items offered for sale by the township residents; and potential exploitation of the space of poverty for the personal enrichment – and redemption – of the tourist. During a township tour the 'real', the 'authentic' South African space is in fact generated within the context of a very self-consciously artificial and staged production of timeless ethnic difference that underlies such a tour, even as the tour emphasizes the progress made since the end of apartheid. As Manfred Rolfes notes of the 'poverty tourism' phenomenon he refers to as 'poorism', such 'staged authenticity' is a performance in which 'authenticity is characterized by facilitating or staging a glance at the back stage for the tourists' (2010: 422).

Irma Booyens discusses the history of township tourism and its immense popularity, and she notes that township tourists 'tend to be educated and culturally sensitive', and that 'the proportion of visitors travelling to South Africa for cultural purposes has increased significantly since 1994' (Booyens 2010: 274), the year that Nelson Mandela became president in South Africa's first democratic elections.[1] Some of the most positive aspects of township tourism are its apparent ability to enhance township economies, its educational potential, and its facilitation of legitimate and meaningful interaction opportunities between township residents and international travellers. Booyens argues, however, that such benefits are not viable given the current models of most tours:

> Tourists are often taken to township areas on superficial journeys and in most cases there is very limited interaction between them and the local residents. Authenticity is therefore easily compromised. There is a constant struggle between market viability and authentic representations of local cultures and tourists are regularly taken on pseudo-trips that do not reflect past or present realities.
>
> (Booyens 2010: 277)

Similarly, Jessica L. Dickson notes that in 2010, while township residents who work for township tourism outfits 'were finding surprising ways to navigate their growing social mobility through relationships with international guests', an examination of public discourse about 'common sense' and safety with regard to township tourism indicated that 'rumor and speculation acted to re-territorialize crime and violence to township spaces ... thereby reaffirming apartheid-era socio-spatial divisions' (Dickson 2012: 32). Regardless of whether one is opposed to or in favor of such tours, however, according to Freire-Medeiros, opponents and supporters alike believe that poverty is unjust, and that 'socially and economically vulnerable human beings count as citizens and should not simply be gazed upon' (2012: 3).

So what was I to make of the fact that the first thing my Xhosa tour guide told me was *to gaze upon* Langa's residents, to take pictures, and to treat the experience – in his words – 'like a safari'? And what of the title of P.K. Stowers' (2012) article in *AtlantaBlackStar*, 'The new safari: South African township tours'? On one hand, many of the companies that take tourists into townships also run safaris that take tourists to see wild animals, but the comparison of humans living in townships to animals witnessed, photographed and historically killed on safaris, at the very least, should allow for an ecofeminist lens through which to consider the place of post-apartheid township tourism within the context of a racist colonial history that rhetorically constructed indigenous South Africans *as* animals. Furthermore, such rhetorical eliding of human and animal within the context of the contemporary township tour requires recognition of the position of the township tour within the traditions of the colonial enterprise of big-game hunting, contemporary photographic safaris, 'human zoos', and so-called ecotourism in Africa more broadly. This rhetoric serves to undermine *ubuntu*'s more holistic philosophy. The history of big-game-hunting safaris in Africa and such safaris' current connections to contemporary notions of supposedly more socially responsible tourism models – like township tourism and, more specifically, ecotourism, a model that promises, according to the Ecotourism Society, 'responsible travel to natural areas that conserves the environment and improves the well-being of local people' (quoted in Duffy 2002: 6) – are issues that are deeply implicated in an imperialist model of colonial exploitation, one that persisted after many African nations had gained independence from their former colonizers.

According to Brian Herne in *White Hunters: The Golden Age of African Safaris*, the term 'white hunter' originated in British East Africa after the turn of the twentieth century, but 'big game hunting was already popular in other parts of the "Dark Continent", notably in South Africa' (2001: 3). Herne's text examines the history of the white hunter in Africa, from the first safari business to the 1960s and 1970s during which increased hunting regulations and conservation measures began to impede sport killing. While Herne's text celebrates the legacies of these white hunters, Edward J. Steinhart's *Black Poachers, White Hunters: A Social History of Hunting in Colonial Kenya* conversely focuses on the ways that indigenous African peoples' hunting practices were literally and rhetorically (via the dualism of hunter/poacher) criminalized in order for white safaris to thrive. Steinhart asserts that 'the struggles over the definition and control of hunting and the politics and revenues which it yielded may be key to understanding the contests of power that went on for seven decades between settlers, officials, and Africans' (2006: 18). Furthermore, this Western demonstration of domination of nature paralleled 'European racial and class domination over black Africans' (Duffy 2002: 294); therefore colonized subjects and hunted animals occupy the same space in the colonial milieu in which big-game hunting came of age – and an ecofeminist reading allows us to see how conflation of subject positions remains present in the contemporary rhetoric of the township tour *as* safari.

To complicate matters further, if the colonial philosophy described above traditionally equated indigenous human life with animal life and valued neither, then the more supposedly environmentally conscious wildlife refuge system has benefited animals and corporations at the expense of indigenous human populations. For example, when the Ndumo Game Reserve was established in 1924, the Tonga people of South Africa were forced to leave the area and were denied access to water within the reserve (Honey 1999: 367). Rosaleen Duffy, in her study *A Trip Too Far: Ecotourism, Politics & Exploitation*, comments that 'in the developing world, there is an added layer to the politics of tourism because of memories of colonial control', and in places like Kenya, 'conservation and tourism schemes have replicated the colonial system of separating people and the environment' (Duffy 2002: 101). Furthermore, most of the income generated by such reserves benefits the private corporations that run the wilderness and photographic safaris, with minimal income being generated for indigenous populations that are often displaced and disenfranchised by these business ventures. Like hunting and township tourism, according to Duffy, ecotourism in Africa is dependent upon the 'politically laden image of the destination country' and, in the contemporary moment, 'host societies are packaged and commodified for consumption by an external audience, promising the exotic, the unspoiled, the pristine and – even worse – the primitive' (2002: xii).

In the case of the township tour, what is being packaged is not an unspoiled and pristine landscape devoid of humans but rather a landscape scarred and damaged by the legacy of apartheid, a space of abject poverty and privation where humans have been forced to live *like animals* in an ever present – and, for the sake of the tourist – highly choreographed struggle for freedom and human dignity. And such tours do little to address the structural inequalities that still exist in post-apartheid South Africa or the gender-based violence that shapes current South African reality. Such tourism evokes images of turn of the twentieth-century 'human zoos' that put Africans on display throughout Europe: 'exhibiting Africans as animals, uncivilized, primitive, animistic made it sound justified to colonize them. It was also a source of entertainment for the European of the time to see how "backward Africans were"' (Mwesigire 2014).[2]

Alternately, the township tour offers catharsis and redemption for the tourist (who, by virtue of the fact that she or is he is almost always white and therefore racially implicated in South Africa's history of apartheid), and an opportunity for the new South Africa to present itself as democratic, progressive and liberated from its oppressive history. For example, one of the hallmarks of the Cape Capers tour is the one-man play 'Isandulela – The Dawn, the story of an old person on the day of our first National Election on 27 April 1994' (Cape Capers 2006b), staged by the Siyasaga Township Theatre in Langa's Community Center.[3] At first glance, then, it might be easy to dismiss township tourism for its staged nature, but such tours also necessarily require that the political and social space of South African townships and their residents be included in the story of the new South Africa; according to Dickson, 'township tourism highlights the historical roles of spaces of exclusion and resistance, and their contested representation within national narratives of development and transformation' (2012: 35). Tourists are invited into the personal spaces of township residents, including their homes; tour guides and residents alike share their stories, even as much of the movement across the racial boundaries is one way, allowing affluent whites into the space of the township. But one can also assert that movement across racial and spatial boundaries provides an opportunity to enact *ubuntu*, to acknowledge a shared humanity that requires shared responsibility.

If, for white tourists, the township becomes elided with the jungle, a journey into the forbidden zones of darkest Africa via its situation as safari, the tour nonetheless flips the colonial narrative of Christian salvation and conquest of African 'savages' to offer non-African tourists an opportunity for an imaginary redemption for the evils done in the name of European imperialism. Within this discourse, the bodies, voices and lives of black township women in particular occupy a complex and fraught position; even as a result of the township tourism industry, township women may in fact have greater special mobility and access to social and physical spaces beyond the confines of the township.[4] But such mobility often depends upon their willing objectification as subjects worthy of a voyeuristic external scrutiny largely informed (but not acknowledged within the context of the tour) by their status as victims of a predatory sexual milieu that places them at consistent risk of both rape and HIV/AIDS.

Despite the fact that the 1996 Constitution gave South African women unprecedented rights, particularly in terms of reproductive freedom (with provisions offering safe circumstances in which to terminate unwanted pregnancy, and in terms of inclusivity in the decision-making mechanisms of the country), Mary Hames notes that often these laws fail to realize that 'women in different race groups are differently privileged', and that 'Black African women, in particular, have historically been the most marginalized' (2006: 1314). For the majority of black South African township women, just as for black South African women living in rural areas, 'even the notion of liberal citizenship is still a pipe dream':

> the realities of existence in urban informal settlements are those of extreme deprivation. Without an extended support system, living in contexts where crime and violence are a constant menace, where floods and fires threaten lives, and suffering from a chronic lack of employment, life for these women is exceptionally hard and hostile.
>
> (Hames 2006: 1325)

In the presentation and performance of the township tour as staged for an external audience, women's health and safety are omitted from the narrative of township life in the new South Africa; the success of that narrative depends on women's complicity with the agreed-upon tourist text of upward mobility, progress and hope that is propagated in large part because of and by the township tourist industry itself. In what follows, I offer an ecofeminist reading of several counter-narratives that tacitly engage with *ubuntu* and challenge the township gaze.

## Eland, *Mother to Mother*, and 'Fatty Boom Boom'

Stacy Vorster's provocative 'Inner-city safaris and wild public art' decon-structs the meaning of animal iconography in *Eland*, Clive van der Berg's 2007 huge concrete sculpture of the South African antelope that stands at the entrance to Johannesburg at the Nelson Mandela Bridge. She claims that to read such animal iconography as 'nostalgic calls for an imagined pre-urban South Africa' is sentimental and fails to recognize the ways that such art works 'transform existing tropes to perform a ritual of loss and recovery, thus enacting the liminality of a post-trauma South Africa and a cathartic sense of memento mori' (Vorster 2013: 147). Her argument and *Eland* itself situate South African animals as at once absent from the urban landscape and simultaneously present as a spectre that haunts the South African imaginary as intimately linked with the landscape and with mechanisms of imperialism and colonization that compartmentalized animals and humans. In the context of apartheid-era South Africa, animals were excised from urban landscapes through their destruction via big-game hunting, their subsequent placement in wildlife preserves, or their dismissal – as is the case with cattle, as I discuss below – as inconsequential. Similarly, black South Africans were removed from both urban and rural areas via their (dis)placement in townships. In Vorster's reading of *Eland*, the ghosts of displaced and hunted animals haunt South African history – and the recognition of the connection between human and animal displacement and haunting is central to an ecofeminist understanding of the politics that created and maintain various spaces (urban, township, rural) in contemporary South Africa.

In many ways, South African Sindiwe Magona's 1998 novel *Mother to Mother* (Magona 1998a) enacts Vorster's 'liminality of a post-trauma South Africa' in its engagement with various animal and human displacements and hauntings, and the narrative in many ways constitutes an explicit ecofeminist reading of both township space and relegation to it. Magona's novel imagines a series of letters from a South African Xhosa township mother, Mandisa, to the American mother whose daughter her son has killed. The novel is Magona's fictional chronicling of Wednesday August 25, 1993, the historical day when the historical American Fulbright scholar Amy Biehl was murdered in the township of Guguletu; despite Magona's identification of Biehl in the preface to the book, the murdered woman remains nameless throughout the work. Biehl, who was white, was murdered by an angry black mob when she drove several black friends from the University of the Western Cape, where she was studying, to their home in Guguletu township. Three black men were charged with her murder, and the case drew international attention to the powder keg of township violence by the legacy of South Africa's sanctioned racism, even as apartheid was in its final hours, about to give way to democracy only months later.[5]

Despite its dependence on a historical event, Magona's narrative is a work of fiction that conflates the three men charged in Biehl's killing into one character.[6] The novel paints a scathing portrait of the mob mentality that leads to Biehl's murder, as well as to the black-on-black killings and violence against women that remain endemic to life in South African townships in general and in Guguletu, a township created in the 1960s to alleviate over-crowding in Cape Town's oldest township Langa,[7] in particular. In one sense, the Amy Biehl case – as covered in the news media and fictionalized in Magona's novel – brought into sharp relief for a Western audience one consequence of a long and violent history of sanctioned racism in South Africa, but conversely, coverage of it supported and enlivened a familiar mythological narrative of black male predation and white female victimization. Biehl's status as 'conventionally' pretty, blonde, upper-class, highly educated and white (not to mention American) was at once responsible for the media's attention to her murder as politically motivated even as it also played on her status as a white, Western, female conquest for the menace of black South African township men. But Magona's novel, via Mandisa's letters – which begin with 'my son killed your daughter' (Magona 1998a: 1) – links the murdered girl to her murderer as members of a community of fighting against an unjust history. Magona renders both Mandisa's son and the girl he murders as sacrificial animals, and Mandisa employs animal metaphors throughout the narrative. When she learns that a white woman has been killed, Mandisa says, 'is it not enough that we kill each other as though the other is an animal ...?' (45); her son is a 'pit bull' (38); scared people are 'like blind-starving donkeys' (39). The murdered woman is a scapegoat, 'the sacrifice' of her race (210), and her death is consistently linked in Mandisa's narrative to another historical sacrifice, the Xhosa Cattle-Killing of 1856–57.

According to J.B. Peires in his foundational and comprehensive work on the Cattle-Killing, *The Dead Will Arise* (1989), in 1856 the young female prophet Nongqawuse claimed that if the Xhosa killed all of their cattle:

> two suns would rise red in the sky over the mountain of Ntaba kaNdoda where they would collide and darkness would cover the earth ... Then the righteous dead ... and the new cattle would rise ... The English ... would retreat into the sea, which would rise up in two walls to engulf them and open a road for them.
>
> (Peires 1989: 98)

The Xhosa slaughtered over 400,000 cattle but the prophecies remained unfulfilled; mass starvation resulted causing the Xhosa population to drop from 105,000 in January of 1857 to 25,916 a year later (ibid.: 319). And as a result of the killing, over 600,000 acres of Xhosa land was lost to whites. In an interview with David Attwell and Barbara Harlow, Magona has said that there are two versions of the story of the killing: 'there's one version that we were taught in school, there's another version that we African people believe' (Attwell and Harlow 2000: 289). Mandisa's grandfather Tatomkhulu describes the deep resentment that must have driven the Xhosa to kill their cattle; in his retelling of Xhosa history, the Cattle-Killing is an act of bravery as opposed to the act of ignorance and superstition described by Mandisa's white teachers. Tatomkhulu refers to his ancestors' environmental consciousness, their respect for their land and their animals. They were, he says, 'Readers of Nature's Signs' who 'allowed themselves fallacious belief' (Magona 1998a: 176); he notes that 'cattle are not for food', that 'when one is hungry, there is corn in the field' (177). According to her grandfather, nothing was wasted by Mandisa's Xhosa ancestors who also 'diligently tended their fields' (178), cared for the land, and utilized every part of any animal they killed. He says that the sacrifice of the cattle and crops 'was to drive abelungu [whites] to the sea, where, so the seer had said, they would all drown ... Such noble sacrifice. But then, the more terrible the abomination, the greater the sacrifice called for' (178).[8]

The historical and symbolic role of cattle in indigenous South African cultures is not limited to the Xhosa Cattle-Killing; it is omnipresent, from the time that the Khoikhoi people broke with the hunter San, for whom 'control over hunting for the distribution of meat, and particularly trade in ivory, were mechanisms for asserting power, stamping territorial authority, and defining gender roles' (Beinart and Coates 1995: 19). Sometime before the fifteenth century, the Khoikhoi began to cultivate livestock, and in the communal culture of the Khoikhoi people, 'livestock was by far the most valued form of private property in a society where land was never divided among individuals' (Elphick 1977: 59). Despite the value placed on livestock, according to Richard Elphick, 'neither sheep nor cattle were regularly slaughtered. Slaughter was undertaken chiefly to celebrate special occasions ... or as a sacrifice to combat illness among humans or stock' (1977: 60). Furthermore, in the case of the Cattle-Killing, the fact that animal sacrifice was practiced to save livestock as well as humans clearly indicates the value placed upon livestock animals by the Xhosa, a value that is at least structured upon a sense of respect for the inherent value of the animal.

By the late 1600s, however, the Khoikhoi lost their livestock in large part because of the Dutch East India Company's policies of robbery and military action, as well as by virtue of the Dutch colonizers' 'spread of new diseases, interdiction of chiefly aggrandizement, expropriation of pastures, [and] demand for Khoikhoi labor' (Elphick 1977: 174). As the Cape settlers moved inland, they appropriated not only large tracts of land, but also any livestock that was on that land (Ohlson and Stedman 1994: 21). The contested role of cattle in South Africa was still apparent well into the twentieth century, when 'voluntary' removals forced black South Africans to leave their farms and sell their cattle for mere pittance to Boer (Dutch) farmers. Because 'cattle are a measure of a man's success in the villages' (Goodman 1999: 325), the loss of cattle that one had cared for and seen increase over generations was not only a devastating financial blow, but was also akin to the loss of a kind of ancestral memory, the loss of a history dependent upon human and animal co-dependency and interaction.

Despite the very clear historical significance of cattle in the lives of indigenous South Africans, cattle are not associated, in the Western imagination, with African culture, space and history – and they are certainly absent from townships and from wildlife preserves where tourists travel on various kinds of 'safaris'. In fact, because of their familiarity and non-exotic, unromantic nature, despite their immense importance within South African history, cattle play no role in the story told about Africa by the West. From Joseph Conrad's 1899 depiction of the 'heart of darkness' as a 'blank space' on a map (Conrad 2007/1899: 8), the unnamed Congo as 'an empty stream, a great silence, an impenetrable forest' (41), the Western discourse of 'Africa' has been homogenizing, a narrative of empty space uninhabited by humans, vast and filled with unfamiliar and exotic animals – elephants, lions, cape buffalo, leopard and rhinoceros (considered the 'big five') – ripe for, in particular, white male consumption. While cattle and their significance within African societies remain largely absent from most Western discourse about Africa, in her analysis of *Eland*, Stacey Vorster notes that the image of the safari and the great white hunter still looms large, so much so that 'street-wise South Africans ... may take delight in the naivety of many uninitiated tourists (who all too often assume we have wild animals stalking around outside hotels)' (2013: 148). Even such cities as Johannesburg 'can be imagined as a game drive of sorts, as a result of the inherited animal iconography as well as the few instances that have been installed more recently'. Nonetheless, she notes, such iconography is dependent upon white Western mythology and 'relies on out-dated and over-used mythologies of Africa, such as Joseph Conrad's "heart of darkness" filled with wild beasts and savage natives' (ibid.: 148–49).

South African Zef group Die Antwoord's 2012 video for their song 'Fatty Boom Boom' satirizes this outdated mythology via a send-up of the Western assumption that wild animals roam through even the most urban spaces in South Africa, and it explicitly critiques and disrupts the view of the supposedly 'real' South Africa offered by the tourist gaze. In addition to constituting a send-up of US pop singer Lady Gaga (who at one point asked Die Antwoord to open for her), the video links township tourism with safari, depicting a black South African tour guide driving a fake Lady Gaga (wearing her iconic meat dress, which entices a lion to devour her at the end of the video) through what he calls the 'concrete jungle', the urban space of Johannesburg where, in the video, lions, panthers and hyenas are situated beside shopkeepers and piles of trash. The video, like Magona's novel, blatantly criticizes the naivety of the white, Western woman (who, in this case, is actually a man in drag) for her presumption that, via the tourist gaze, South Africa is a space that is accessible to her and that its culture is something she can appropriate for commercial gain. In Die Antwoord's video, she becomes prey for the animal, the victim of her own entitlement.

The space mocked in this video is the staged space of the township tour; like the township space of Magona's novel, it is historically defined by deep and layered othering via the racist mechanisms of South Africa's colonial history, its disruption of indigenous gender roles, and its legacy of displacement and relocation of indigenous human and animal populations – a legacy that removes both parties from their abilities to have productive relationships with either the land or each other. In what has constituted the most controversial aspect of the video, white singer ¥o-landi Vi$$er appears covered entirely in black body paint, and the video alternates between images of the band members covered in either black or white paint. The band's use of blackface was heavily criticized as racist. Adam Haupt notes that

> Yo-Landi and [fellow white musician] Ninja 'go native' by blackening up for profit and sport. It is white privilege that provides Die Antwoord with the means to 'borrow' from aspects of black cultural expression and project colonial notions of blackness
>
> (Haupt 2012)

Another way to read such performativity is as an affront to the racial divisions and distinctions that have marred South African history; it is at once a transgression of boundaries and an acknowledgement of a shared humanity. In that the band also appears in stark white paint, it is possible to read black and white as a false binary, only maintained in the service of oppression.

Unlike the contemporary township tour, Magona's novel invites the reader into the space of the black apartheid-era South African township and situates that space as at once a locus of displaced disenfranchisement and also a breeding ground for inhuman and inhumane violence, a place where it is impossible for *ubuntu* to thrive. In its maternal representation of the violence done to and by black South Africans over the course of hundreds of years of history, Mandisa gives voice to township women's complex and dangerous position while also invoking the Xhosa Cattle-Killing as a narrative of potential cultural healing. Mandisa describes how her knowledge that the whites stole the land from black South Africans seems to be 'knowledge with which [she was] born' (Magona 1998a: 173) because of the pervasive presence of Xhosa oral history as it is told to Mandisa by her grandfather. In its presentation of township space as a ruined landscape, its attention to the dehumanization of the people who live in this space, and its invocation of the Cattle-Killing as one nation's attempt to return to a precolonial moment, Magona's narrative constitutes an ecofeminist manifesto that both implicitly and explicitly posits that all oppressions – from the ground up, as it were – are linked and reinforcing of one another.

According to Mandisa's account (which is based on Magona's experience), the physical space of the township is a 'congested' place where 'the streets are narrow, debris-filled, full of gullies alive with flies, mosquitoes, and sundry vermin thriving in pools of stagnant water' (27) in which children play. Furthermore, the land is not arable but sandy, unable to 'hold down anything, not even wild grass ... It would take a hundred years of people living on it to ground the sand and trample some life into it so that it would support plant and animal' (28). Such a description illustrates the reality of the township as a place that cuts residents off not only from access to South Africa's urban centres but also from access to usable land on which to maintain crops and livestock. Mandisa characterizes Guguletu as 'grey', 'ugly. Impersonal', noting that it is 'both big and small. The place sprawls as far as the eye can see. It is vast ... All that space. But even as you look you suddenly realize that it will be hard to find any place where you can put your foot down' (27). The implication is clear, that the residents of the township do not 'own' the space, and the township does not consist of land that residents can tend to sustain their existence.

Beyond the double-bind of the female colonial subject, Siphokazi Koyana argues that township *mothers* experience a third layer of othering, the 'triple jeopardy of the black working mother' (Koyana 2002: 51). Such women cannot, by virtue of their race and social position, attain the standard of a white, nuclear family; second, they must conform to the 'Eurocentric legal system' (ibid.: 51) that privileges the work of men; and third, they are expected to conform to 'traditional black patriarchy' (ibid.: 51). Furthermore, while South African women experienced patriarchy precolonially, the reality for South African women in the precolonial period was markedly different from their postcolonial status. According to Judith Stevenson:

> women were central to pre-colonial economies and carried important, culturally sanctioned roles. Public space was not dominated by males, although the social organization included parallel male–female domains. Women exerted political, social, and economic influence through women's collectives, such as age grades, agricultural and market relationships, and secret societies. Through such collectives, women wielded considerable power and were able to challenge patriarchal authority.
>
> (Stevenson 2011: 140)

The power of black South African male dominance over black South African women, however, is the result of 'the Christian model of womanhood given to them by nineteenth-century missionaries', which required that black women not 'take leadership roles in ... public affairs. They were to remain in the home as mothers and wives' (ibid.: 143).

This triple jeopardy of township women is apparent in the current political and social milieu, shaped as it is by the spectre of both pervasive rape and the AIDS crisis, the discourse of which haunts Magona's novel, particularly with regard to Mandisa's protection of her own daughter Siziwe from assaults that can result not only in pregnancy but in death. When Mandisa returns to Guguletu after hearing that there has been trouble in the township, she comments on her concern for her daughter: 'a girl-child, she is more vulnerable than the other two children' (Magona 1998a: 40); she notes, 'every day, one hears of rapes. Rapes, not a rape' (38). According to Lydia Polgreen, 'a 2009 study by the Medical Research Council found that one-quarter of men admitted to raping someone, and nearly half of those men said they had raped more than once' (Polgreen 2013), and most rapists go unpunished – even in the face of overwhelming evidence of their guilt. By way of explanation, 'analysts point to the history and culture of South Africa, a deeply patriarchal society that devalues crimes against women', a place where 'the police do not take rape allegations seriously' (ibid.).

## *Ubuntu* and ecofeminism

In order to address this legacy, in *No Future without Forgiveness* Archbishop Desmond Tutu famously defined the South African philosophy of *ubuntu* for a Western audience, noting that at its core this philosophy recognizes that 'a person is a person through other persons'. *Ubuntu* asserts that 'what dehumanizes you inexorably dehumanizes me'; *ubuntu* 'gives people resilience, enabling them to survive and emerge still human despite all efforts to dehumanize them' (Tutu 1999: 31). The significance of such a philosophy as an instrument to enable healing in post-apartheid South Africa is profound: in a country as potentially irrevocably damaged and fractured, and with a population so consistently dehumanized, the need to reclaim one's humanity – one's very humanness – via a recognition of humanity in others is essential. Nonetheless, *ubuntu* still seems to be largely absent in a country where human beings consistently – and increasingly – commit violent acts against one another.[9] While the reasons for violence in South Africa are complex, based in a colonial history that has propagated and enforced various dualisms that serve to instrumentalize indigenous South Africans, one way to begin to understand and potentially address the complexity of this legacy of violence is to situate it within the above ecofeminist framework that allows for a nuanced and holistic reading of the 'reality' of South African townships as spaces much more historically complex than the staged performance of the township tour. Such a reading can then build upon *ubuntu*'s recognition of one's humanity as inherently linked with the humanity of others in order to recognize the ways that South Africa's systematic and legalized *dehumanization* of indigenous peoples was enacted through their displacement from the land, their animals and their conceptions of gender roles.

The township tour offers an image of tentative democratic hope, even as it belies a history of violent and nuanced othering that underscores both the construction of townships and the structural inequities that plague township residents in the present. Die Antwoord's 'Fatty Boom Boom' mocks and then holds up to the light simplistic and reductive conceptions of species, race and gender as these categories are presumed to exist and be understood by external audiences and for external consumption. Stacy Vorster's reading of *Eland* invokes the absent animal bodies that haunt South African history, even as she discourages the impulse to idealize an imagined and sentimental past as some sort of answer to the absences and displacements of the current moment. And Sindiwe Magona, in *Mother to Mother*'s attention to the linkages between the destruction of a nation's animals, a people's subsequent displacement into state-sanctioned townships, gender-based violence, and the dehumanization of black South Africans draws upon the Xhosa Cattle-Killing in order to imagine how what on the surface might look like an extreme act of random violence might in fact be the product of centuries of racist oppression. These texts provide a framework for offering potential township tourists ecofeminist tools for viewing township spaces and residents within a more fully nuanced and complex historical trajectory than that offered by the tour itself.

In Magona's 'Mama Africa' (1998b), a story that appeared in *The New Internationalist*'s 'Red and Green: Eco-Socialism Comes of Age' issue immediately after the publication of *Mother to Mother*, the narrator implores all Africans to recognize that 'life is a chain' and to realize the interconnectedness between all beings. The narrative indicates that the way to shift South Africa's history from oppression and violence to a lived ethic of *ubuntu* is through an ecofeminist recognition of the interconnections between humanity and nature. Mama Africa implores, 'when a child is born, plant a tree to mark the event. Help both grow strong and healthy. Let the child know the tree that is her life.' The need for recognition between various types of life is Magona's plea, and Mama Africa calls for this recognition:

> Sibanye! We are one. All nature is linked. What happens to any part of that chain cannot but affect when happens to another. People and forests, rivers, seas, mountains, deserts and wetlands; beasts of the forest and those of the home ... everything is one – connected, mutually dependent.
>
> (ibid.)

Magona's novel enacts this vision as well, restoring cattle to the story of indigenous South African displacement from rural to township space, and her narrative demonstrates the Xhosa belief in inherent value of the animal. In linking the sacrifices of Amy Biehl and her killer to the sacrifice of cattle during the killing, Magona's novel ingeniously suggests that the violence against the land that began with colonial intrusion resulted in violence done to the Xhosa's most valued livestock animals – and that the slaughter of those animals, in turn, is responsible for township violence between human beings, for the triple jeopardy of township mothers, South Africa's rape epidemic and, ultimately, Amy Biehl's murder as retributive justice. For the outsider gazing into the space of the township, a recognition and respect of both history and Mama Africa's mandate is essential, an act not of *retributive* but of *restorative* justice; it is an opportunity to negotiate the linked oppressions that define South Africa's past, even as it offers the opportunity to move in productive ways into the present.

## Notes

1  Manfred Rolfes notes that in terms of 'slum tourism', 'it is estimated that 40,000 such tourists visit Rio de Janeiro each year, while in Cape Town, the figure is … within a range of about 300,000 visitors' (Rolfes 2010: 421) per year.
2  To commemorate the 200th anniversary of its constitution, Norway has recreated a human zoo: 'the outdoor exhibition called European Attraction Limited which was set up in the capital, Oslo, in Frogner Park, has recreated a notorious 1914 Norwegian human zoo. The original Congo village, or Kongolandsbyen, was inhabited by about 80 people, actually Senegalese, who were put on display for public entertainment for five months' (RT 2014). The installation has sparked outrage.
3  Cape Capers' web page links to a video of its Langa township tour, which contains this performance. http://www.youtube.com/watch?v=YWQpFvlnLNM
4  See Jessica L. Dickson's (2012) 'Revisiting "township tourism": multiple mobilities and re-territorialization of township spaces in Cape Town, South Africa' for her analysis of the ways in which participation in the township tourist endeavor affords certain township women the opportunity to 'traverse the social boundaries of race, gender, sexuality, and the policing of their elders … with impunity, and even … admiration' (35).
5  For an excellent examination of the Biehl case within the larger context of late apartheid-era violence, see *Long Night's Journey into Day*, Deborah Hoffmann and Frances Reid's 2000 documentary about South Africa's Truth and Reconciliation Commission.
6  The three are Vusumzi Ntamo, 23 at the time of conviction; Mongezi Manqina, 22; and Mzikhona Nofemela, 19. All three were charged and convicted, but they later sought and were granted amnesty under the Truth and Reconciliation Commission. Amy Biehl's parents attended the hearings of their daughter's killers and supported their bids for amnesty.
7  Langa was established in 1927 under the terms of the 1923 Urban Areas Act, which forced black South Africans to live in locations separate from white South Africans.
8  I have argued in *Wilderness into Civilized Shapes* (Wright 2010) that the narrative's treatment of the Xhosa as environmentally responsible prior to colonization is mythological, but that mythology nonetheless does productive work in terms of imagining an alternative Xhosa future.
9  Robyn Dixon notes that after consistently cutting violent crime rates since 1995, the country's national crime statistics for 2012–13 'are the worst in a decade, analysts said. The figures show increases in the crimes South Africans fear most: murder; attempted murder; violent, armed house robbery; and carjacking' (Dixon 2013).

## References

Ashcroft, W., Griffiths, G. and Tiffin, H. (1998) *Key Concepts in Postcolonial Studies*, London: Routledge.

Attwell, D. and Harlow, B. (2000) 'Interview with Sindiwe Magona', *Modern Fiction Studies* 46(1): 282–295.

Beinart, W. and Coates, P. (1995) *Environment and History: The Taming of Nature in the USA and South Africa*, London: Routledge.

Booyens, I. (2010) 'Rethinking township tourism: towards responsible tourism development in South African townships', *Development Southern Africa* 27(2): 273–287.

Boswell, B. (2011) 'Re-memory and an African ecofeminist poetic of healing in Malika Ndlovu's Poetry', *Scrutiny2* 16(2): 32–41.

Cape Capers (2006a) 'Responsible tourism policy', available at http://www.tourcapers. co.za (accessed 1 October 2013).

Cape Capers (2006b) 'Township experience', available at http://www.tourcapers.co.za (accessed 1 October 2013).

Conrad, J. (2007/1899) *Heart of Darkness and the Congo Diary*, New York: Penguin.

Cornelissen, S. (2005) 'Producing and imagining "place" and "people": the political economy of South African international tourist representation', *Review of International Political Economy* 12(4): 679–699.

Dickson, J.L. (2012) 'Revisiting "township tourism": multiple mobilities and the re-territorialization of township spaces in Cape Town, South Africa', *Anthropology Southern Africa* 35(1–2): 31–39.

Die Antwoord (2012) 'Fatty Boom Boom', *Ten$Ion*, Zef Recordz.

Dixon, R. (2013) 'Violent crime on the rise again in South Africa', *Los Angeles Times*, 19 September, available at http://www.latimes.com/world/worldnow/la-fg-wn-south-africa-crime-20130919-story.html (accessed 12 October 2013).

Duffy, R. (2002) *A Trip Too Far: Ecotourism, Politics & Exploitation*, London: Earthscan.

Eddo-Lodge, R. (2013) 'A white family had a month in a South African township, but what next?' *The Guardian*, 5 September, available at http://www.theguardian.com/commentisfree/2013/sep/05/white-family-month-south-african-township (accessed 5 October 2013).

Elphick, R. (1977) *Kraal and Castle: The Founding of White South Africa*, New Haven: Yale University Press.

Freire-Medeiros, B. (2012) *Touring Poverty*, New York: Routledge.

Gaard, G. (1993) 'Living interconnections with animals and nature', in *Ecofeminism: Women, Animals, Nature*, edited by Gaard, G., Philadelphia: Temple University Press, 1–12.

Gaard, G. (2010) 'New directions for ecofeminism: toward a more feminist ecocriticism', *Interdisciplinary Studies in Literature and Environment* 17(4): 643–665.

Goodman, D. (1999) *Fault Lines: Journeys into the New South Africa*, Berkeley: University of California Press.

Hames, M. (2006) 'Rights and realities: limits to women's rights and citizenship after 10 years of democracy in South Africa', *Third World Quarterly* 27(7): 1313–1327.

Haupt, A. (2012) 'Die Antwoord's revival of blackface does South Africa no favours', *The Guardian*, 22 October, available at http://www.theguardian.com/global/2012/oct/22/die-antwoord-blackface-south-africa (accessed 3 January 2015).

Herne, B. (2001) *White Hunters: The Golden Age of African Safaris*, New York: Holt.

Hoffmann, D. and Reid, F. (dir.) (2001) *Long Night's Journey into Day* [DVD], San Francisco: Iris Films.

Honey, M. (1999) *Ecotourism and Sustainable Development: Who Owns Paradise?*, Washington, DC: Island Press.

Ilhaam, A. (2009) 'The nature of the future: an ecocritical model', *Ethics & the Environment* 14(2): 139–151.

Koyana, S. (2002) '"Why are you carrying books? Don't you have children?": revisiting motherhood in Sindiwe Magona's autobiographies', *English Studies in Africa* 45(1): 45–55.

Li, H. (1993) 'A cross-cultural critique of ecofeminism', in *Ecofeminism: Women, Animals, Nature*, edited by Gaard, G., Philadelphia: Temple University Press, 272–294

Magona, S. (1998a) *Mother to Mother*, Boston: Beacon.

Magona, S. (1998b) 'Mama Africa: a parable', *New Internationalist* November, available at http://newint.org/features/1998/11/05/mama (accessed 19 October 2013).

Mutekwa, A. and Musanga, T. (2013) 'Subalternizing and reclaiming ecocentric environmental discourses in Zimbabwean literature: (re)reading Doris Lessing's *The Grass is Singing* and Chenjerai Hove's *Ancestors*', *Interdisciplinary Studies in Literature and Environment* 20(2): 239–257.

Mwesigire, B. (2014) 'Exhibiting Africans like animals in Norway's human zoo', This Is Africa, 25 April, available at http://thisisafrica.me/exhibiting-africans-like-animals-norways-human-zoo 2014 (accessed 16 May 2014).

Ohlson, T. and Stedman, J. (1994) *The New is Not Yet Born: Conflict Resolution in Southern Africa*, Washington, DC: Brookings Institution.

Peires, J.B. (1989) *The Dead will Arise: Nongqawuse and the Great Xhosa Cattle-Killing Movement of 1856–1857*, Johannesburg: Ravan.

Polgreen, L. (2013) 'Dropped charges in deadly rape provoke fury in South Africa, and pessimism', *The New York Times*, 8 June, available at http://www.nytimes.com/2013/06/09/world/africa/rape-and-murder-stirs-fury-in-south-africa.html?pagewanted=all&_r=0 (accessed 12 October 2013).

Rich, J. (2012) 'Embracing the spirit of ubuntu', *Huffington Post*, 22 October, available at http://www.huffingtonpost.com/dr-judith-rich/ubuntu_b_1803189.html (accessed 3 January 2015).

Rolfes, M. (2010) 'Poverty tourism: theoretical reflections and empirical findings regarding an extraordinary form of tourism', *GeoJournal* 75: 421–442.

RT (2014) '"Human Zoo" project in Norway sparks racism row', RT, 6 May, available at http://rt.com/news/159320-norway-human-zoo-racism (accessed 16 May 2014).

Siwiwe Tours (2010) 'Cape Town township tours: about Langa', available at http://www.townshiptourscapetown.co.za/about-langa (accessed 5 October 2013).

Steinhart, E. (2006) *Black Poachers, White Hunters: A Social History of Hunting in Colonial Kenya*, Athens, OH: Ohio University Press.

Stevenson, J. (2011) '"The mamas were ripe": ideologies of motherhood and resistance in a South African township', *Feminist Formations* 23(2): 132–163.

Stowers, P.K. (2012) 'The new safari: South African township tours', *AtlantaBlackStar*, 26 September, available at http://atlantablackstar.com/2012/09/26/the-new-safari-south-african-township-tours (accessed 19 October 2013).

Tutu, D. (1999) *No Future without Forgiveness*, New York: Random House.

Urry, J. (1990) *The Tourist Gaze: Leisure and Travel in Contemporary Societies*, London: Sage.

Vorster, S. (2013) 'Inner-city safaris and wild public art', *Critical Arts* 27(2): 147–162.

Wright, L. (2010) *Wilderness into Civilized Shapes: Reading the Postcolonial Environment*, Athens, GA: University of Georgia Press.

# 9 From 'cli-fi' to critical ecofeminism

## Narratives of climate change and climate justice

*Greta Gaard*

*In the month that I begin to write about climate change, my body begins to sweat.*

*I wake in the night, flooded with heat. The warmth begins at the base of my skull, then curls up my head and around my neck like smoke curling under a closed door. The heat pours down my neck and shoulders, arms, spine, leaving me sweating, then chilled.*

*Nothing is wrong. This sudden heat is a step toward my own mortality, natural and inevitable.*

*I think about what it is like to be a body, overheating.*

## Introduction

How can feminists and ecocritics empathize with *earth others*[1] and use that empathy to motivate our scholarship? To date – eschewing both empathy and empirical data – the United States business, government and media have resisted the dire warnings echoing from environmentalists to politicians, NASA scientists, and the United Nations' Intergovernmental Panel on Climate Change (IPCC), a group of over 300 scientists and government officials whose reports in 1990, 1995, 2001, 2007 and 2013 confirm the fact that anthropogenic (human-created) greenhouse gas emissions could, if left unchecked, raise global average temperatures by as much as 5.8°C (or 10.4°F) by the end of this century. From the grassroots, Idle No More indigenous activists, Occupy activists, forest-dwellers in Brazil, women farmers and scientists in India, along with citizens and leaders of low-lying nations all affirm the urgency of global climate change – its immediate effects as a humanitarian and ecological crisis – as possibly the most pressing issue on the international environmental agenda. Yet first-world citizen-consumers have been slow to listen, and slow to demand institutional changes, lulled into complacency, in part, by propaganda from the mainstream media, and the half-truths of climate change science fiction ('cli-fi'). This chapter offers an empathic, empirical and embodied intervention.

Given the proven power of narrative to shape public opinion and to mobilize social movements,[2] I propose bringing a critical ecofeminist standpoint – bridging feminist animal studies, posthumanism, material feminism, ecofeminism and feminist ecocriticism – to illuminate the strengths and shortcomings of literary narratives that present the problem of climate change from a (masculinist) technological-scientific perspective. Provided with a more complete restor(y)ing of climate change causes and effects, authors and readers of literature, as well as activists and ecocritics will have a greater potential to shape and contribute to activist and policy-making discourses around climate justice.

   Ecocritics have already observed the disjunction between the environmental sciences and the environmental humanities (Buell 2005; Garrard 2004), noting the dominance of environmental sciences in defining environmental problems and controlling the discourse around their solutions. These enviro-science analyses offer incomplete descriptions without the perspective of the environmental humanities: fields such as ecopsychology, public health, environmental philosophy, environmental politics, environmental economics and ecocriticism provide critical information that augments and often transforms our understanding of environmental problems – particularly in the case of climate change. To begin, I explore a variety of climate change narratives that fail to challenge the underpinnings of colonialism, neoliberalism, speciesism and gendered fundamentalisms.[3] By expanding the genres and geographies of ecocritical analysis to include artists of color and of diverse sexualities, and addressing in narratives and analyses the climate-changing practices of animal food production and consumption, a critical ecofeminist perspective may offer a more inclusive restor(y)ing of climate change narratives.

## Climate change fiction and 'cli-fi' science fiction

Despite a wealth of feminist environmental writing from the 1980s to the present, ranging from environmental justice-themed science fiction by Octavia Butler (i.e. *The Xenogenesis Trilogy, Parable of the Sower*), Ursula LeGuin (*The Word for World is Forest, Always Coming Home, Buffalo Gals and Other Animal Presences*) and Marge Piercy (*Woman on the Edge of Time*) to futurist apocalyptic and post-apocalyptic novels such as Starhawk's *The Fifth Sacred Thing*, Cormac McCarthy's *The Road* and Margaret Atwood's *MaddAdam* trilogy, the feminist fiction confronting climate change has yet to be written.[4] To date, the prominent texts of climate change fiction and science fiction discussed herein are largely male-authored and non-feminist at best, or anti-feminist and sexist at worst – problematic in that feminist research has traced the root causes of climate change to humanist, colonialist, antidemocratic and anti-ecological beliefs and practices (MacGregor 2010).

   In climate change fiction, the most literary representative of the genre is T.C. Boyle's *A Friend of the Earth* (2000), its title a reference to the US-based international organization Friends of the Earth, founded in 1969 by David Brower. Set somewhere around Santa Barbara, California, in the year 2025, this fictional narrative suggests that global warming is a consequence of economic, cultural and political forces that have produced unsustainable population growth, irreversible loss of biodiversity, deforestation, species extinction and an end to social supports such as health care and social security. Although the narrative ends on a comedic note, promising re-creation of the heteronuclear family and thus the perpetuation of the human species, the overwhelming tone of *A Friend of the Earth* is one of cynicism and despair: its narrative solution is withdrawal from society, since civic engagement hasn't worked. Boyle's analysis of global warming includes the ecological, social, cultural, economic and political causes and consequences, though with a focus on the white middle class; the book omits discussion of diversity such as gender, race, sexuality and nation when addressing climate change problems or solutions. But climate change is not an equal opportunity disaster, undifferentiated in its impacts on diverse nations, communities, genders.

In climate change science fiction (first called 'cli-fi' in 2007 by journalist Dan Bloom), the message is sometimes reversed: according to skeptic Michael Crichton's *State of Fear* (2004), climate change is a hoax produced by environmentalists so determined to promote fear of climate change that they use exotic technologies to start natural disasters (crumbling a massive Arctic glacier, triggering a tsunami) and are willing to see innocent people die, just to make their case. Crichton's narrative portrays the 'experts' – who include PhDs, scientists, intellectuals and feminists – as spectacularly corrupt and terribly wrong. His heroic skeptic, John Kenner, is companioned by a trusty Nepalese sidekick, Sanjong, echoing the racist and not-too-subtle homoerotic pairing of The Lone Ranger and Tonto from US westerns of the 1940s that celebrated the epic myth of Euro-American colonialism. In Crichton's novel, the pair work together to provide charts, graphs and other 'hard' data to disprove global warming. By the novel's conclusion, one environmentalist has been fed to cannibals, and the skeptics have become suddenly irresistible to women, all in nine days. If the narrative itself isn't sufficiently alarming, ecocritics may find the book's popularity with the uncritical and unscientific public even more disturbing, and be appalled by its use as a textbook for the honors seminar 'Scientific Inquiry: Case Studies in Science' at SUNY-Buffalo.[5]

Kim Stanley Robinson's climate change trilogy, *Forty Signs of Rain* (2004), *Fifty Degrees Below* (2005), *Sixty Days and Counting* (2007), is a welcome counterpoint to Crichton's polemic, at least from an ecocritical standpoint. The first text in the series sets up the problem of global warming when Washington, DC is hit hard with two days of rain, portions of the city are flooded and animals are released from zoos so they don't drown. The second text shows the more developed consequences of global warming: the Gulf Stream has stalled, causing frigid winter temperatures in the Eastern United States and Western Europe. As people starve, multinational corporations find ways of making a profit (which is the same plot as in Nathaniel Rich's *Odds Against Tomorrow*). Antarctica's ice shelves collapse, and low-lying nations sink under the waters. In Washington, DC, environmental scientists must overcome government inertia to put in place policies that may save the world.

While the second novel focuses on the market failures of capitalism and democracy in the West, the third novel's narrative suggests that the world would be better if scientists took over politics. Scientists fill the White House, but the book does not explore the benefits and drawbacks of a scientocracy (science's false claims of objectivity and its universalizing tendencies, as well as the corporate control of science, being chief among them), and seems to promote the idea that everything would be better if only the right *man* were President. Indeed, all of Robinson's main plots revolve around men, the main characters are men, and the proposal that a male-centered ecosocialist scientocracy will solve problems of climate change without addressing problems of social injustice, not to mention simple gender parity, seems limited at best.

A spate of 'cli-fi' novels has appeared in the years 2011–13, effectively defining this new genre. Novels that take climate change as a fact and set their plot around characters who must deal with the fallout include Paolo Bacigalupi's *The Windup Girl* (2009), Ian McEwan's *Solar* (2010), Barbara Kingsolver's *Flight Behavior* (2012), Daniel Kramb's *From Here* (2012) and Nathaniel Rich's *Odds Against Tomorrow* (2013). A review essay by Rebecca Tuhus-Dubrow (2013) discusses seven of these novels, and a website on 'Cli-Fi Books' run by a British Columbia micropress, Moon Willow, was launched in August 2013, and renamed simply 'Eco-Fiction' by 2015 (Woodbury n.d.). A reviewer for *The New York Times*, Richard Pérez-Peña (2014) notes that cli-fi fits 'a long tradition of speculative fiction that pictures the future *after* assorted catastrophes' and omits analysis of the catastrophe's root causes and solutions: cli-fi addresses adaptation and survival, but 'if the authors are aiming for political consciousness-raising, the effort is more veiled than in novels of earlier times'. Recent feminist ecocritical analyses of climate change narratives concur with Pérez-Peña, for example Christa Grewe-Volpp's (2013) discussion of Octavia Butler's *Parable of the Sower* (1993) and Cormac McCarthy's *The Road* (2006) as climate change post-apocalyptic novels that depict characters struggling to survive in degraded environments, and Katie Hogan's (2013) queer green analysis of climate change references in Tony Kushner's apocalyptic play *Angels in America* (1994), linking illnesses that are simultaneously social, ecological and psychological. As this ecocritical scholarship shows, the focus of cli-fi narratives remains confined within the apocalyptic failure of techno-science solutions and uninformed by the global climate justice movement.[6] After reading such narratives, cli-fi readers take home the message that climate change is a failure of technology and science, not a failure of species justice or environmental justice, and thus their actions after reading these books might include renewed faith in techno-science solutions and individual carbon footprint reduction, rather than working for system-wide eco-justice changes.

## Climate change nonfiction writing

In the field of literary nonfiction, the majority of texts provide narratives that make environmental sciences more accessible through the lens of environmental literature, yet offer little information about environmental politics, sociology, climate justice or ecosocial strategies for response. Two examples of this approach include Tim Flannery's *The Weather Makers* and Elizabeth Kolbert's *Field Notes from a Catastrophe: Man, Nature, and Climate Change*. Flannery's volume contains 36 short essays on the consequences of global warming, and in the final third of the book he poses solutions that involve individual, national and international actions to reduce carbon dioxide. The core of his message explores how we can shift from fossil fuels to a hydrogen-based economy, and while he acknowledges that the US administration has been influenced by coal industry donations to the Republican party, thereby undermining political action, Flannery's environmental science solutions obscure the powerful influence of environmental economics, politics and culture.

In refreshing contrast, Elizabeth Kolbert's work returns to the view that human politics is at the core of our responses to climate change. Her essays provide international snapshots of how global warming is affecting people, places and species. She interviews scientists and skeptics, bringing scientific data to a humanities audience, and exposing the fallacies of global warming skeptics. Yet her conclusion to the final chapter on the 'Anthropocene' (a geological epoch) offers no solutions but despair: 'It may seem impossible to imagine that a technologically advanced society could choose, in essence, to destroy itself, but that is what we are now in the process of doing' (Kolbert 2006: 187). While there is a wealth of nonfiction handbooks countering Kolbert's despair with suggestions for 'what YOU can do to stop global warming', these too are limited by their focus on individual actions in the absence of environmental context: they fail to address strategies for countering the power of multinational corporations overriding democratic decisions at the level of community, state and nation.[7]

## Children's and young adult climate change narratives

Children's environmental literature has tremendous potential for communicating messages about ecosocial justice, community empowerment and strategies for ecodefence (Gaard 2009). But as of 2014, children's climate change literature has not realized this potential. Several texts focus on climate change effects in the Arctic (Bergen 2008; Rockwell 2006; Tara 2007), using polar bears or penguins as protagonists, and building on children's cross-species empathy to instill awareness. The solutions offered range from empathy to action, yet they articulate only environmental science's approach to climate change (i.e. switch energy sources, plant trees, bicycle, reduce consumption, and 'write representatives in Congress' – but the letters' content is unspecified). And there is an eco-skeptic presence in children's literature as well. Holly Fretwell's *The Sky's Not Falling: Why It's OK to Chill about Global Warming* (2007) assures children that human ingenuity combined with an 'enviropreneurial' spirit will lead to a bright environmental future, not one where people ruin the Earth.

Children's films with climate change themes have not fared much better. Both *Happy Feet* (2006) and *Wall-E* (2008) use the narrative trajectory of heterosexual romance to tell stories framed by the consequences of climate change. In *Happy Feet*, climate change and its root cause, elite humans' overconsumption of nature, manifest not only through ice cracking, but also through the problem of human overfishing, and the resultant scarcity of fish and increase of garbage in the Arctic. In *Wall-E* the Earth is completely covered with garbage, and the romance between robots Wall-E and Eve begins when a human spaceship sends a probe to see if Earth can be reinhabited by the refugee population of humans who have become obese, chair-bound consumers, ruled and pacified by a single corporation. In both narratives, children are invited to identify with childlike and disempowered male heroes who succeed in ecodefence and heterosexuality alike. In both films, the human change of consciousness is magical – the penguin simply confronts the overfishing, garbage-throwing humans with the plastic ring from a six-pack; Wall-E befriends the chair-bound consumers' obese leader, who 'speaks truth to power' and inspires the populace to return to Earth. In fiction, simply learning the facts about environmental devastation is sufficient to inspire action; in reality, rationalism is rhetorically insufficient, climate change facts are distorted by narrative manipulation and a masculinist techno-science framework, and planetary elites (sometimes including ecocritics and our readers) are invested in current colonialist and neoliberal economic benefits and thus seem apathetic or reluctant to change.

In young adult (YA) fiction, there's been a 'boom in dystopian fiction' with post-apocalyptic scenarios, prompted by the immense popularity of Suzanne Collins's *The Hunger Games* trilogy (2008, 2009, 2010), whose clear cli-fi backdrop was stripped from the books' adaptation into a major motion picture (2012). Writing in *The New Yorker*, reviewer Laura Miller (2010) argues that

> dystopian fiction may be the only genre written for children that's routinely less didactic than its adult counterpart. It's not about persuading the reader to stop something terrible from happening – it's about what's happening, right this minute, in the stormy psyche of the adolescent reader.
>
> (Miller 2010)

Evidence supporting this view can be found in Mindy McGinnis's *Not a Drop to Drink* (2010) and Saci Lloyd's *The Carbon Diaries 2015* (2010), both of which present 16-year-old protagonists struggling to survive environmental degradation, sociopolitical breakdown and hormonal transitions of adolescence at the same time. Whether it is mandated water rationing (McGinnis) or carbon rationing (Lloyd), both books offer female survivalist characters reminiscent of Jean Hegland's prescient novel *Into the Forest* (1996), narrating the survivalist struggles of two teenage sisters after the collapse of civilization, by which they have lost electricity, telephones, mail, automobile fuel, commodified foods and their parents.

Disagreeing with *The New Yorker*'s Laura Miller, *New America Foundation* essayist Torie Bosch argues 'there is a strong didactic element' in dystopian YA fiction, as 'young people today are constantly told that their good behaviour can – must – make up for the environmental sins of their forefathers': YA novels such as Caragh O'Brien's *Birthmarked* (2010) and Lauren Oliver's *Delirium* (2011) as well as *The Hunger Games* 'are all about empowering teenagers, especially girls, to speak up and act against injustice' (Bosch 2012). In this thread, a very promising novel by Ann Brashares, *The Here and Now* (2014), depicts a time-travelling teenage protagonist, 17-year-old Prenna James, whose 'back-from-the-future' travels with her mother and a few hundred others transport them from the climate change ravages of 2090 back to New York city in 2010, where the environmental crises of the future might still be averted. The narrative makes frank observations of a community living in 'a paradise they are unwilling to relinquish even if that means dooming the future' and raises the question, 'if a terrible future can be avoided, isn't it morally right to try?' (Clare 2014). Linking climate change with first-world overconsumption, Brashares's *The Here and Now* seems many steps closer toward providing an accurate portrayal of climate change causes and interventions, and offers young adult readers narrative inspiration for environmental activism.

## Climate change documentary and film

In Al Gore's *An Inconvenient Truth* (2006), a narrative synthesis of rationalism and empathy succeeded in bringing the topic of climate change to a popular audience. The film's impact can be seen in the fact that President Bush mentioned climate change in both his 2007 and 2008 State of the Union addresses, but not in 2006; and an internet search for the term 'global warming' yielded only 129 articles for 2005, the year before the film's release, but 471 articles for 2007, the year after the film was produced (Johnson 2009: 44). Laura Johnson attributes Gore's popular success to his capacity for moderating apocalyptic rhetoric with scientific rationalism and constructions of audience agency: at the same time that Gore gestures toward present and future climate change disasters, he simultaneously endorses new technologies and political activism. His message offers no images of either the global elites and economics responsible for global warming, the ground-zero victims of global climate change, or the activist citizens who are leading the battles for climate justice; he makes no connections between a meat-based diet and its environmental consequences. Thus the film avoids invoking oppressor guilt, though still encouraging action. From a feminist and environmental justice standpoint, Gore's analysis is woefully incomplete. While narratives that inspire environmentally minded action are surely laudable, Gore's limited solutions will not address or rectify all climate injustices.

Science fiction films build on Gore's apocalyptic tenor, but without its rhetorical balance, they actually undermine the credibility of climate scientists. *Waterworld* (1995), *The Day After Tomorrow* (2004), *A.I. Artificial Intelligence* (2001), *Elysium* (2013) and *Snowpiercer* (2013) depict white male heroes working to restore life or love against a backdrop of climate change consequences. The Mariner hero of *Waterworld* battles with evil pirates and eventually succeeds in his quest to bring an orphan girl, her female caretaker and a male hydroelectric power expert, among others, to 'Dryland' (Mt. Everest) while the Mariner returns to the sea/frontier; on 'Dryland', one assumes, the mundane tasks of sustaining life are unsuited to heroic actions characteristic of the Mariner (aptly cast as Kevin Costner). *The Day After Tomorrow* offers a similar narrative of father-figure rescuing child, as paleoclimatologist Professor Jack Hall tries to save the United States from the effects of climate change and its rapidly returning Ice Age while also trying to save his son Sam, who has taken refuge in the New York Public Library, far north of the line of projected safety from freezing.[8] Both films present climate change consequences as too far-fetched to be credible: the entire planet flooded? The next Ice Age, in a week?

The more complicated films of the five also offer some eerie plausibilities. *A.I.* (for Artificial Intelligence) offers an 11-year-old cyborg boy as a hero whose primary quest is to regain a mother's love. The film raises questions about human identity in a future affected by climate change, and suggests readings of humans as cyborgs, the Earth as a rejecting mother, and climate change as the ultimate rejection from the Earth/mother – a new twist on mother-blaming. *Elysium* provides a white male hero (Matt Damon) living on the impoverished Earth (crowded and overpopulated largely by people of color), whose poverty and romance with a Latina single mother compel him to infiltrate the elites on the Earth-satellite Elysium – led by the evil white woman, ably portrayed by Jodi Foster – to download the entire operating system for the elites' instantaneous health care, and through his suicide transferring that health care to an open democratic access that will not only save those suffering on Earth, but immediately heal the dying daughter of his beloved Latina. *Snowpiercer* also depicts class divisions, albeit aboard a Noah's Ark Train speeding on a globe-spanning track encircling an ice-age planet, conditions produced by the failure of geo-engineering in solving the climate crisis. The film's white working-class hero leads a rebellion, breaking through the train's many class divisions and uncovering the hedonism of the first-class elites, the train's exploitation of children, and its violent population reduction methods, all ending in the train's explosion, an avalanche, and the edenic return to a frozen (but soon-to-thaw) world for the security system engineer's teenaged daughter and a pre-teen boy. The unabashed irony of all these narratives is their race and gender reversal: around the world, it is poor women, rural women and women of color who are most affected by global climate change effects, and it is women who are working as grassroots heroes to mitigate and adapt to the results of a global environmental crisis created by the world's elites, largely, white men (Women's Environmental Network 2007).

Has ecocriticism been unable to contribute to ongoing conversations about global warming, simply for a lack of worthy literary and cultural artifacts? The few ecocritics who have explored global warming believe so. 'Literary writing has not kept pace with the developments in science and public policy pertaining to climate change, peak oil, population pressure, and the food crisis' writes Patrick D. Murphy (2008: 14). 'American fiction writers have a rather dim track record on the topic of climate change' Scott Slovic concurs (2008: 109). But I wasn't ready to give up so easily. Still seeking narratives with an awareness of intersectionality and an approach that could bridge the environmental sciences and the environmental humanities, I turned to ecofeminist theory, environmental justice analyses, critical animal studies and feminist ecocriticism.

## Getting the full story: from environmental sciences to environmental humanities and feminist ecocriticism

> *To say the earth's warming is natural, inevitable, is to dismiss the effect of elite overconsumption and waste. Breathe in the shimmering air exuded by a thousand cars, creeping along crowded freeways. Trace the line of brown diffusing into sky behind the jet airplane, watch smokestacks pumping thick grey clouds into a clotted sky. Breathing, drinking, consuming, my body embodies effects from the rising levels of greenhouse gases, airborne and waterborne pollutants. My body also rides in cars, looks out the window of airplanes, switches on lights and uses computers powered with coal and the energy of choked rivers.*
>
> *I am part of the problem.*
> *My face flushes with heat.*

From the aforementioned intersectional standpoints of feminist environmental justice ecocriticism, climate change can be seen as an environmental justice problem with material consequences for the environmental sciences. In her essay 'From heroic to holistic ethics', ecofeminist and vegan activist Marti Kheel (1993) develops her theory of the truncated narrative, a theory that foregrounds the rhetorical strategy of omission: 'Currently, ethics is conceived as a tool for making dramatic decisions at the point at which a crisis has occurred. Little if any thought is given to why the crisis or conflict arose to begin with' (1993: 256). In Western ethics, values are debated on an abstract or theoretical plane, and problems are posed in a static, linear fashion, detached from the contexts in which they are formed: 'we are given

truncated stories and then asked what we think the ending should be'
Kheel explains (ibid.: 255). Creating 'ethics-as-crisis' conveniently creates an
identity for the ethical actor as hero, an identity well suited to what Val
Plumwood (1993) defines as the Master Model. 'Western heroic ethics is
designed to treat problems at an advanced stage of their history', Kheel
argues, and

> run counter to one of the most basic principles in ecology – namely, that
> everything is interconnected ... By uprooting ethical dilemmas from the
> environment that produced them, heroic ethics sees only random, iso-
> lated problems, rather than an entire diseased world view. But until the
> entire diseased world view is uprooted, we will always face moral crises
> of the same kind.
>
> (Kheel 1993: 258–59)

As an alternative to truncated ethical narratives and heroic ethics, Kheel
proposes retrieving 'the whole story behind ethical dilemmas' uncovering
the interconnections of social and environmental perspectives, policies, economics and decision-making, including all those affected by the ethical
'crisis'. With the whole story restored, we can work more effectively for
solutions to current ecosocial problems, and prevent others in the future,
thereby eliminating the need for heroes – though as Kheel wryly observes,
'prevention is simply not a very heroic undertaking' (ibid.: 258).

Kheel's theory describing truncated narratives helps illuminate the 'story'
of climate change causes and solutions – stories that surface in the popular
media, in science, literature and culture. Upon initial inquiry, the stories we
receive about the causes of climate change are narrated by the environmental
sciences, which suggest that climate change is primarily a problem of transportation and energy production; on further inquiry, environmental sciences
and environmental politics reveal climate change is a problem exacerbated
by processes of industrialized animal-based agriculture, as documented by
the United Nations' Food and Agricultural Association report, *Livestock's
Long Shadow* (Steinfield et al. 2006). From environmental politics, we then
learn the 'subplot' of both these 'cover stories'[9] is the deeper problem of
first-world industrialized nations' overconsumption and waste of global
nature and all those associated with nature – indigenous people, the 'two-
thirds' (or 'developing') nations, nonhuman animals and ecosystems. An
embedded subplot to the first-world/two-thirds-world narrative is the powerful presence of multinational corporations, whose economic force and
global trade agreements have the capacity to overpower democratic decisions
made at all levels – city, state and nation. Finally, at the bottom of these
narrative hierarchies lie the inequalities of gender, race and species, which
are present at almost every level of society and nation.[10] Inspired by Kheel's
theory, I have compiled 'Facts that restore the truncated narrative of climate
change' in Box 9.1.

## Box 9.1 Facts that restore the truncated narrative of climate change

*Transportation, energy production, animal-based agriculture*

Independent environmental scientists and the United Nations Intergovern-mental Panel on Climate Change (IPCC n.d.) describe climate change as produced by an excess of greenhouse gases, primarily carbon dioxide, emitted as a by-product of human industrialized activities – burning fossil fuels in cars, and creating energy with coal-fired power plants. The well known focus on the social problems of transportation and energy production often obscures the fact that methane, another greenhouse gas that is 23 times stronger than carbon dioxide, also contributes to climate change, with industrialized animal agriculture playing a significant role in its production.

The United Nations Food and Agriculture Organization (FAO) (Steinfield et al. 2006) and the popular US-based journal *Scientific American* (Fiala 2009) concur that industrialized animal-based food production ('factory farming') contributes significantly to climate change. Moreover, industrial food pro-duction has hidden environmental costs in its use of insecticides and fertilizers, deforestation, water pollution and water consumption, feed given to cattle, fuel for farming, transportation and refrigeration. *Scientific American* (Fiala 2009) concluded that worldwide meat production of beef, chicken and pork emits more greenhouse gases than all forms of global transportation or industrial processes. The FAO report suggests that giving up the average 176 lb of meat consumed annually, per person, in developed countries is one of the greenest lifestyle changes individuals can make. 'Why is vegetar-ianism still considered a personal lifestyle decision when it has such enormous global ramifications?' asks Marti Kheel (2009: 49). She concludes, 'the impact of diet on the environment is the inconvenient truth that Gore and other environmentalists fail to voice'.

*Industrialized versus developing nations*

An environmental politics perspective emphasizes that climate change is a global environmental problem predominantly produced by industrialized nations, and suffered primarily by developing nations, along with the poorer classes, marginalized within the industrialized nations. For example, with only 4 per cent of the world's population, the United States emits 25 per cent of the world's carbon dioxide (Center for Progressive Reform 2008). Yet climate change talks have been repeatedly stalled by finger-pointing and foot-dragging, as each of the more industrialized nations refuses to lead the way in greenhouse gas reductions. No one wants to be first in reducing what the elites see as their rightful standard of living.

While climate change will affect the entire global environment, its impacts will be felt hardest by those least able to make adaptations for survival.

People living in poverty are more likely to live in unplanned, temporary settlements, which are erected on unsuitable land – prone to the risks of flooding, storm surges and landslides. Most eke out a precarious economic existence through subsistence farming or fishing, and have no savings or assets to insure them against external shocks. Often, they lack sanitation and their limited access to clean water, poor diet and inadequate health-care provisions undermine their resistance to infectious diseases. Moreover, their lack of social status and the informal nature or remoteness of their settlements means that they do not receive adequate warnings of impending disasters, and relief efforts are least likely to reach them. Lack of education and official neglect means that they have little alternative after disasters but to remain in, or return to, the same disaster-prone areas, with diminished assets, and await the next calamitous event.

### Inequalities of genders and sexualities

A feminist environmental perspective confirms that women are the ones most severely affected by climate change and natural disasters due to social roles, discrimination and poverty. Around the world, women's gender roles restrict women's mobility, impose tasks associated with food production and caregiving, and simultaneously obstruct women from participating in decision-making about climate change, greenhouse gas emissions, and decisions about adaptation and mitigation. In developing countries, women living in poverty bear the burden of climate change consequences, as these create more work to fetch water, or to collect fuel and fodder – duties traditionally assigned to women. As rural areas experience desertification, decreased food production, and other economic and ecological hardships, these factors prompt increased male out-migration to urban centers with the promise of economic gain and wages returned to the family; these promises are not always fulfilled. In the short term, and possibly long term as well, male out-migration means more women are left behind with additional agricultural and household duties such as caregiving. These women have even fewer resources to cope with seasonal and episodic weather and natural disasters.

Gender inequalities mean that women and children are 14 times more likely than men to die in ecological disasters (Aguilar 2007; Aguilar et al. 2007). For example, in the 1991 cyclone and flood in Bangladesh, 90 per cent of the victims were women. The causes are multiple: warning information was not sent to women, who were largely confined in their homes; women are not trained swimmers; women's caregiving responsibilities meant that women trying to escape the floods were often holding infants and towing elder family members, while husbands escaped alone; moreover, the increased risk of sexual assaults outside the home made women wait longer to leave, hoping that male relatives would return for them. Similarly, in the 2004 tsunami in Aceh, Sumatra, more than 75 per cent of those who died were women. The deaths of so many mothers leads to increased infant mortality, early marriage of girls, increased neglect of girls' education, sexual assaults, trafficking in women and child prostitution. Even in industrialized countries, more women than men died during the 2003 European heat wave, and during Hurricane Katrina in the USA, African-American women – the poorest population in that part of the country – faced the greatest obstacles to survival (Aguilar et al. 2007).

Transgendered persons and gay/lesbian/bisexual/transgender/queer persons (GLBTQ) already live on the margins of most societies, denied rights of marriage and family life, denied health-care coverage for partners and their children, denied fair housing and employment rights, immigration rights and more. Climate change exacerbates pressures on marginalized people first, with economic and cultural elites best able to mitigate and postpone impacts; as a global phenomenon, homophobia infiltrates climate change discourse, distorting our analysis of climate change causes and climate justice solutions, and placing a wedge between international activists. Two examples will suffice: at the First Worldwide Peoples' Conference on Climate Change and Mother Earth held in Cochabamba, April 19–22, 2010, Bolivian President Evo Morales claimed that the presence of homosexual men around the world was a consequence of eating genetically modified chicken: 'The chicken that we eat is chock-full of feminine hormones. So, when men eat these chickens, they deviate from themselves as men' (ILGA 2010). This statement exemplifies a dangerous nexus of ignorance, speciesism and homophobia that conceals the workings of industrial agribusiness. A second example is the invisibility of GLBTQ people in the wake of Hurricane Katrina, an unprecedented storm and infrastructure collapse which occurred just days before the annual queer festival in New Orleans, 'Southern Decadence', a celebration that drew 125,000 revellers in 2006 (Southern Decadence New Orleans n.d.). The religious right quickly declared Hurricane Katrina an example of God's wrath against homosexuals, waving signs with 'Thank God for Katrina' and publishing detailed connections between the sin of homosexuality and the destruction of New Orleans. It is hard to imagine GLBTQ people not facing harassment and discrimination during and after the events of Katrina, given the fact that Louisiana, Alabama and Mississippi lack any legal protections for GLBTQ persons and would have been unsympathetic to such reports. Yet in statements of climate justice to date, there is no mention of the integral need for queer climate justice.

Restoring many of the missing components from global warming's truncated narrative, the 27 Bali Principles of Climate Justice (2002)[11] redefine climate change from an environmental justice standpoint, using as a template the original 17 Principles of Environmental Justice (Energy Justice Network 1991) created at the First National People of Color Environmental Leadership Summit. They connect the unsustainable consumption and production practices of the North (first-world industrialized countries) and the elites of the South (two-thirds world, 'developing' countries) with the environmental impacts felt most harshly by those in the South and the impoverished areas of the North. The principles address the categories of gender, indigeneity, age, ability, wealth and health; they provide mandates for sustainability in energy and food production, democratic decision-making, ecological econom-ics, gender justice and economic reparations to include support for adaptation and mitigation of climate change impacts on the world's most vulnerable populations. The missing pieces from this statement – the role of indus-trialized animal agriculture, and the specific climate justice impacts on LGBT people – still need inclusion. With these two additional elements completing the story by correcting its heterosexism and speciesism – in effect, its *humanism* – the intersectional analysis provided by the Bali Principles offers the best articulation for restoring the truncated narrative of climate change.

## Climate justice narratives: a feminist ecocritical perspective

> *The earth is not a woman, not a single body but billions. I think of heavy white bears, swimming in search of solid ice. Unable to sleep on this hot summer night, I rumble downstairs, get a glass of ice water and hold it to my forehead. I think of migrating birds and butterflies, disoriented by diminished wetlands and early blooming flowers, and of people sitting on rooftops or suffocating in attics, surrounded by floodwater from broken levees. I think of women who cannot swim, women who wait at home for help that never comes, women who drown attempting to bring elders and children to safety.*
>
> *We are, all, bodies of knowledge.*

The interdependence among human, animal and environmental health is a knowledge legacy of the feminist, anti-toxics and environmental justice movements of the twentieth century. Beginning with Rachel Carson's (1962) research exposing the links between pesticides and human/animal/environ-mental health, and augmented by Lois Gibbs' activism exposing childhood cancer clusters in her working-class community atop Hooker Chemical's dump at Love Canal; by the feminist anti-toxics movement of the 1980s, the breast cancer and environment activism of the 1990s (Brady 1991; Clorfene-Casten 1996), and the environmental justice movement of the 1990s and beyond; and by the research linking cancer and environmental toxins as reported in Theo Colborn et al.'s *Our Stolen Future* (1996), Sandra Steingraber's *Living Downstream* (1997), and Tyrone Hayes et al.'s work on the endocrine-disrupting effects of atrazine (2002) – the scientific and experiential grounds for what material feminist Stacy Alaimo (2008) terms 'transcorporeality' are over 50 years strong. Our physical selves are more accurately conceived of as material *flows* rather than discrete and bounded bodies, and thus we must also 'reimagine "climate change" and the fleshy, damp immediacy of our own embodied existences as intimately imbricated', argue Astrida Neimanis and Rachel Loewen Walker: 'the weather and the climate are not phenomena "in" which we live at all – where climate would be some natural backdrop to our separate human dramas – but are rather of us, in us, through us' (Neimanis and Walker 2014: 559). This transcorporeality, as Neimanis reiterates, is 'embodied, but never essentialised'; it is always articulated 'in ways that cannot be dissociated from politics, economics, coloniality and privilege – and my [our] embeddedness therein' (Neimanis 2013: 103).

Given the persistence of feminist, antiracist and environmental theories confirming our transcorporeality with human and more-than-human natures, and our responsibilities/response-abilities to and with these transcorporeal bodies, I found it hard to explain the absence of women, people of color, and eco-queers as authors of the cli-fi narratives I had surveyed (though white women do figure more prominently as authors of children's books). As Michael Ziser and Julie Sze found, mainstream global climate change narratives are characterized by 'the elision of specific race- and class-based environmental injustices', and redeploy 'traditional U.S. environmental tropes in ways that soft-pedal environmental justice goals' (Ziser and Sze 2007: 387). To date, few ecocritics have asked this question: if global warming narratives in fiction, nonfiction, science fiction and film alike have been largely the domain of white men, what genre are queers and artists of color using to address global warming? As ecocritic Stephen Siperstein suggests, we must be 'willing to expand our vision of the genre' (2014). In climate justice documentaries, short stories, music videos and popular songs, eco-critics may discover more inclusive and intersectional narratives that restore the truncated narratives of climate change, and offer strategies for mitigating the effects of climate injustices.

Perhaps the first climate justice documentary to reach a global audience, *The Island President* (2011), offers an environmental justice (humanities) counterpart to the 'inconvenient truth' of Al Gore's environmental science. This film traces President Mohamed Nasheed of the Maldives as he fights to compel industrialized nations to face up to the impact of their climate-changing emissions on the most low-lying countries in the world. While the people of the Maldives visit neighboring island countries to seek refuge and resettlement possibilities, Nasheed meets with global dignitaries who attend the Copenhagen Climate Summit in 2009 where, at the last moment, he makes a speech that salvages an agreement. Though the Copenhagen summit is widely regarded as a failure, it was the first time that India, China and the USA had agreed to reducing emissions. This documentary is all the more stirring in light of the fact that in February 2012, President Nasheed was forced to resign under threat of violence, in a coup d'état perpetrated by security forces loyal to the former dictator, and the dictator's half-brother won the Presidential elections in November 2013. The links between a lack of democracy and climate injustice are clear not just in the Maldives, but throughout the two-thirds world.

In the short story 'Cayera' by Filipino writer Honorio Bartolomé De Dios (2007), a gay beautician, Bernie, and her friends join a movement against logging operations and the construction of an industrial plant in the agricultural village of San Martin. Although the town's elite know Bernie as a trusted aide, her inclusion in the movement is questioned on the basis of her sexuality. Although she and her friends are mocked by the eco-heterosexual marchers in the rally, Bernie later transforms her beauty parlor into a hiding place for rebels, whom she transforms into women to protect them from the military. 'Pageantry and performance thus become sites of resistance', Nina Somera (2009) concludes, arguing that climate change 'aggravates longstanding inequalities and peculiar situations that strike one's layers of identities – as a tenant farmer, industrial worker, lesbian mother, landless widow, indigenous woman and so on'.

Marvin Gaye's 1971 popular hit, 'Mercy Mercy Me (The Ecology)' was remade in 2006 by the Dirty Dozen Brass Band, giving the song a New Orleans jazz flavour, and an album cover depicting a solitary, naked man pulling a canoe through a flooded urban landscape, unmistakably targeting this song to the events surrounding Hurricane Katrina. Gaye asks, 'What about this overcrowded land? How much more abuse from man can she stand?'[12] In the context of global warming catastrophes and climate justice, Gaye's lyrics gain new resonance. Hurricane Katrina was an event that made visible the arrogance of culture's attempt to control nature, along with the indifference of urban planners and engineers to the structures of safety allegedly protecting poor people and people of color – particularly women of color (Seager 2006), and the ways these social hierarchies affect the land, water and nonhuman animals.

Another exemplary artist, India Arie produced two songs on her *Testimony Volume 2* album (2009) that address global warming from an intersectional, climate justice perspective. The first song, 'Better Way', contrasts the government's response to Hurricane Katrina and the politically motivated war in Iraq against the media manipulation and sheer indifference of elected politicians, particularly then-President George W. Bush: 'Is it democracy or is it the oil? It's in the news every day, we're a paycheck away, and the President's on the golf course.'[13] In the tradition of black spirituals, Arie (like Martin Luther King) positions herself as both Moses figure and feminist lyricist with her refrain, 'Let my people go!' Her proposed solution to these and other problems of social, environmental and climate injustice is a reconception of human identity as interdependent, with inclusivity and care presented as the sole strategy for human survival: 'I know there's gotta be a better way, and we gotta find it – we gotta stand together, or we can fall apart'.

Another song on Arie's album, 'Ghetto' argues for an interdependent self-identity that makes connections across nationality, class and race. Her work persuasively articulates the problems of global justice to first-world listeners (the 'you' of the lyrics) by exposing the third world within the first world: 'to be hungry in L.A. is just like starving in Bombay. Homeless in Morocco is a shelter in Chicago.'[14] Contrasting definitions of the ghetto as 'a place of minority, and poverty, and overpopulation', Arie insists that 'we live on this earth together', and that from outer space, the whole world can be seen as a ghetto because 'it's a small world after all'. Arie's lyrics playfully reverse the white supremacist erasure and commodification of difference through the Disneyland 'small world' metaphor, and the disembodied 'eye in the sky' techno-science metaphor of space exploration, whereby the blue ball of Earth equalizes (and erases) all social hierarchies; mindful of difference, Arie uses these same dominant metaphors strategically, to draw listeners together.

Another climate justice music video, Kool Keith's ('Dr. Octagon') 'Trees Are Dying' (2007) presents an African-American boy age 11 or 12 as its rap narrator, dressed as a schoolteacher in a white shirt, black plaid bow tie, red plaid suspenders, white pants and converse high-tops. The boy poses as teacher and newscaster, standing in front of a blackboard where a map of the United States is chalked over with heat-wave temperatures – 186 to 202°F – and a hurricane spiral marking the Gulf of Mexico. The blackboard bursts into flames and his back catches on fire. As he dances and narrates, we see other women and children costumed as trees, stiffly marching through a field of clear-cut stumps, falling backwards against headstones, and dancing a ring-around-the-roses circle of death in front of nuclear reactors spewing smoke into the skies. A crew of children dressed as scientists mix smoking fluids and pour them into a planet Earth bubble that explodes and rolls away; a frenzy of cars drives across the screen and onto a six-lane freeway, each car with a bull's horns strapped to the hood. A white, high-heeled shoe stamps down a building, introducing a robotic white woman wearing a business suit, acting the role of Godzilla; she attempts unsuccessfully to jam a tree branch into a copier machine, as children in white scientists' coats mill around her, working at other copying machines, and papers fly in the air. Significantly, the majority of the actor-dancers are black pre-teen children, the landscape and sky are persistently grey, and refrains such as 'apathy kills' and 'car-car-carbon dioxide' and 'like the elephants, trees are dyin' repeat in lyrics and in superimposed text. The music video's rich metaphorical twists on popular culture make clear connections among species extinction, defor-estation, unsustainable transportation and energy production, corporate-driven colonization of nature, white supremacy, adult supremacy and an apathetic gerontocracy.

Along with an intersectional analysis of the root causes of climate change in social, economic and global injustices, these hip-hop lyrics and music video offer a sensory re-connection that is unavailable via other media such as literature and cinematic narrative: they make viewers want to dance. In contrast to the immobilizing sense of futility, apathy or denial often inspired by informational overkill from environmental science and cli-fi literature alike, climate justice musical narratives offer a more inclusive and a more popularly accessible medium, one that energizes its audiences and invites movement toward action and activism alike.

## Critical ecofeminism and climate change

A recent branch of environmental feminist theory – variously called 'material feminism' (Alaimo and Hekman 2008), 'eco-ontological feminism' (Blair 2008), and 'eco-ontological social/ist feminist thought' (Bauman 2007) – offers a strategy for building on key contributions of ecological feminist and environmental justice perspectives: the centrality of an interdependent self-identity and the value of embodied knowledge, present in issues of race, class, gender, sexuality, age and ability, as well as issues of environmental health. According to this branch of environmental feminist thought, the essentialism–social constructionism debates of the 1990s and the ascendancy of social constructionism have misrepresented ecofeminism and essentialism as synonymous categories, denouncing and discarding both in order to emphasize the shaping forces of culture in organizing human identity and experiences.[15] Twenty years later, feminists are acknowledging that the suspect term was *essentialism*, and are now arguing for a 'feminist politics of the-body-in-place ... founded in an affirmation of our dependence on the earth' (Mann 2006: 129). Material feminism, write Stacy Alaimo and Susan Hekman, explores 'the interaction of culture, history, discourse, technology, biology and the "environment", without privileging any one of these elements' (2008: 7). Similarly, critical ecofeminism envisions human identity as continually becoming-with earth others; it involves 'see[ing] creativity and agency in the other-than-human world around us' (Plumwood 2009). Thus 'the potential for us to respond meaningfully to climate change', writes Jennifer Blair, will 'depend on a re-conception of subjectivity and a re-conception of the ways in which humans perceive and effect change in the material world' (Blair 2008: 319). The problem is that 'no matter what information about global warming the media communicates, people seem to need to feel the heat themselves in order to respond to the phenomenon in meaningful, change-driven ways' (ibid.: 320). I suggest that climate justice narratives – in documentary, literature and music – offer artistic media capable of putting people in motion *and* feeling the heat.

What are ecocritics *doing* about climate change? Certainly, we are bringing our position as educators to serve the larger work of connecting literature with contemporary environmental issues, problems and solutions. In our scholarship, our essay-writing and presentations, we can also address the truncated narratives of climate change, provide narrative data that bridge the environmental sciences with the environmental humanities to fill in these omissions, and interrogate Western culture's preference for heroes and crisis over everyday citizen action and apocalypse-prevention. In our classes, we can expand our range of genre and media, ensuring that we include texts by women, eco-queers and artists of color when we read narratives of global climate change and climate justice, and encouraging pedagogies from service learning to creative writing exercises as avenues for students to gain experiential education that re-connects them with the beauty, the danger and the ecosocial contexts influencing our material embodiment.

As environmentalists and ecocritics have noted, if everyone must experience the effects of climate change first-hand in order to take meaningful action, our actions will come too late to make a difference. In this context, narrative offers a powerful potential for creating an 'entangled empathy' (Gruen 2012), the affective mode that offers an avenue for understanding across differences. When the narratives of climate change are presented not just as a techno-science story but also as a matter of a transcorporeality that explicitly embodies and values the intersecting differences of gender, sexuality and species with differences of race, class, ecology and nation, then cli-fi readers will have a more complete story of climate injustices and a more effective road map for activist responses.

*Awake in the cricket-murmuring darkness of late summer, I am not alone.*

## Notes

1 The term 'earth others' is Val Plumwood's (2012), and it articulates the philosophical animism or 'animist materialism' that she was developing at the time of her premature death. Her ideas anticipate new materialisms and critical animal studies, and firmly ground my articulation of a critical ecofeminism.

2 For example, Harriet Beecher Stowe's *Uncle Tom's Cabin* (1852) provoked an outcry against slavery, Upton Sinclair's *The Jungle* (1906) mobilized legislation to regulate the meatpacking industry, Rachel Carson's *Silent Spring* (1962) launched the environmental movement and campaigns to ban the use of DDT, and Edward Abbey's *The Monkey Wrench Gang* (1975) launched EarthFirst! and its famous tactics of 'monkeywrenching'.

3 Thanks to the popularity of cli-fi, the field is proliferating at such a rate that any survey inevitably will be incomplete. I recommend Dan Bloom's 'Cli-Fi Central' Facebook page, Andrew Dobson's review of cli-fi narratives at http://www.andrewdobson.com/eco-apocalypse-novels.html and the Eco-Fiction website at http://eco-fiction.com for their rich resources, as of January 2015.

4 These feminist environmental justice texts have been discussed from an ecofeminist literary perspective (see Alaimo 1998; McGuire and McGuire 1998; Armbruster 1998) and a feminist ecocritical perspective (Grewe-Volpp 2013; Hogan 2013; Stein 2013).

5 Clyde Freeman Herreid (2005) reports on his use of Crichton's *State of Fear* as a primary text for his honors seminar in 'Scientific Inquiry: Case Studies in Science'. The fact that Crichton's novel is a work of science fiction, not researched fact, does not preclude it from use in Herreid's University Honors Program course at The State University of New York, Buffalo.

6 A notable exception would be the recent publication of Naomi Oreskes and Eric M. Conway's *The Collapse of Western Civilization* (2014).

7 Facts well known to anti-globalization eco-activists since the battle against the General Agreement on Tariffs and Trade (GATT) in the mid-1990s are now summarized in Naomi Klein's *This Changes Everything: Capitalism vs. The Climate* (2014).

8 There are some enjoyable moments to the film, from a progressive ecocritical standpoint: the students in the library are burning Nietzche's books to stay warm; there's a President who refuses to listen to global warming science, and a Vice President who says action will cost too much; and US citizens are portrayed as

climate refugees crossing the border into Mexico by fording the Rio Grande, offering a wry twist on anti-immigrant sentiments.

9 By 'cover story' I mean the story that is on the cover of a rather thick stack of narratives about the causes and solutions to global warming. I do not mean that the 'cover story' is covering all the narratives, only that it has gained so much prominence that it functions to obscure other intersectional narratives that are also accurate descriptions of experiential fact.

10 I qualify this claim about the omnipresent inequalities of gender and sexualities with the word 'almost' to acknowledge the presence of traditional indigenous societies whose gender role differences are unmarked by differential valuations. Such societies are already quite marginalized in the global economy.

11 The principles were developed by an international coalition of groups – which includes CorpWatch, Third World Network, Oil Watch and the Indigenous Environmental Network, among others – at the final preparatory negotiations for the Earth Summit in Bali in June 2002.

12 The complete lyrics to 'Mercy Mercy Me' can be found at http://www.metro lyrics.com/mercy-mercy-me-lyrics-marvin-gaye.html.

13 Complete lyrics to India Arie's 'Better Way' can be found at http://www.lyrics mode.com/lyrics/i/indiaarie/better_way.html.

14 Complete lyrics for India Arie's 'Ghetto' can be found at http://www.azlyrics. com/lyrics/indiaarie/ghetto.html.

15 There are many branches of ecofeminist theory (Gaard 1998; Sturgeon 1997; Merchant 1995), including branches that are liberal, socialist, anarchist, radical feminist, womanist and cultural feminist; the latter is the branch most often charged with essentialism. Vegan and vegetarian ecofeminists are now arguing that the anti-essentialist backlash against ecofeminism is motivated by a deeper backlash against ecofeminism's defense of inter-species justice (see Gaard 2011).

# References

Aguilar, L. (2007) *Women and Climate Change: Women as Agents of Change*, Gland, Switzerland: International Union for Conservation of Nature, available at http://cmsdata.iucn.org/downloads/climate_change_gender.pdf (accessed 10 April 2014).

Aguilar, L., Araujo, A. and Quesada-Aguilar, A. (2007) *Fact Sheet on Gender and Climate Change*, Gland, Switzerland: International Union for Conservation of Nature, presented at the UNFCCC COP 13, Bali, December 2007, available at http://gender andenvironment.org/resource/gender-and-climate-change (accessed 14 January 2015).

Alaimo, S. (1998) '"Skin dreaming": the bodily transgressions of Fielding Burke, Octavia Butler, and Linda Hogan', in *Ecofeminist Literary Criticism: Theory, Interpretation, Pedagogy*, edited by Gaard, G. and Murphy, P.D., Urbana, IL: University of Illinois Press, 123–138.

Alaimo, S. (2008) 'Trans-corporeal feminisms and the ethical space of nature', in *Material Feminisms*, edited by Alaimo, S. and Hekman, S., Bloomington: Indiana University Press, 237–264.

Alaimo, S. and Hekman, S. (eds) (2008) *Material Feminisms*, Bloomington: Indiana University Press.

Arie, I. (2009) 'Better Way' and 'Ghetto', *Testimony Volume 2*.

Armbruster, K. (1998) '"Buffalo gals, won't you come out tonight": a call for boundary-crossing in ecofeminist literary criticism', in *Ecofeminist Literary Criticism: Theory, Interpretation, Pedagogy*, edited by Gaard, G. and Murphy, P.D., Urbana, IL: University of Illinois Press, 97–122.

Atwood, M. (2003) *Oryx and Crake*, New York: Random House.

Atwood, M. (2009) *The Year of the Flood*, New York: Doubleday.

Atwood, M. (2013) *MaddAddam*, New York: Random House.

Bacigalupi, P. (2009) *The Windup Girl*, San Francisco: Night Shade Books.

Bali Principles of Climate Justice (2002) available at http://www.ejnet.org/ej/bali.pdf (accessed 10 September 2013).

Bauman, W.A. (2007) 'The "eco-ontology" of social/ist ecofeminist thought', *Environmental Ethics* 29(3): 279–298.

Bergen, L. (2008) *A Story About Global Warming*, New York: Little Simon/Little Green Books.

Blair, J. (2008) 'Media on ice', *Feminist Media Studies* 8(3): 318–323.

Bosch, T. (2012) 'Climate change in *The Hunger Games*: how dystopian young-adult fiction is tackling the social consequences of global warming', *Slate*, 21 March, available at http://www.slate.com/articles/arts/future_tense/2012/03/the_hunger_games_birthmarked_delirium_ya_fiction_on_climate_change_.html (accessed 10 April 2014).

Boyle, T.C. (2000) *A Friend of the Earth*, New York: Viking Books.

Brady, J. (1991) *1 in 3: Women with Cancer Confront an Epidemic*, San Francisco: Cleis Press.

Brashares, A. (2014) *The Here and Now*, New York: Delacorte Press.

Buell, L. (2005) *The Future of Environmental Criticism: Environmental Crisis and Literary Imagination*, Malden, MA: Blackwell.

Butler, O. (1993) *Parable of the Sower*, New York: Warner Books.

Butler, O. (2000) *The Xenogenesis Trilogy*, New York: Time/Warner Books.

Carson, R. (1962) *Silent Spring*, New York: Houghton Mifflin.

Center for Progressive Reform (2008) *International Environmental Justice and Climate Change*, available at http://www.progressivereform.org/perspintlenvironJustice.cfm (accessed 10 April 2014).

Clare, C. (2014) 'Back from the future: The Here and Now by Ann Brashares', *The New York Times*, 4 April, available at http://www.nytimes.com/2014/04/06/books/review/the-here-and-now-by-ann-brashares.html?_r=0 (accessed 10 April 2014).

Clorfene-Casten, L. (1996) *Breast Cancer: Poisons, Profits, and Prevention*, Monroe, ME: Common Courage Press.

Colborn, T., Dumanoski, D. and Myers, J.P. (1996) *Our Stolen Future*, New York: Penguin/Plume.

Collins, S. (2008) *The Hunger Games*, Danbury, CT: Scholastic Press.

Collins, S. (2009) *Catching Fire*, Danbury, CT: Scholastic Press.

Collins, S. (2010) *Mockingjay*, Danbury, CT: Scholastic Press.

Crichton, M. (2004) *State of Fear*, New York: HarperCollins.

De Dios, H.B. (2007) 'Cayera', in *Ladlad 3: An Anthology of Philippine Gay Writing*, edited by Garcia, J.N. and Remoto, D., Pasig, The Philippines: Anvil Publishing.

Energy Justice Network (1991) 'Principles of environmental justice', available at http://www.ejnet.org/ej/principles.html (accessed 26 January 2013).

Fiala, N. (2009) 'How meat contributes to global warming', *Scientific American* 4 February, available at http://www.scientificamerican.com/article.cfm?id=the-green house-hamburger (accessed 10 September 2013).

Flannery, T. (2006) *The Weather Makers*, New York: Atlantic Monthly Press.

Fretwell, H. (2007) *The Sky's Not Falling! Why It's OK to Chill about Global Warming*, Los Angeles, CA: World Ahead Media.

Gaard, G. (1998) *Ecological Politics: Ecofeminists and the Greens*, Philadelphia, PA: Temple University Press.

Gaard, G. (2009) 'Toward an ecopedagogy of children's environmental literature', *Green Theory and Praxis* 4(2): 11–24.

Gaard, G. (2011) 'Ecofeminism revisited: rejecting essentialism and re-placing species in a material feminist environmentalism', *Feminist Formations* 23(2): 26–53.

Garrard, G. (2004) *Ecocriticism*, New York: Routledge.

Grewe-Volpp, C. (2013) 'Keep moving: place and gender in a post-apocalyptic environment', in *International Perspectives in Feminist Ecocriticism*, edited by Gaard, G., Estok, S. and Oppermann, S., New York: Routledge, 221–234.

Gruen, L. (2012) 'Navigating difference (again): animal ethics and entangled empathy', in *Strangers to Nature: Animal Lives and Human Ethics*, edited by Zucker, G., New York: Lexington Books, 213–234.

Hayes, T.B., Collins, A., Lee, M. et al. (2002) 'Hermaphroditic, demasculinized frogs after exposure to the herbicide atrazine at low ecologically relevant doses', *Proceedings of the National Academy of Sciences, USA* 99(8): 5476–5480.

Hegland, J. (1996) *Into the Forest*, New York: Bantam/Calyx Books.

Herreid, C.F. (2005) 'Using novels as bases for case studies: Michael Crichton's state of fear and global warming', *Journal of College Science Teaching* 34(7): 10–11.

Hogan, K. (2013) 'Queer green apocalypse: Tony Kushner's *Angels in America*', in *International Perspectives in Feminist Ecocriticism*, edited by Gaard, G., Estok, S. and Oppermann, S., New York: Routledge, 235–253.

ILGA (2010) 'Bolivian President: eating estrogen-rich chicken makes you gay', International Lesbian, Gay, Bisexual and Trans and Intersex Association, 15 April, available at http://ilga.org/bolivian-president-eating-estrogen-rich-chicken-makes-you-gay (accessed 10 September 2013).

IPCC (n.d.) *The IPCC Assessment Reports*, Intergovernmental Panel on Climate Change, available at http://www.ipcc.ch (accessed 10 September 2013).

Johnson, L. (2009) '(Environmental) rhetorics of tempered apocalypticism in "An Inconvenient Truth"', *Rhetoric Review* 28(1): 29–46.

Kheel, M. (1993) 'From heroic to holistic ethics: the ecofeminist challenge', in *Ecofeminism: Women, Animals, Nature*, edited by Gaard, G., Philadelphia, PA: Temple University Press, 243–271.

Kheel, M. (2009) 'Communicating care: an ecofeminist perspective', *Media Development* February: 45–50.

Kingsolver, B. (2012) *Flight Behavior*, New York: HarperCollins.

Klein, N. (2014) *This Changes Everything: Capitalism vs. The Climate*, New York: Simon & Schuster.

Kolbert, E. (2006) *Field Notes from a Catastrophe: Man, Nature, and Climate Change*, New York: Bloomsbury.

Kool Keith/Dr. Octagon (2007) 'Trees Are Dying', available at http://www.youtube.com/watch?v=XtsdtNdk5ao (accessed 10 September 2013).

Kramb, D. (2012) *From Here*, London: Lonely Coot.

LeGuin, U. (1987) *Buffalo Gals and Other Animal Presences*, Santa Barbara, CA: Capra Books.

LeGuin, U. (1985) *Always Coming Home*, New York: Harper & Row.

LeGuin, U. (1976) *The Word for World is Forest*, New York: Putnam Books.

Lloyd, S. (2010) *The Carbon Diaries 2015*, New York: Holiday House.

MacGregor, S. (2010) 'Gender and climate change: from impacts to discourses', *Journal of the Indian Ocean* 6(2): 223–238.

Mann, B. (2006) *Women's Liberation and the Sublime: Feminism, Postmodernism, Environment*, New York: Oxford University Press.

McCarthy, C. (2006) *The Road*. London: Picador.

McEwan, I. (2010) *Solar*, New York: Random House/Anchor Books.

McGinnis, M. (2013) *Not a Drop to Drink*, New York: Katherine Tegan Books.

McGuire, C. and McGuire, C. (1998) 'Grass-roots ecofeminism: activating utopia', in *Ecofeminist Literary Criticism: Theory, Interpretation, Pedagogy*, edited by Gaard, G. and Murphy, P.D., Urbana, IL: University of Illinois Press, 186–203.

Merchant, C. (1995) *Earthcare: Women and the Environment*, New York: Routledge.

Miller, L. (2010) 'Fresh hell: what's behind the boom in dystopian fiction for young readers?', *The New Yorker*, 14 June, available at http://www.newyorker.com/arts/critics/atlarge/2010/06/14/100614crat_atlarge_miller?currentPage=all (accessed 10 April 2014).

Murphy, P.D. (2008) 'Terraculturation, political dissolution, and myriad reorientations', *Tamkang Review* 39(1): 3–18.

Neimanis, A. (2013) 'Feminist subjectivity, watered', *Feminist Review* 103: 23–41.

Neimanis, A. and Walker, R.L. (2014) 'Weathering: climate change and the "thick time" of transcorporeality', *Hypatia* 29(3): 558–575.

O'Brien, C. (2010) *Birthmarked*, New York: Macmillan/Roaring Brook Press.

Oliver, L. (2011) *Delirium*, New York: HarperCollins.

Oreskes, N. and Conway, E.M. (2014) *The Collapse of Western Civilization: A View from the Future*, New York: Columbia University Press.

Pérez-Peña, R. (2014) 'College classes use arts to brace for climate change', *The New York Times*, 31 March, available at http://www.nytimes.com/2014/04/01/education/using-the-arts-to-teach-how-to-prepare-for-climate-crisis.html?_r=0 (accessed 10 April 2014).

Piercy, M. (1985) *Woman on the Edge of Time*, New York: Fawcett Books.

Plumwood, V. (1993) *Feminism and the Mastery of Nature*, New York: Routledge.

Plumwood, V. (2009) 'Nature in the active voice', *Ecological Humanities Review* 46 (May), available at http://www.australianhumanitiesreview.org/archive/Issue-May-2009/plumwood.html (accessed 8 July 2014).

Plumwood, V. (2012) *The Eye of the Crocodile*, edited by Shannon, L., Canberra: Australian National University E-press.

Rich, N. (2013) *Odds Against Tomorrow*, New York: Farrar, Straus, Giroux.

Robinson, K.S. (2004) *Forty Signs of Rain*, New York: Bantam.

Robinson, K.S. (2005) *Fifty Degrees Below*, New York: Bantam.

Robinson, K.S. (2007) *Sixty Days and Counting*, New York: Bantam.

Rockwell, A. (2006) *Why Are the Ice Caps Melting? The Dangers of Global Warming*, New York: Collins.

Seager, J. (2006) 'Noticing gender (or not) in disasters', *Geoforum* 37: 2–3.

Siperstein, S. (2014) 'Climate change fiction: radical hope from an emerging genre', available at http://eco-fiction.com/climate-change-fiction-radical-hope-from-an-emerging-genre/ (accessed 14 January 2015).

Slovic, S. (2008) 'Science, eloquence, and the asymmetry of trust: what's at stake in climate change fiction', *Green Theory and Praxis: The Journal of Ecopedagogy* 4(1): 100–112.

Somera, N. (2009) 'Que[e]r[y]ing the climate debates', *Women in Action*, 2: 81–84.

Southern Decadence New Orleans (n.d.) 'The history of Southern Decadence', available at http://www.southerndecadence.net/history.htm (accessed 14 January 2015).

Starhawk (1993) *The Fifth Sacred Thing*, New York: Bantam Books.

Stein, R. (2013) 'Sex, population, and environmental eugenics in Margaret Atwood's *Oryx and Crake* and *The Year of the Flood*', in *International Perspectives in Feminist Ecocriticism*, edited by Gaard, G., Estok, S. and Oppermann, S., New York: Routledge, 184–202.

Steinfield, H. et al. (2006) *Livestock's Long Shadow: Environmental Issues and Options*, Rome: Food and Agriculture Organization of the United Nations, available at ftp:// ftp.fao.org/docrep/fao/010/A0701E/A0701E00.pdf (accessed 8 July 2014).

Steingraber, S. (1997) *Living Downstream: An Ecologist Looks at Cancer and the Environment*, Boston, MA: Addison-Wesley.

Sturgeon, N. (1997) *Ecofeminist Natures: Race, Gender, Feminist Theory and Political Action*, New York: Routledge.

Tara, S.L. (2007) *Snowy White World to Save*, Dallas, TX: Brown Books.

Tuhus-Dubrow, R. (2013) 'Cli-Fi: birth of a genre', *Dissent* (Summer), available at http://www.dissentmagazine.org/article/cli-fi-birth-of-a-genre (accessed 8 July 2014).

Women's Environmental Network (UK) (2007) *Women's Manifesto on Climate Change*, 15 May, available at http://www.wen.org.uk/climatechange/resources/manifesto.pdf (accessed 10 April 2014).

Woodbury, M. (n.d.) 'Exploring eco- and climate fiction', available at http://eco-fiction. com/climate-fiction (accessed 14 January 2014).

Ziser, M. and Sze, J. (2007) 'Climate change, environmental aesthetics, and global environmental justice cultural studies', *Discourse* 29 (2/3): 384–410.

## Film references

*A.I. Artificial Intelligence* (2001) directed by Steven Spielberg, Dreamworks Studios.

*An Inconvenient Truth: A Global Warning* (2006) directed by Davis Guggenheim, Paramount Studios.

*The Day After Tomorrow* (2004) directed by Roland Emmerich, 20th Century Fox.

*Happy Feet* (2006) directed by George Miller, Animal Logic/Warner Brothers.

*The Hunger Games* (2012) directed by Gary Ross, Lions Gate Films.

*The Island President* (2011) directed by John Shenk, Afterimage Public Media.

*Wall-E* (2008) directed by Andrew Stanton, Pixar Animation Studios.

*Waterworld* (1995) directed by Kevin Reynolds, Universal Pictures.

# 10 Using gender theories to analyse nature resource management

*Christine Katz*

## Introduction

Nature has been and often is conceptualized as nurturing, untouched, virgin, undiscovered, unoccupied, waiting for exploration and detection, and requiring protection and care. At the same time, nature has been construed as wild, untamed, threatening, as something which needs to be conquered, controlled and stemmed. Both sets of constructions are loaded with images of femaleness. Women historically and in the present day are linked to nature through the ways in which female behaviour, societal gender roles and tasks are naturalized. Feminist research has identified and analysed the historical relationship between the domination of nature and discrimination against women/femininity (Merchant 1980/1987; Bleier 1984; Keller 1985, 1995; Harding 1986; Hubbard 1990; Haraway 1995; von Winterfeld 2006; Braidotti et al. 1994; Schultz 2006). On one hand, an often implicit reference to nature through, for example, reference to biological determination, legitimizes the subordination and devaluation of attributes assigned to the feminine, of tasks and responsibilities allocated to the female sphere and the exclusion of women or femininity from realms coded as masculine. On the other hand, referring to women/femininity or to supposedly female capabilities/attitudes such as reproductivity or nurturing in symbolic terms facilitates the exploration, protection and control of nature.

Conceptions of nature/women have undergone several reinterpretations.[1] The most profound was in the seventeenth century during the emergence of the natural sciences, changing from an organic to a mechanistic guiding principle accompanied by changes in images of femininity alongside industrial and political transformations in societies. Since that time, control and instrumentalization have been the maxims of nature management, assisted by schematization, modelling and mathematization (Merchant 1980/1987; Gloy 1995, 1996). Many ecosystematic models of nature present it as a resource, construed as a reified system of functional processes and energetic flows, a system in which organic shape and structural qualities have become irrelevant (e.g. Sachs 1992, 1993; Trepl 1987; Katz 2004). The lives of individual organisms have little importance, while the loss of species which have no obvious function for maintaining the system (so called redundant species, Filser 2000) is accepted. In wealthy Western nations, female reproductivity is facing a corresponding shift into something which requires continuing technical control and external expert support thus devaluing body knowledge and corporeal potency (Duden 2002). Although feminist theories differ conceptually, feminist critiques of these conceptualizations of nature tend to agree that they require an emotionally distanced, independent, rational (explorer or protector) subject. With its claims for control, instrumentalization, paternalism and hegemony, this model of nature demonstrates clearly masculine characteristics.

How conceptions of nature and women, as well as societal nature and gender relations, relate to each other, and how these interrelations are structured and organized, and with what impact on nature and women or gender respectively, are key questions in studies on gender and the environment – be they labelled as ecofeminism (Diamond and Orenstein 1990), ecological feminism (Warren 1994), feminist environmentalism (Agarwal 1992), social ecofeminism (Heller 1990), critical feminist eco-socialism (Plumwood 2002), or gender and the environment (Schultz 2006) (see Gaard 2011). Other strands of literature place more emphasis on intersectional claims, trying to integrate perspectives on animal rights/interspecies justice, queer ecology, racism and sustainability (Hofmeister and Katz 2011; Katz 2006; Gaard 2010, 2011; Mortimer-Sandilands and Erickson 2010). There are differences in the conceptualization and meaning of 'matter' and 'materiality' in feminist debates on environmental issues but adequate consideration of the material dimensions of nature and gender presents an ongoing challenge and risks accusations of essentialism (Mellor 1997; Alaimo 2010). Much conceptual work on gender/women and environment/nature highlights the symbolic order and its specific implications for individual women, men, others and nature which structures this interrelation and represents a logical system of heteronormative oppression, expressed and reflected in gendered symbols, images or models and in structures which exclude 'otherness' (Hofmeister et al. 2013; Plumwood 1992, 1993; Mortimer-Sandilands and Erickson 2010; Mellor 2015).

Much of the empirical research on gender and nature relations focuses on land use, agriculture and forestry (Mölders 2010; Sachs 1996; Cummings et al. 2002; Lyrén 2004; Howard 2003; Leach 1991; Flintan 2003; Brandth and Haugen 1998; Hehn et al. 2010). This literature has focused mostly on gender identity and structure by examining working and social conditions of women and the interplay between them in gendered power relations (Katz and Mölders 2013a; Lidestav and Reed 2010; James 1991; Lewis 2005; Gibson et al. 2000; Carroll et al. 1996, Colfer 2005). However, there is a lack of empirical analyses based on (de-)constructive theories and/or conceptualizing gender as a process category (as in 'doing gender'); nor are there any sustainability (or intersectional) approaches integrating ecological, social, economic and cultural aspects, or focusing on the interconnection between their symbolic-discursive, material relations and the patterns of dominance which they reflect and reproduce (Saugeres 2002; Sachs 1996).

In this chapter, I reflect on different perspectives on the linkages between gender and nature depending on which concept of gender is applied in research on nature management (Hofmeister et al. 2013: 47 ff.). Furthermore, focusing on the working practice of German foresters, I will discuss the approach 'doing gender' (West and Zimmerman 1987; Gildemeister and Wetterer 1992) and how it interacts with 'doing nature' (Poferl 2001) as an effective and necessary way of identifying interconnected hegemonic patterns in the linkages between gender and nature in their symbolic and material dimensions. I scrutinize the gendered dynamics of different management practices and the gendered application of power towards nature and femininity. Concluding this chapter, I discuss the transformative potential of nature management practices centred on reproductive principles.

## Gender concepts in research on forest nature management: perspectives on identity concepts and structural frames

Forestry in Germany is a male-dominated sector offering state employment and with the attractive status of official civil service. Up to the 1970s, no women had been hired as official civil servants in forestry and thus women had no access to occupational career opportunities within this sector of employment (Hehn 2010). Since then, records show an increasing number of women have studied forestry or had forestry-related continuing education. However, this has not led to more women holding leading positions in forestry (Kühnel 2006; Lewark et al. 2006). There is still a lack of women in top positions in the forestry service and in hunting unions, as well as in the timber industry. Where they are employed within forestry, women predominate in book-keeping and other areas of office work, public relations and forest-related environmental education (Westermayer and Blum 2010). Furthermore, over 70 per cent of women hold part-time positions (Katz and Mayer 2010).

This 'ceiling effect' in the forest sector persists without any signs of change (Katz 2011) despite structural reforms in German forestry during the past decade, accompanied by flexibilization and strong economization. Moreover, many work areas are organized as add-on or out-service work – such as forest-related environmental education – and mostly are performed only part time and by women. This situation is characterized as marginalization through gender, according to labour studies and research on professionalization (Mayer 2010; Rabe-Kleberg 1996; Gildemeister and Wetterer 2007; Ridgeway and England 2007). The situation is aggravated by the way women are linked symbolically with nature. Due to their perceived reproductive and nurturing capacities, women are supposed to be closer to nature, particularly suited to carrying out private, caring and educational tasks, and to be more physically fragile in comparison with men (Orland and Scheich 1995;

Termeer 2005). This perception supports their exclusion from traditionally male occupational fields (see Katz and Mölders 2013b; Beer 1984; Colfer 2005).

Gender research on German (and Middle European) forestry of the past 20 years has investigated the individual and structural restrictions for women employed within this sector and their exclusion from certain forest-related occupations and responsibilities (Lyrén 2004; Lidestav and Reed 2010; Hehn et al. 2010; Nadai and Seith 2001).[2] Most of these studies mobilize an identity concept of gender that is oriented to differences between men and women (Lidestav and Reed 2010). As such, identity is produced based on sex/gender – irrespective of any other social or other biological determinants (Hofmeister and Katz 2011). Research grounded in this identity approach has produced knowledge about gendered patterns of admission into forest professions, about gendered earnings and about career options in German forestry, which is shown to be a stable male domain (Nadai and Seith 2001; Hehn et al. 2010). Not only gender differences, but also the barriers and prejudices facing men and women who wish to work outside traditional roles and areas of employment, are scrutinized. Such gender differences and barriers are considered and interpreted as structurally embedded, as expressions as well as the results of both gendered power relations and the politics of gendered attribution (Hehn 2010; Nadai and Seith 2001; Mayer 2010; Katz 2011).

Forest-related gender research shows how unequal power relations and narrow options for women are due to structural problems resulting from the gender hierarchy in forest-related professions. Thereby, gender is conceptualized as a structural category rather than solely an attribute of each individual man or woman (Hofmeister et al. 2013: 62), and this results in different behaviour patterns distinguished by sex/gender (Beer 1984; Becker-Schmidt 2007/1993; Hofmeister et al. 2013: 62). In these analyses, gender refers to the structural power relations and the continuing validity of socially important conditions that prevent equality between men and women, even though gender roles change and evolve, as do gender-coded attributions of tasks and activities. For instance, male foresters who agree to transfer to environmental-education positions following the merger of forest districts are downgraded in their salary bracket (Katz 2011). This is because 'reproductive' activities such as office and administrative work, or environmental education, are paid a lower salary. Reproductive work refers to those activities which are not within the scope of conventional economic calculations, such as child and health care, housework and grocery shopping, which are unpaid and mostly carried out by women (Bock and Duden 1976; Dalla Costa and Jones 1973). The reproductive sphere is understood to also include work or working fields that are poorly paid and/or of low social prestige and with a tendency to become de-professionalized. These activities are connoted as female (social work, elementary education, caring, cleaning, communicating or mediating). It also includes reproductivity in nature and environmental regenerativity (e.g. Biesecker and Hofmeister 2006, 2010). Such a logic maintains gendered inequalities within forestry. Other studies classify the prevailing gender relations with reference to the 'hidden standard' defined by the male working environment (Westermayer and Blum 2009, 2010). Claims for and measures taken to improve equality are then focused and oriented towards women's strategic adaptation to an unchanged masculine work environment.

There is a need for research based on gender conceptualized as a process of 'doing gender' (West and Zimmerman 1987; Gildemeister and Wetterer 1992), which examines the active (re-)production and alteration of gender roles and hierarchies through social practices with reference to structural conditions. In the following, I show how 'doing gender' is interdependently linked to 'doing nature' (Poferl 2001) in forest nature management. I examine how the interconnections between gender and nature are realized and sub-stantiated, and how they materialize in forest management practice. I discuss also how concepts of nature and the professional behaviour of foresters and forest management practices are gendered, and what this means for gender and nature relations.

## Doing gender while doing nature in forestry

Thirty per cent of Germany's land area is covered with woodland – one-third consists of deciduous forest, two-thirds is dominated by coniferous forests (pure and mixed sites). From the end of the fourteenth century, spruce and pine trees were increasingly planted. One hundred per cent of the growth is harvested,[3] mostly with the help of big harvesters. In recent decades, the German forest service has implemented a variety of reforms accompanied by substantial personnel reductions (Katz and Westermayer 2010). Today 2 per cent of people in paid work are employed in forestry, which generates 3 per cent of German gross domestic product. Nowadays, woodlands and forestry are under significant economic pressure due to the worldwide increase in demand for timber as well as the current requirement for fuelwood in Germany. The effects of this development on timber-related politics are heavily debated (Politische Ökologie 2013).

Several changes of direction have occurred in silviculture (the process of tending, harvesting and regenerating a forest) in the past 50 years. Apart from monocultural, age-class forestry[4] which was introduced extensively after the Second World War and is still used, most forest districts practise so-called sustainable forestry, which aims to grow mixed (in age, species and structure) and stable forests with a high productivity rate. Ecological or nature-oriented forestry (in Germany known as *Prozessschutz-Konzept*: pro-tection of natural processes) focusing on minimally invasive methods (e.g. cutting single, selected trees) emphasizes the economic advantages of using natural forest dynamics and mindful observation of development and process, instead of fixed forestry models and methods based on human intervention

(Fähser 1988, 1995; Kaiser and Sturm 1999). These three forest-management approaches co-exist, though on different scales. Less than 5 per cent of German woodland is managed according to the ecological process-protection approach.[5]

Forest nature management is gendered in terms of working relations (structural conditions and individual effects), symbolic meanings, attributes, professional responsibilities and in the practice of 'doing nature' (Lidestav and Reed 2010; Nadai and Seith 2001; Katz and Mayer 2006). In these nature–gender interactions, the material visibility of the human–nature relation reveals its dominance structure and gender coding (Katz 2011). In the following, I point out how power relations are expressed in doing gender while doing nature: first via the presence of persons; second via the visibility of physical/corporeal exertion; and third via the status of nature – the visibility of reproductivity (Katz 2010, 2011, 2015).[6]

First, the merger of forest districts due to reforms of the forest sector was accompanied by an increase in responsibilities for staff, including individual accountability for where and when they worked and flexibility as to whether work is part or full time depending on what requires to be done. As a result, power over and in nature management processes has become visible through the presence of staff/foresters. Foresters consider being permanently on call as necessary for developing connections to the forest as nature, and for building relationships with other stakeholders that make forestry more than just profit- and resource-oriented. Continuous presence offers productive and useful opportunities to engage with local communities through demonstrating the work of forestry and affinities with nature to gain acceptance of forest management strategies. However, constant presence and availability blurs the boundaries between work and private life and this has gendered implications for men and women. Foresters with children separate their professional and private lives such that they are more pragmatic about, or even distance themselves from, their forest activities. While many male foresters are able to practise forestry in relational ways that are localized, situated, and without a clear dissociation of private life from work life, women organize a spatiotemporal split between those two realms – paradoxically, something that gender research has shown to be connoted as masculine (Beer 1984; Notz 2004). Gender research has found continuous availability to be characteristic of the realities of women's paid and unpaid reproductive work. Therefore, although the situation in forestry offers a clear break with the symbolic gender order, other axes of imbalance and inequality are emerging due to different life realities. Situated, context-oriented and relational concepts of forest work are far more difficult for women to realize. The flexibility that enables intense engagement with local forest-related needs (the constant visibility and availability that are necessary for the effective management of environmental and social relations) is subject to conditions outside the direct working context. It is the gendered and segregated division of work and its gendered structures which hinders women (and men) involved in reproductive caring tasks from having the full cooperative, communicative, relation-oriented, contextualized, personal presence demanded by forest management practices. Even when both women and men equally value being outdoors and engaged in their forest work, social structures and distribution of tasks still contribute to the exclusion of women, even though gender roles and gendered attributions have changed.

Second, Vera Hoffman's research (1998) on forest work demonstrates the gender coding of power in the interrelation between gender and the nature of the forest through the visible physical attributes of foresters. The claimed physical superiority of man, his muscular strength set against the hardship and riskiness of forest work, especially logging, are still given as reasons for classifying forest work as a purely male profession. Yet, if this assumption of the necessity of physical toughness is based on calorie consumption (Hoffman 1998), the forest work carried out by women, such as planing off and hacking timber or planting, involving bending down or kneeling in uncomfortable and exhausting positions for long periods, is no less strenuous than the work undertaken by men. Physical strength, however, is still a desirable qualification for forest work, especially for manual timber work, even though it is now assisted by machinery. The physical strength of the male body represents here the visible control or conquest of nature/the forest. Those physical activities are marked with attributions such as danger, working alone and stamina, thus labelling this working sector as an exclusively masculine one. In logging activities and timber work, the relationship of men's power over nature becomes more obvious in comparison with the physical effort of women, whose hard labour often consists of continuous, smaller tasks. Their physical effort is not as evident in, for example, felling a tree. The powerful, shaping effect on nature of their work remains invisible or can even be interpreted as a gesture of humility, because it is done predominantly with a bent-over and flexed posture (Katz 2011, 2015). Furthermore the nurturing aspects of women's work, such as planting a tree, detract from the demanding effort invested. In conclusion, the power that shapes or controls nature materializes via physical work when men are doing it, but is hidden when women are involved.

The introduction of the chainsaw in the 1950s makes clear how the visibility of power relations is instrumentalized by gender-coded attributes in reference to physical conditions. Developed as a facilitator of timber work, the chainsaw was designed to support physically weaker persons (such as women). But instead, women were not allowed to use them up to the 1970s, due to the supposed danger of this technology. Use of chainsaws demonstrated the powerfully dominant relationship over nature in the forest in another, more effective and modern, physical manner. It also resulted in a significant social upgrading of the whole working sector, supporting its performance as a solely male domain.

Third,[7] the visible impacts of gendered power relations are evident even in areas of work such as office-based decision-making that are less physically challenging. Masculine power to shape nature is apparent in the ways in which the forest is managed and regulated to achieve operational goals. Logging yields or the creation of specific forest conditions are visible manifestations of that power. The greater the intensity of intervention in the way the forest grows, the more apparent the power and control that is being wielded. Clear cutting in combination with the age-class forestry techniques outlined above are extreme examples of this in conventional forestry. This approach conceptualizes the forest/nature as requiring continuous external control, and forestry as an active task of supervision required to meet production targets that optimize benefits against costs. The relationship with the forest and with nature is one of authority and control and is characterized by an obvious and measurable claim over the creativity of nature. This is reflected in an interventionist and intensive regulation of the reproductive forces of nature in the forest (e.g. by planting, technically assisted care measures, fencing, cleaning and thinning). All these require active control by a distant agent whose actions strive to achieve maximum efficiency with resources according to the principles of 'Economic Man' (Mellor 2015).

Process-oriented, open-ended nature management approaches are based on conceptions of nature that characterize it as a self-regulating and self-regenerating actor, available and productive for forestry purposes without any external manipulation. Nature in this understanding is conceptualized as an active counterpart, as equal co-designer. The main intention of this approach is not to regard the forest solely as a product wherein maximum cost efficiency is achieved through direct and intensive intervention in and constant regulation of reproductive processes. It is more concerned with learning about and working with the conditions that enable the maximum reproductive potential of nature to unfold by itself. In order to practise this kind of relational, adaptive forest management, at least 10 per cent of the forest area is unmanaged and kept as a 'reference area', whose productivity functions as a benchmark for tree-felling which is not to be exceeded (McAfee et al. 2010: 408 ff.). Economic benefit is achieved by 'minimizing the input rather than maximizing the output' (ibid.: 409). This process-oriented approach can be sustained only when at least 10 per cent of the trees remain unfelled (e.g. as bird breeding places or as habitat for other species).

This is a relational approach to forestry where nature and foresters interact as design partners. Invisible, silent activities, including 'allowing to be', 'observing' and 'relating', are required, activities that require a continuous and physical contact with nature to absorb and perceive the natural dynamics of the forest using all the senses. The quality of a forest is seen as something that cannot be measured by mechanical or empirical quantitative tests, but must be appreciated in its complexity and entirety.

With the process-oriented management approach, we see no shaping power through its intervention methods as they are not invasive and are barely visible, or through sudden alterations in the appearance of the forest. The quality of this approach is evident in the amount of timber produced,

which meets economic targets, but also and particularly through the production process, which allows growing and dying, enfolding and self-organization
at the same time, thus providing diversity in structure, dynamics, species and
functions. Only practised observers can recognize the economic and ecological
potential and changes that result from the creative waywardness of the forest
itself. However, process-oriented and relational nature management practices
are difficult to validate and justify in an economy that focuses on exploitation
and utilization and that is geared towards measurable and visible success.
Such practices are clearly judged in ways similar to evaluations of unpaid
family care and subsistence work. For this reason, it may be difficult for the
tasks and competencies related to process-oriented forestry to be understood as 'real' forest work. Furthermore, the concept of process-oriented
forestry seems alien to the common understandings of a forester who visibly
and audibly keeps the forest in order through constant organizing activities,
assisted by a variety of technical equipment, and who promotes forest
growth and redesigns it at his own discretion.

## Conclusion

In this chapter, I have tried to show that using the (de-)constructive approach
of 'doing gender' and combining it with 'doing nature' will enrich current
knowledge about the production (process, structure and individual dimensions) of injustice, inequality and dominance in nature and gender relations.
By adopting a doing gender, doing nature perspective, we can assess the
quality of different nature management practices and their transformative
power towards more sustainable ways of dealing with nature. This approach
brings to the fore the gendered dimensions in the role of 'reproductivity'
and how it is valued.

(In-)visibility and relatedness are categories that represent core elements of
the gendered division of labour with an essential structurizing function in
nature management practices. On one hand, these categories are involved in
reproducing and contesting common gendered distinctions such as the dissociation of public/occupational and private spheres, of product-oriented
and relational working tasks, of nature as an object to be shaped and foresters
as managing agents. On the other hand, existing and powerful socio-structural
and gender hierarchical conditions and frames prevent the dissolution of
dominance relations that perpetuate gendered inequalities within forestry,
hampering equal participation in roles and positions at decision-making
levels.

In conventional forestry, reproductivity must be technologically controlled
and modified to be deemed utilizable for economic objectives. Analogous to
the regenerative and reproductive potentials of nature, the accomplishment
of reproductive tasks in society is seen to be gratis and devalued in economic
terms, a low-budget, 'add-on product' which is continuously available
(Biesecker and Hofmeister 2006, 2010). Reproductive capability, know-how

and experience are still associated with women and femaleness as 'natural attributes' and thus seen as biologically determined characteristics which are detached from structural power. Gender research has exposed these connections as expressions and constituents of societal power relations. In the underlying system of dualisms, female-connoted categories such as reproductivity, attentiveness and relatedness, and activities like social caring or educating, are devalued against male connoted capitalistic, profit-maximizing productivity of goods, thus constituting a hierarchical structure of dominance and subordination. This system of oppression not only forms a symbolic order but is also reflected in structures and resources leading to discrimination, marginalization and exclusion of individuals who do not meet the male-connoted norms (e.g. Plumwood 1992).

What can be learned and concluded? A nature resource management practice such as forestry, which aims to be sustainable and gender equitable, needs to move its orientation away from a logic of exploitation, and needs to change its traditional culture of masculinity with its controlling, regulating and optimizing phantasy of nature understood as a mechanistic model (Katz 2015). To achieve this, it will not be sufficient to increase the number of women in forest service organizations.

If we want to realize methods of nature management where the otherness of nature is respectfully acknowledged, where nature is seen as co-designer during the production process, and where nature is allowed to develop by itself, we require concepts and working approaches that differ from the current technocratic system of intense interventions and imposed regulations. Another logic must be established, different from the structure of understanding that 'takes its paradigm from scientific objectivity … grounded in the disembodied Cartesian subject that feminists have shown so often and clearly to be typical of androcentric philosophizing' (Glazebrook 2005: 76). These 'eco-logics' represent instead 'new ways of thinking about nature' (2005: 76) through which quiet and relational activities come to the fore, which necessitate soft skills such as being able to be part of and to embed into processes. The practical knowledge needed to achieve this cannot be generated if the designing forester is not engaging and relating with nature as a co-designer in the forest. The required competencies therefore have to be introduced and developed through education, as they are not a question of personality traits. This characterizes a new type of forest profession whereby nature informs claims of knowledge, and the required competencies of foresters are based on connectedness, self-reflexion, embeddedness and embodiment within nature being cultivated (Katz 2015). Such competency is drawn 'on the physicality of environmental elements as well as of the thinker', thus allowing 'nature's temporality to resonate within knowledge itself' (Glazebrook 2005: 76).

Thinking about nature in a new and different way, as being active and capable of acting (Haraway 2006; Latour 2001), would imply its integration into the negotiation process as an actor involved in its own management.

That being so, other options regarding the use of forests would open up, options beyond those centred merely on capital-oriented and value-added principles (Katz and Mölders 2013a: 277). For this, there must first be an appreciation of reproductive activities, both in the forest and in foresters' personal lives. A culture of acknowledgement is required, which will be created and lived by both men and women, and in mutual interaction with conducive structural conditions.

## Notes

1 Various concepts of gender have been introduced since the 1970s – although not in a linear way as most are applied concurrently (e.g. Hofmeister et al. 2013): difference and identity concepts focusing on biological (men/women) and socially construed difference (gender), radical constructivistic (linguistic turn) and process-oriented concepts of 'doing gender' (Butler 1999/1990; West and Zimmerman 1987) and the feminist approach in new materialism (materialistic turn, Alaimo and Hekman 2008).
2 Most of the gender research on forest and nature resource management is based on a gender approach which is difference-oriented (caused by socialization) and/or focused on 'female approaches' to resource management (Cummings et al. 2002; Lyrén 2004; Flintan 2003). In most agrarian Southern countries, women are responsible for managing domestic resources – although they lack land and access rights and official roles. Consequently they are directly affected by changes in soil fertility or soil availabilty due to environmental problems and/or due to exploita-tive, economic concepts that concentrate on maximizing short-term profit. Gender studies on nature management and land use from and looking at the Southern countries are often focused on cases (Lidestav and Reed 2010) that suggest an alternative (and more sustainable) approach to nature resource management by women (e.g. Shiva 1989) but without appealing to essentialist concepts.
3 In Germany less than 2 per cent of forests are excluded from cultivation.
4 Trees of the same age and species are grown together alongside similar areas of older or younger trees. The most mature trees are then clear cut.
5 A reassessment of forest structures, dynamics, and the associated socio-economic observations of this process-protection approach found that the annual timber yield increased by 15 per cent and the annual profit increased by 20 per cent while damage from natural disturbances (e.g. windthrow, insects) decreased. So, in comparison with conventional forestry, this concept not only improved ecological values, but was also economically viable and produced higher yields (Fichtner 2009, DBU 2008).
6 These results are based on a literature review and empirical qualitative research on professional actors working in the fields of forest nature management con-ducted by the author. This research was funded by German ministries: the Research Union for Women-/Gender Research in Science, Technology and Medicine of the Federal Science Ministry of Lower-Saxony (2001–03) and the State Ministry of Education and Research (research programme 'Sustainable Forestry' 2005–09). Twenty-two expert interviews (with foresters, heads of forest offices, forest experts from the German forest service and ministries) were conducted and analysed through a qualitative content analysis of 'cases'; an inductive procedure was applied and types were identified in terms of nature conception/management and gender (Kelle and Kluge 2009; Mayring and Gläser-Zikuda 2008).
7 This argument was made originally in Katz (2011: 184).

# References

Agarwal, B. (1992) 'The gender and environment debate: lessons from India', *Feminist Studies* 18(1): 119–158.

Alaimo, S. (2010) *Bodily Natures: Science, Environment and the Material Self*, Bloomington: Indiana University Press.

Alaimo, S. and Hekman, S. (eds) (2008) *Material Feminisms*, Bloomington: Indiana University Press.

Becker-Schmidt, R. (2007 [1993]) 'Geschlechterdifferenz – Geschlechterverhältnis: soziale Dimensionen des Begriffs, Geschlecht', in *Zeitschrift für Frauenforschung*, Jg. 11, H.1/2, S.37–46, zitiert nach: Hark, S. (Hrsg.): *Dis/Kontinuitäten. Feministische Theorie. 2. aktualisierte und erweiterte Auflage*, Wiesbaden, 115–127.

Beer, U. (1984) *Theorien geschlechtlicher Arbeitsteilung*, Frankfurt a.M./New York: Campus Verlag.

Biesecker, A. and Hofmeister, S. (2006) *Die Neuerfindung des Ökonomischen. Ein (re) produktionstheoretischer Beitrag zur Sozial-ökologischen Forschung*, München: Oekom.

Biesecker, A. and Hofmeister, S. (2010) 'Focus: (re)productivity: sustainable relations both between society and nature and between the genders', *Ecological Economics* 69(8): 1703–1711.

Bleier, R. (1984) *Science and Gender: A Critique of Biology and its Theories on Women*, New York: Pergamon.

Bock, G. and Duden, B. (1976) 'Arbeit aus Liebe – Liebe aus Arbeit: Zur Entstehung der Hausarbeit im Kapitalismus', in *Frauen und Wissenschaft. Beiträge zur Sommeruniversität für Frauen im Juli 1976*, Berlin: Gruppe Berliner Dozentinnen, 118–152.

Braidotti, R., Charkiewicz, E., Häusler, S. and Wieringa, S. (eds) (1994) *Women, the Environment and Sustainable Development: Towards a Theoretical Synthesis*, London: Zed Books.

Brandth, B. and Haugen, M. (1998) 'Breaking into a masculine discourse: women and farm forestry', *Sociologia Ruralis* 38(3): 427–442.

Butler, J. (1999 [1990]) *Gender Trouble: Feminism and the Subversion of Identity*, New York: Routledge.

Carroll, F.O., Freemuth, J. and Les, A. (1996) 'Women forest rangers', *Journal of Forestry* 94(1): 38–41.

Colfer, C.J.P. (2005) 'The struggle for equity in forest management', in *The Equitable Forest: Diversity, Community and Resource Management, Resources for the Future*, edited by Colfer, C.J.P., Washington, DC: Resources for the Future/CIFOR, 1–18.

Cummings, S., v. Dam, H. and Valk, M. (2002) *Natural Resource Management and Gender: A Global Source Book*, Amsterdam: Royal Tropical Institute.

Dalla Costa, M. and Jones, S. (1973) *Die Macht der Frauen und der Umsturz der Gesellschaft*, Berlin: Merve Verlag.

DBU (2008) *Abschlussbericht zum Projekt Nutzung ökologischer Potenziale von Buchenwäldern für eine multifunktionale Bewirt-schaftung*, Deutsche Bundesstiftung Umwelt, Flintbek: Landesamt für Natur und Umwelt Schleswig-Holstein.

Diamond, I. and Orenstein, G.F. (eds) (1990) *Reweaving the World: The Emergence of Ecofeminism*, San Francisco: Sierra Club Books.

Duden, B. (2002) *Geschichte des Ungeborenen. Zur Erfahrungs- und Wissenschaftsgeschichte der Schwangerschaft 17–20 Jahrhundert*, Göttingen: Vandenhoeck and Ruprecht.

Fähser, L. (1988) 'The ecological orientation of the forest economy', *Natural Resources and Development* 28: 71–99.

Fähser, L. (1995) 'Nature-oriented forestry in Lübeck', *International Journal of Ecoforestry* 11(1): 7–11.

Fichtner, A. (2009) *Einfluss der Bewirtschaftungsintensität auf die Wachstumsdynamik von Waldmeister-Buchenwäldern (Galio-odorati – Fagetum)*, Kiel: Mitteilung d. Arbeitsgemeinschaft Geobotanik.

Filser, J. (2000) 'Redundanz von Arten, funktionellen Gruppen und ganzen Nahrungsnetzen in Abhängigkeit von äußeren Bedingungen: Definitions- und Verständnisproblematik am Beispiel von Bodenorganismen', in *Funktionsbegriff und Unsicherheit in der Ökologie*, edited by Jax, K. and Breckling, B., *Theorie in der Ökologie Bd. 2*, Frankfurt a.M.: Peter Lang Verlag, 31–44.

Flintan, F. (2003) *Engendering Eden. Volume I. Women, Gender and Integrated Conservation and Development Projects. Lessons Learnt and Ways Forward*, London: International Institute for Environment and Development.

Gaard, G. (2010) 'New directions for ecofeminism: toward a more feminist ecocriticism', *Interdisciplinary Studies in Literature and Environment* 17(4): 1–23.

Gaard, G. (2011) 'Ecofeminism revisited: rejecting essentialism and re-placing species in a material feminist environmentalism', *Feminist Formations* 23(2): 26–53.

Gibson, C., Ostrom, E. and McKean, M.A. (2000) 'Forests, people and governance: some initial theoretical lessons', in *People and Forests: Communities, Institutions and Governance*, edited by Gibson, C., McKean, M.A. and Ostrom, E., Cambridge, MA: Massachusetts Institute of Technology, 227–242.

Gildemeister, R. and Wetterer, A. (1992) 'Wie Geschlechter gemacht werden. Die soziale Konstruktion der Zweigeschlechtlichkeit und ihre Reifizierung in der Frauenforschung', in *Traditionen – Brüche. Entwicklung feministischer Theorie*, edited by Knapp, G.A. and Wetterer, A., Freiburg i.Br.: Kore Verlag, 202–254.

Gildemeister, R. and Wetterer, A. (2007) *Erosion oder Reproduktion geschlechtlicher Differenzierungen? Widersprüchliche Entwicklungen in professionalisierten Berufsfeldern und Organisationen*, Münster: Westfälisches Dampfboot.

Glazebrook, T. (2005) 'Gynocentric eco-logics', *Ethics and the Environment* 10(2): 75–99.

Gloy, K. (1995) *Das Verständnis der Natur, Bd. I: Die Geschichte des wissenschaftlichen Denkens*, München: Beck Verlag.

Gloy, K. (1996) *Das Verständnis der Natur, Bd. II: Die Geschichte des ganzheitlichen Denkens*, München: Beck Verlag.

Haraway, D. (1995) *Die Neuerfindung der Natur. Primaten, Cyborgs und Frauen*, edited by Hammer, C. and Stieß, E., Frankfurt a.M.: Campus Verlag.

Haraway, D. (2006) 'Monströse Versprechen. Eine Erneuerungspolitik für das un/an/geeignete Andere', in *Monströse Versprechen. Coyote-Geschichten zu Feminismus und Technowissenschaft*, 2nd edn, edited by Haraway, D., Hamburg: Argumente Verlag, 11–81.

Harding, S. (1986) *The Science Question in Feminism*, Ithaca/New York: Cornell University Press.

Hehn, M. (2010) 'Arbeit adelt – und Ihr bleibt bürgerlich! Frauenausschluss aus deutschen Forstverwaltungen im Wandel der Zeit', in *Abschied vom grünen Rock? Forstverwaltungen, waldbezogene Umweltbildung und Geschlechterverhältnisse im Wandel*, edited by Hehn, M., Katz, C., Mayer, M. and Westermayer, T., München: Oekom Verlag, 33–60.

Hehn, M., Katz, C., Mayer, M. and Westermayer, T. (eds) (2010) *Abschied vom grünen Rock? Forstverwaltungen, waldbezogene Umweltbildung und Geschlechterverhältnisse im Wandel*, München: Oekom Verlag, 33–60.

Heller, C. (1990) 'Toward a radical eco-feminism', in *Renewing the Earth: The Promise of Social Ecology*, edited by Clark, J., London: Green Print, 160–170.

Hoffmann, V. (1998) *Die Arbeitssituation der Waldarbeiterinnen in Deutschland. Agrarwissenschaftliche Forschungsergebnisse*, Hamburg: Verlag Dr. Kovač.

Hofmeister, S. and Katz, C. (2011) 'Naturverhältnisse. Geschlechterverhältnisse. Nachhaltigkeit', in *Handbuch Umweltsoziologie*, edited by Groß, M., Wiesbaden: VS Verlag, 365–398.

Hofmeister, S., Katz, C. and Mölders, T. (eds) (2013) *Geschlechterverhältnisse und Nachhaltigkeit. Die Kategorie Geschlecht in den Nachhaltigkeitswissenschaften*, Opladen, Berlin, Toronto: Barbara Budrich Verlag.

Howard, P.L. (2003) *Women and Plants: Gender Relations in Biodiversity Management and Conservation*, London: Zed Books.

Hubbard, R. (1990) *The Politics of Women's Biology*, New Brunswick, NJ: Rutgers University Press.

James, C. (1991) 'Women in the forest service: the early years', *Journal of Forestry* 89(3): 14–17.

Kaiser, M. and Sturm, K. (1999) *Dem Öko-Wald gehört die Zukunft. Wirtschaftsvergleich unterschied-licher Waldbaustrategien (in Mitteleuropa)*, Hamburg: Greenpeace.

Katz, C. (2004) 'Die Einbeziehung des Menschen bei der Erforschung gesellschaftlicher Natur-/Umweltbeziehungen: Das Beispiel Humanökologie', in *Naturverständnisse in der Nachhaltigkeitsforschung*, edited by Rink, D. and Wächter, M., Frankfurt, New York: Campus Verlag, 73–102.

Katz, C. (2006) 'Gender und Nachhaltigkeit. Neue Forschungsperspektiven', *GAIA* 15(3): 206–214.

Katz, C. (2010) 'Natur ist was man daraus macht! Naturvorstellungen von forstlichen Akteuren in der waldbezogenen Umweltbildung', in *Abschied vom grünen Rock? Forstverwaltungen, waldbezogene Umweltbildung und Geschlechterverhältnisse im Wandel*, edited by Hehn, M., Katz, C., Mayer, M. and Westermayer, T., München: Oekom Verlag, 61–94.

Katz, C. (2011) 'Im Wald: Doing Gender While Designing Nature. Geschlechteraspekte der Gestaltungspraktiken eines Naturraums', in *räumlich_körperlich – Feministische Zugänge zu Natur und Materie. Forum Frauen- und Geschlechterforschung*, edited by Scheich, E. and Wagels, K., Forum Frauen- und Geschlechterforschung, Band 32, Münster: Westfälisches Dampfboot, 176–197.

Katz, C. (2015) 'Die Geschlechterperspektive in der Naturgestaltung: Was bringt sie für das Handlungsfeld Wald?', in *Nachhaltigkeit anders denken – Veränderungspotenziale durch Geschlechterperspektiven*, edited by Katz, C., Thiem, A., Heilmann, S., Koch, L., Moths, K. and Hofmeister, S., Wiesbaden: VS Verlag.

Katz, C. and Mayer, M. (2006) 'MännerWeltWald – Natur- und Geschlechterkonstruktionen in Handlungsmustern von Waldakteuren/innen', in *Frauen-MännerGeschlechterforschung. State of the Art, Schriftenreihe der Sektion Frauen- und Geschlechterforschung in der Deutschen Gesellschaft für Soziologie*, edited by Aulenbacher, B., Bereswill, M., Löw, M., Meuser, M., Mordt, G., Schäfer, R. and Scholz, S., Münster: Westfälisches Dampfboot, 241–253.

Katz, C. and Mayer, M. (2010) 'Bildung für nachhaltige Entwicklung als Leitkonzept für die waldbezogene Bildungsarbeit', in *Abschied vom grünen Rock?*

Forstverwaltungen, waldbezogene Umweltbildung und Geschlechterverhältnisse im Wandel, edited by Hehn, M., Katz, C., Mayer, M. and Westermayer, T., München: Oekom Verlag, 191–208.

Katz, C. and Mölders, T. (2013a) 'Schutz, Nutzung und nachhaltige Gestaltung. Geschlechteraspekte im Umgang mit Natur', in *Geschlechterverhältnisse und Nachhaltigkeit*, edited by Hofmeister, S., Katz, C. and Mölders, T., Opladen, Berlin, Toronto: Barbara Budrich Verlag, 269–277.

Katz, C. and Mölders, T. (2013b) 'Natur zwischen Schutz, Nutzung und nachhaltiger Gestaltung – feministische Ansichten', *Zeitschrift Ariadne* 64: 66–73.

Katz, C. and Westermayer, T. (2010) 'Einleitung', in *Abschied vom grünen Rock? Forstverwaltungen, waldbezogene Umweltbildung und Geschlechterverhältnisse im Wandel*, edited by Hehn, M., Katz, C., Mayer, M. and Westermayer, T., München: Oekom Verlag, 9–24.

Kelle, U. and Kluge, S. (2009) *Vom Einzelfall zum Typus: Fallvergleich und Fallkontrastierung in der qualitativen Sozialforschung*, Wiesbaden: VS Verlag.

Keller, E.F. (1985) *Reflections on Gender and Science*, New Haven: Yale University Press.

Keller, E.F. (1995) 'Origin, history and politics of the subject called "Gender and Science" – a first person account', in *Handbook of Science and Technology Studies*, edited by Jasanoff, S.E.A., Thousand Oaks, CA: Sage, 80–94.

Kühnel, A. (2006) *Zugangsvoraussetzungen für die Berufstätigkeit im höheren Forstdienst in Baden-Württemberg seit dem Ende des zweiten Weltkriegs – dargestellt unter besonderer Berücksichtigungvon Geschlechtergerechtigkeit*, Freiburg: Diplomarbeit an der Fakultät für Forst- und Umweltwissenschaften der Universität Freiburg.

Latour, B.(2001) *Das Parlament der Dinge: für eine politische Ökologie*, Frankfurt a.M.: Suhrkamp Verlag.

Leach, M. (1991) 'Engendered environments: understanding natural resource management in the West African forest zone', *IDS Bulletin* 22(4): 17–24.

Lewark, S., Steinert, S., Hehn, M. and Mutz, R. (2006) *Studium und Berufstätigkeit forstwissenschaftlicher Absolventinnen und Absolventen. Verbleibanalyse 2006 für deutschsprachige Studiengänge der Forstwissenschaft und erste Ergebnisse für die Fakultät für Forst- und Umweltwissenschaften der Universität Freiburg*, Arbeitswissenschaftlicher Forschungsbericht Nr. 5, Freiburg: Institut für Forstbenutzung und forstliche Arbeitswissenschaft d. Universität Freiburg.

Lewis, J.G. (2005) 'The applicant is no gentleman: women in the forest service', *Journal of Forestry* 105(5): 259–263.

Lidestav, G. and Reed, M.G. (2010) 'Preface: Gender and forestry', *Scandinavian Journal of Forest Research* Supp 9: 1–5.

Lyrén, L. (2004) *Gender and Forestry. A Bibliography*, Umea: Forestry Library, Swedish University of Agricultural Sciences (SLU), available at http://www.bib.slu.se/bib liotek/skogs/genus/genderandfor.pdf (accessed 20 December 2014).

Mayer, M. (2010) 'Forstliche Bildungsarbeit zwischen Nische und Professionalisierung', in *Abschied vom grünen Rock? Forstverwaltungen, waldbezogene Umweltbildung und Geschlechterverhältnisse im Wandel*, edited by Hehn, M., Katz, C., Mayer, M. and Westermayer, T., München: Oekom Verlag, 101–120.

Mayring, P. and Gläser-Zikuda, M. (2008) *Die Praxis der qualitativen Inhaltsanalyse*, Weinheim: Beltz Verlag.

McAfee, B.J., de Camino, R., Burton, P.J., Eddy, B., Fähser, L., Messier, C., Reed, M.G., Spies, T., Vides, R. et al. (2010) 'Managing forested landscapes for socio-ecological resilience', in *Forests and Society – Responding to Global Drivers of Change*, IUFRO

World Series Vol. 25, edited by Mery, G., Katila, P., Galloway, G., Alfaro, R.I., Kanninen, M., Lobovikov, M. and Varjo, J., Tampere, Finland: Tammerprint Oy, 401–435, available at http://www.iufro.org/science/special/wfse/forests-society-global-drivers (accessed 27 July 2015).

Mellor, M. (1997) *Feminism and Ecology*, Cambridge/New York: Polity Press.

Mellor, M. (2015) 'Linking gender and sustainability: a material relation', in *Nachhaltigkeit anders denken – Veränderungspotenziale durch Geschlechterperspektiven*, edited by Katz, C., Thiem, A., Heilmann, S., Koch, L., Moths, K. and Hofmeister, S., Wiesbaden: VS Verlag.

Merchant, C. (1980/1987) *Der Tod der Natur. Ökologie, Frauen und neuzeitliche Naturwissenschaft. Übersetzung aus dem Amerikanischen von Holger Fliessbach*, München: C.H. Beck (original: *The Death of Nature: Women, Ecology and the Scientific Revolution*, New York: Harper Collins).

Mölders, T. (2010) 'Von der Frauen-Frage zum Vorsorgenden Wirtschaften – eine (re) produktionstheoretische Interpretation empirischer Befunde zur Gender-Dimension von Agrarpolitik', *Femina Politica* 19(1): 43–55.

Mortimer-Sandilands, C. and Erickson, B. (eds) (2010) *Queer Ecologies: Sex, Nature, Politics and Desire*, Bloomington: Indiana University Press.

Nadai, E. and Seith, C. (2001) *Frauen in der Forstwirtschaft. Hürden, Chancen, Perspektiven*, Schriftenreihe Umwelt Nr. 324, Bern: Bundesamt für Umwelt, Wald und Landschaft (BUWAL).

Notz, G. (2004) 'Arbeit: Hausarbeit, Ehrenamt, Erwerbsarbeit', in *Handbuch Frauen- und Geschlechterforschung. Theorie, Methoden, Empirie*, edited by Becker, R. and Kortendiek, B., Wiesbaden: VS Verlag, 420–428.

Orland, B. and Scheich, E. (eds) (1995) *Das Geschlecht der Natur*, Frankfurt a.M.: Suhrkamp Verlag.

Plumwood, V. (1992) 'Feminism and ecofeminism: beyond the dualistic assumptions of women, men and nature', *Ecologist* 22(1): 8–13.

Plumwood, V. (1997 [1993]): *Feminism and the Mastery of Nature*, London: Routledge.

Plumwood, V. (2002): *Environmental Culture: The Ecological Crisis of Reason*, New York: Routledge.

Poferl, A. (2001) 'Doing gender, doing nature? Einführende Bemerkungen zur Intention des Bandes', in *Geschlechterverhältnisse – Naturverhältnisse. Feministische Auseinandersetzungen und Perspektiven der Umweltsoziologie*, edited by Nebelung, A., Poferl, A. and Schultz, I., Opladen: Leske + Budrich Verlag, 9–17.

Politische Ökologie (2013) '*Wald – Politische Spielräume zwischen Baum und Borke*', *Politische Ökologie* 123.

Rabe-Kleberg, U. (1996) 'Professionalität und Geschlechterverhältnis. Oder: Was ist "semi" an traditionellen Frauenberufen', in *Pädagogische Professionalität. Untersuchungen zum Typus pädagogischen Handelns*, 2nd edn, edited by Combe, A. and Helsper, W., Frankfurt a.M.: Suhrkamp Verlag, 276–302.

Ridgeway, C. and England, P. (2007) 'Sociological approaches to sex discrimination in employment', in *Sex Discrimination in the Workplace: Multidisciplinary Perspectives*, edited by Faye, J.C., Stockdale, M.S. and Ropp, S.A., Malden, MA: Blackwell, 189–211.

Sachs, C. (1996) *Gendered Fields. Rural Women, Agriculture and Environment*, Boulder, CO: Westview Press.

Sachs, W. (1992) *Satellitenblick: die Visualisierung der Erde im Zuge der Weltraumfahrt*, Forschungsgruppe 'Grosse Technische Systeme' des Forschungsschwerpunkts

Technik, Arbeit, Umwelt am Wissenschaftszentrum Berlin für Sozialforschung (WZB), Berlin: Forschungsschwerpunkt des WZB Technik, Arbeit, Umwelt.

Sachs, W. (ed.) (1993) *Global Ecology: A New Arena of Political Conflicts*, London: Zed Books.

Saugeres, L. (2002) 'The cultural representation of the farming landscape: masculinity, power and nature', *Journal of Rural Studies* 18: 373–384.

Schultz, I. (2006) 'The natural world and the nature of gender', in *Handbook of Gender and Women's Studies, K21*, edited by Davis, K., Evans, M. and Lorber, J., London, Thousand Oaks, New Delhi: Sage, 376–396.

Shiva, V. (1989) *Staying Alive: Women, Ecology and Development*, London: Zed Books.

Shiva, V. and Mies, M. (1995) *Ökofeminismus: Beiträge zur Praxis und Theorie*, Zürich: Rotpunkt-Verlag.

Termeer, M. (2005) *Verkörperungen des Waldes. Eine Körper-, Geschlechter- und Herrschaftsgeschichte*, Bielefeld: transcript Verlag.

Trepl, L. (1987) *Geschichte der Ökologie. Vom 17. Jahrhundert bis zur Gegenwart*, Frankfurt a.M.: Athenäum Verlag.

Warren, K.J. (ed.) (1994) *Ecological Feminism*, Boulder, CO: Westview Press.

West, C. and Zimmerman, D.H. (1987) 'Doing gender', *Gender and Society* 2: 125–151.

Westermayer, T. and Blum, S. (2009) 'Erste Ergebnisse der Bedarfserhebung: Vereinbarkeit von Beruf und Familie', *AFZ/Der Wald* 64(1): 34–35.

Westermayer, T. and Blum, S. (2010) 'Fallbeispiel: Geschlechterverhältnisse in einer deutschen Forstverwaltung', in *Abschied vom grünen Rock? Forstverwaltungen, waldbezogene Umweltbildung und Geschlechterverhältnisse im Wandel*, edited by Hehn, M., Katz, C., Mayer, M. and Westermayer, T., München: Oekom Verlag, 147–164.

von Winterfeld, U. (2006) *Naturpatriarchen. Geburt und Dilemma der Naturbeherrschung bei den geistigen Vätern der Neuzeit*, München: Oekom-Verlag.

# 11 Organizing and managing ecofeminism

## Material manifestations of spiritual principles in business

*Ali Young and Scott Taylor*

### Introduction: organization, management and ecofeminism

As this collection demonstrates, ecofeminism is making a gradual return to prominence in practice and academic analysis. We explore here how the movement and its ideas can be understood in the light of conventional modernist organization and management, and the everyday socio-economic practices embedded within those. We do this through an examination of a prominent manifestation of ecofeminism in the contemporary Western arena, two organizations that are both engaged with New Age activities located within the capitalist marketplace (Lau 2000).

Many of the central beliefs, values and commitments at the heart of eco-feminism in the USA and Europe were born amidst an array of counter-cultural emergences in the 1960s and 1970s. They have often been interwoven with allied social movements including feminist spirituality, deep ecology and environmentalism, forms of neo-paganism and the Human Potential Movement (HPM). In contrast to the HPM's internal focus, however, ecofeminism developed as a form of protest against external threats such as nuclear weapons threat and environmental disaster. Its values and principles have also been at the heart of *non-dominant* movements within Western (Northern) cultures, as well as in the regions that the dominant systems in the West have also been responsible for colonizing (Mies and Shiva 1993). Western experiments and explorations have also gradually percolated out from sites of specialist, often academic interests into practice, eventually becoming packaged and sold as commodities as part of a globalized marketplace (Carrette and King 2005; Harner 1980; Kripal 2007; Lau 2000; Puttick 1997; Radford Ruether 1992, 2005; Starhawk 1982, 1987).

Approaching contemporary ecofeminist spiritualities in a way that bears such matters in mind, we emphasize the specific places within which it is embodied, in a move that is also partly reflective of the explicit ecofeminist commitment to avoid universalisms and abstractions (Bullis and Glaser 1992; Glazebrook 2005). To start that process, our own sites or 'places' are significant. We are both Western, able-bodied, white, and either feminist or sympathetic to feminism. One of us (Scott) speaks as a (relatively) senior academic specializing in the current debates over the role of spirituality in the workplace. One of us (Ali) is a more junior academic, and has been a practitioner of feminist spiritualities for more than 30 years in non-commercialized social movements such as the nuclear protest movement and in market-based settings. Ali has personal connections to the organizations we analyse here as an active member of both communities, and has just completed an ethnographic study of one of them for her PhD thesis with Scott as co-supervisor. Our intent is to draw on knowledges and experiences afforded by both of these very different frames to approach a reflexively 'placed' analysis, taking note of Heelas' (2008) observation that studies of New Age activity are often heavy on theory and light on empirics. Although we focus here on the production and consumption of ecofeminist ideas and practices in specific organizational contexts in the USA and Europe, we are aware of their presence in very different forms in places beyond the Global North.

Intellectually, we place our analysis alongside discussion of ecofeminism's promises and potentials in relation to a dominant, globalized, mostly neoliberal capitalism, and the preferred market relations approach to conducting everyday life within that. In *Ecofeminism*, Mies and Shiva (1993) acknowledge the political and material inequalities reflected in the different positions associated with inhabiting such market relations in the Global North and South. Describing the dominant and destructive forces of neoliberal capitalism as engaged in processes that homogenize *and* fragment in life-threatening ways, they suggest that many of those who may be differently located may still have common interests. Expressing both positive engagement and hope, the perspective offered from within this non-dominant framework of ecofeminism is, of course, open to challenge. It is commonly argued that the fragmented and commoditized Western spiritualities associated with New Age capitalism are too easily co-opted and neutered as a force for significant change. Much commentary on New Age spiritualities suggests that engagement in their beliefs and activities from within the material economic comforts of Europe or the USA can only be an act of individualism, reinforcing the commodification of nature and its steady rationalization into processes of production/consumption (Carrette and King 2005). In contrast, a small number of others (e.g. Heelas 2008) put forward more optimistic analyses, to suggest that some contemporary spiritualities offer life-affirming and socially radical potentials. Our focus here is less on macroeconomic relations and more on the possibility that some such spiritualities, including those we categorize as ecofeminist, may represent and reproduce very conventional organizational and managerial structures that are, in turn, framed through neoliberal economics and contemporary capitalism. Some facets of the ecofeminist movement, including contributions of feminist authors and academics as well as those offering therapeutic and spiritual tools (Orbach 1994; Starhawk 1987) for change and empowerment, currently function very effectively within neoliberalism, but are nonetheless still constellated around radical principles – an apparent contradiction, or at least a significant tension.

Our analysis leads towards the possibility that there is an alternative way to view this contradiction or tension to the binary 'capital-affirming or radical' debate. We suggest that some participants in New Age capitalism's ecofeminist praxis may be understood as articulating a collectivist, life-affirming, anti-rationalist position that enables construction of a life of tempered radicalism (Meyerson and Scully 1995; see Starhawk 1987 for a prime example of this). This interpretation is supported by close examination of how ideals, production and consumption intersect in the total social organization of labour (Glucksmann 1995) of some New Age capitalists.

Specifically, we draw on the (auto)biographies of two prominent New Age spiritual communities: that led by Gabrielle Roth (1990), founder of the 5Rhythms movement; and the educational activities of Susannah and Ya'Acov Darling Khan (2009), founders of The School of Movement Medicine. We build on our reading of their actions and beliefs to develop the idea of tempered radicalism, arguing that while ecofeminism in the West should be understood as a conceptual frame with radical spiritual roots, the material and social contexts of organization mean it is also subject to continuous negotiation with, contestation from, and incorporation into the neoliberal marketplace. We are sympathetic to the doubts and difficulties of organizing and managing commercial companies with spiritual inspirations in ways that respect ecofeminist principles and praxis, when the survival of the organization in its social, political and economic place is always in doubt. This tension is, we suggest, indicative of the problematic nature of ecofeminism's interaction with contemporary organization and management. This in turn leads us to conclude with a consideration of whether there is a future for ecofeminism as praxis in the context of more conventional, more formally managed and financially bounded work organizations.

## Placing capitalism: 'the need for a new cosmology'

Proposing an approach to *Capitalism as if the World Matters*, Jonathon Porritt (2005), an environmentalist we categorize as a tempered radical, outlines three different scenarios for our and the planet's futures. These range from technological solutions and continuing economic growth, painful recovery from present ailments and the revision of fundamental ideologies, to total economic and social collapse with no long-term future for humanity (Porritt 2005; see also Homer-Dixon 2006; Lomborg 2001; Lovelock 2006). Depending on our perspective, values, life circumstances and degree of economic and social privilege – what Amanda Sinclair (2010) refers to as our 'place' – we may not perceive or experience contemporary global circumstances as representative of a crisis of unprecedented proportions. This in turn, at individual and socio-cultural level, may influence motivation to take action, as well as our view of what sort of action needs to be taken and for what purpose. If we are interested in changing or challenging the dominant organizational and managerial structures that are so implicated in our current position, as tempered radicals are, one key task is to address issues of long-term strategy and effectiveness, as well as burn-out (Meyerson and Scully 1995).

Whilst burn-out obviously afflicts individuals situated within large mainstream organizational contexts, ecofeminisms generally apply wider lenses that enable critical analysis of the structural factors that generate such a loss of wellbeing in the first instance. Ecofeminist perspectives encourage the idea that 'normal' contemporary organizational forms and practices are embedded within patriarchal structures that are responsible for chronic undervaluation of women and the Earth. D'Eaubonne (1974), the feminist scholar credited by some as the originator of the term 'ecofeminism', argues that the forms of leadership and organization embedded within patriarchy are most likely to lead towards the third scenario outlined by Porritt (2005), resulting in the total destruction of the global ecosystem (Bullis and Glaser 1992; see also Banerjee 2008; Plumwood 1993; Weber 1930). In provocatively comparing modernity with syphilis, Glazebrook (2005) argues that successful intervention in its life-threatening pathology will be achieved only through proper diagnosis of the disease. As long as we fail to connect apparently unrelated symptoms together as a single etiology, we will be unable to treat the root cause of the malaise she defines as phallic logic. Some versions of ecofeminism, particularly those concerning themselves with the development of feminist spirituality, derive inspiration from Eastern, indigenous and 'prepatriarchal' religions. These belief systems often incorporate narrative ideas as well as embodied practices to suggest that the Earth herself is a source of immanent divinity with feminine aspects, recognition of which, those practising such forms of ecofeminist spirituality believe, may have the potential to transform norms of social and economic organization (Christ 2003; Radford Ruether 1992).

Unlike most other religious and spiritual forms associated with either New Age or neoliberalism, the cosmological assumption of immanence associated with ecofeminist spiritualities means that everything is viewed as equally, differently conscious (Plumwood 1993). Within this cosmology, there is no basis for hierarchal orderings or dualisms based on difference as grounds for the presumption of superiority. Rather, the hierarchy and dualisms of the dominant Enlightenment cosmology, which continue to be extended across the globe as part of neoliberal capitalism, are described as leading to interlinked oppressions based on sex, race, class and nature. Within such oppressive hierarchy, that which is perceived as subordinate, such as the feminine, body, emotions and nature, is systematically and persistently devalued (Merchant 1980/1990; Young forthcoming). For example, until very recently nature was usually most notable by its absence in organizational analysis,[1] such that its life-sustaining contributions fail to be accounted for at all in dominant international economic models (Bullis and Glaser 1992: 52; Shrivastava 1994; Stevens 2012).

In contrast to this Enlightenment cosmology derived from the Judaeo-Christian tradition, many ecofeminist cosmologies relate to the world as one interconnected web of life. This challenges the Enlightenment cosmological convention of seeing life as a great chain of being which 'may be summarized as a chain of command from God to man to woman to nature' (Puttick 1997: 153) in which salvation is associated with the afterlife. Ecofeminist commentators argue that the web is deserving of care and respect in the here and now, with spirituality representing the connecting principle of life (Christ 2003). Spirituality as life-affirming engagement therefore becomes a resource in an ongoing endeavour based on a number of principles. These include: accordance of new meaning and value to the Earth as sacred, sentient and alive, rather than approaching the planet as an inert, dead resource; revaluing all labour as important; placing environmental sustainability and social justice at the heart of organization; and humanization of organizational forms and managerial practices (Heelas 2008; Radford Ruether 1992). The hierarchy inherent in the dualisms perpetuated by Enlightenment rationalisms and Christian cosmology tend to generate frameworks of practice that reinforce relationships based on dominance/submission and superiority/inferiority, while the web metaphor that ecofeminism proposes consists only of equal participants (Curry 2011; Mies and Shiva 1993). The spiritual or religious domain does not exist apart from the social, political and economic worlds; instead, ecofeminist principles and values suggest spirituality is geared towards the active protection of life in this world.

As part of the ethic of care that an ecofeminist approach implies, there is recognition that humans are completely embedded in and dependent upon nature (Radford Ruether 2005; Curry 2011; Naess and Sessions 1984; Roszak et al. 1995). This means that the self does not (cannot) exist within the web as an isolated or abstract phenomenon, but is constituted in a network of relationships which influence and affect each other. These relationships play out within concrete, local and embodied processes, including the production of knowledge which is 'grounded in human society, situated, partial, local, temporal and historically specific' (Coffey 1999: 11; see also Glazebrook 2005). Organizing and managing are produced through the emotional, sexual, embodied, gendered experience of human beings. Immanence, placing value in the everyday world, therefore functions as a cosmological alternative to transcendence, and provides a practical framework for acknowledging the importance of embodied experiences. It directly challenges objectification and transcendent abstractions, enabling personal behaviours and direct actions in everyday life to be seen as making important contributions to political process and potential changes in collective assumptions about both management and organization (Bullis and Glaser 1992; Christ 1997; D'Eubonne 1974; Radford Ruether 1992, 2005; Spretnak 1999; Starhawk 1987).

## Organizing labour socially

Ecofeminism also focuses attention on approaches to work with the potential to re-constellate labour in fairer and more sustainable ways. Mies and Shiva

(1993) suggest a 'subsistence perspective' as the basis for identifying and creating ecofeminist form(s) of organizing as an alternative to patriarchal capitalism arranged around competition, economic growth and the exploitation of labour to extract surplus value. Ecofeminist organizing can be based on the satisfaction of human needs through the creation of use-values, rather than the purchase of commodities. This will, it is hoped, encourage new relationships with nature based on respect, cooperation and reciprocity, reliable community based on mutual respect between men and women, grassroots democracy, and synergistic approaches to problem solving rooted in the understanding that everything is interconnected. It would also encourage approaches to technology that incorporate social and power relations, a re-integration of work and culture, resistance to attempts to privatize the commons, and for men to be involved in the caring and nurturing (unpaid) domains of life.

These principles are echoed in the concept of 'total social organization of labour' (Glucksmann 1995). Glucksmann points out that the application of the term work only to paid labour, alongside its separation from all spheres other than the market economy, is a distinctive feature of modern organization. She goes on to also challenge understandings of work and labour based on a range of abstracted false dichotomies, such as public/private, work/leisure, home/work, paid/unpaid, production/consumption and commodity/non-commodity. Her argument has several aims. It problematizes reification of the term 'work' as only applicable to paid labour carried out in the market economy. In doing so, we focus on the ascription of value to activities conducted in spheres such as the private or domestic, which have been viewed as less important than activity in the public or marketplace. This simultaneously makes it easier to analyse connections between spheres that may otherwise be seen as independent of each other, and enables exploration of the relationships, interconnections and *inter*dependencies of work conducted at different and apparently disparate sites. Understanding labour as socially organized in this way is, above all, founded on relationality and 'the interconnectedness of all institutions as they stand in relation to each other' (Glucksmann 1995: 68). Glucksmann's framework provides a crucial link between everyday experience in workplaces and at home, that enables analysis of the modernist structures that continue to frame contemporary management and organization.

## Retrieving a lost past, caring for the future in the present

The colonialisms and exploitations carried out in the name of the Global North on the South are just one macro-political manifestation of these unharmonious and unrespectful relations. There are also significant issues in thinking across geographies in this way, as noted above. Immanence in the context of the subsistence production that the majority of the world's women inhabit is still obviously very different from many lives led in the

North. Ecofeminism often appears more engaged with struggles to prevent the material survival base in the South from being subject to the destructive processes associated with imposed colonialisms. This is evident in the Chipko movement in India, the work of Wangari Maathai in Kenya, and Fundación Pachamama in Ecuador. The North has already been subject to waves of cultural and material destruction in its industrialization processes, perhaps creating a nostalgic desire for what has been lost. In many instances this has resulted in precisely the creative solutions and cultural re-weavings typical of ecofeminism and feminist spirituality, intent on finding new narratives and practices that can support the ongoing struggles to restore value to the Earth, the feminine, and all people of the Earth (Christ 1997, 2003; Eisler 1987; Radford Ruether 1992; Starhawk 1987). Whilst it is possible to see cultural adoption of practices from outside the West as a form of colonial appropriation, it is arguable that their success or plausibility may depend on the context. It may be possible to view all efforts towards supporting cooperation and revaluing the profaned as part of a conjoined network of wider shared concerns to encourage an ethic of care rather than one of violence (Carrette and King 2005; Mies and Shiva 1993).

However, it is also possible that in a Western context, since its radical origins in the 1960s and 1970s, ecofeminism has become one of what Carrette and King (2005) suggest are spiritualities bought and sold in Western cultures. Their argument suggests that spiritualities work within and alongside the dominant neoliberal paradigm and its idealized notion of a globalized 'free' marketplace populated by perfectly rational economic actors. Contemporary spiritualities associated with counter-cultural activities and the HPM have often been critiqued, particularly by Marxist (and often male) intellectuals. For example, Lasch (1979) and Schur (1976) offer strong criticism of the 'dangerous narcissism' and 'self-absorption' that can result from spending too much time focused upon the self. Clark et al. (1981) argue that contemporary spiritualities risk encouraging psychological regression; Bird (1980) suggests a loss of moral accountability; Sennett (1977) warns against the tyranny of the intimate; and Wilson (1976) damns the whole movement as culturally irrelevant.

In this long tradition, two of the most recent extended critiques are those by Carrette and King (2005) and Lau (2000). Lau points out that the transposition of bodily practices (aromatherapy, yoga, tai-chi and macrobiotics) from their original cultural contexts into the marketplace as commodities may repeat the sins of a Western Orientalism that romanticizes nature, the past and 'other' cultural forms. She further argues that in correlating personal benefits with planetary wellbeing through the use of co-opted symbolism and associations, the marketplace successfully transforms what is essentially product for profit into pseudo-political action. Carrette and King (2005) focus more on structural dynamics in their critique of market-based spiritualities; their analysis is pessimistic for the radical future of spiritual movements.

Others such as Heelas (2008), Roszak (1978) and Kripal (2007) take a different approach, arguing for the potentially positive social merit of practice in this area. They all note the significance of feminism in ecopsychology, the HPM and contemporary spiritualities. Beckford (1984) also suggests that some of the more positive potentials might include improvements in both individual and collective life, a renewal of religious imagination, encouragement of a value framework that encourages a shared ethical stance and a renewed populism (see also Wuthnow 1978).

Empirically, there is less scholarship available, but two who do engage in this way also address gender and feminism in detail (Kripal 2007; Puttick 1997). Both have been involved as participants in different counter-cultural sites. Puttick (1997) is clear that comparative research on gender roles in new religious movements shows the continuation of a pattern subordinating women that is common to established religious institutions, even when stated ideology might indicate otherwise. In other words, even in purportedly radical new religious movements, women continue to be associated with power-lessness, profanity and the secular. The state of being female generally and specifically continues to be seen as an obstacle to enlightenment and leader-ship (spiritual and otherwise) by women. Unsurprisingly, exceptions to this tend to be the women's spirituality movement and neo-paganism, where priests in mixed gender communities and priestesses, theoretically at least,[2] have equal status.

Kripal's (2007) assessment of how democracy, capitalism, religion and inequality were interconnected in the HPM community at Esalen also con-tains fascinating observations. Acknowledging the validity of criticisms of contemporary spiritualities for their involvement in the marketplace, he also notes that women practitioners dominate most of these movements, some-times by as much as two to one. He describes the consequences of stepping outside the confines of traditional religious and patriarchal organizational structures to inhabit what he calls 'the religion of no religion', as those who do so give up:

> intricate webs of wealth and prestige built up over centuries, usually within hierarchical social systems that have systematically silenced and suppressed female voices.
>
> (Kripal 2007: 40)

Pointing out that livelihoods must be made regardless, Kripal queries who is actually served by criticisms of the relationships between the market and HPM, suggesting that they echo criticisms of self-empowering women throughout history. These are exemplified by attacks on both medieval female mystics and nineteenth-century spiritualists, echoed in the contemporary era in polemics against the spiritual marketplace and the New Age by already empowered men (Hess 1993). While Kripal acknowledges that the early days at Esalen were far from a model of gender equality, he further remarks:

This would all change at Esalen, but only gradually. In time, strong female voices, real institutional empowerment, and above all, more reciprocal child-rearing practices would appear. Men would rear and raise children. Women would lead, teach and administer ... Such an egalitarianism is never perfect ... gender imbalances, socioeconomic injustices, and essentialist assumptions of all sorts remain ... Still, the ideal remains, and ideals matter: the enlightenment of the body is the enlightenment of every body, regardless of gender, sexual orientation, race, class, or religion.

(Kripal 2007: 462)

## 'Strong female voices' in practice

Gabrielle Roth was one of those at Esalen who took enlightenment of the body as her life's work. She founded the 5Rhythms movement in the USA and represented precisely the kind of strong female voice highlighted by Kripal, who met her at Esalen when she worked there as a masseur. She advocated a path to 'enlightenment' through valuing and incorporating the body into psychological and spiritual practices (Roth 1990, 1999, 2004). Roth was a professional contemporary dancer who incurred an injury that ended her career, before moving to Esalen in the 1970s (Roth 1990; Kripal 2007). While there, Roth was a student of a charismatic and reputedly somewhat authoritarian spiritual teacher, Oscar Ichazo, whose work she taught for a time (Roth 1990; Kripal 2007). Surrounded by the great and the good of the personal growth world, including Abraham Maslow, she met and was encouraged by Fritz Perls, the (in)famous Gestalt guru, and Gregory Bateson, anthropologist and author of *Steps to an Ecology of Mind* (1972) as well as sometime husband to Margaret Mead. Encouraged by both, Roth gradually began sharing her skills and expertise as an expressive dancer in the arena of the body.

In *Maps to Ecstasy – Teachings of an Urban Shaman*, Roth recalls an encounter with filmmaker Alejandro Jodorowsky who suggested that she needed to 'cut her father's balls off' (Roth 1990: 20). We assume that he referred to a metaphorical need to free herself from the influence of male-dominated leadership and authority. Roth presumably took his advice because, some time later, she did indeed begin formatting, teaching and then very successfully selling her own work under the brand of '5Rhythms'. More than a million people are now estimated to have been involved with 5Rhythms practice (Kieft 2012).

Roth was a complex figure. On one hand rumoured to be anorexic, battling with this Western dancer's disease for most of her life; on the other completely persuaded (perhaps precisely because she understood it so intimately on a personal level) of the urgent need for Western culture to heal its pathological relationships with both body and feminine. This was a conviction to which she would dedicate most of her life. Roth's teaching and written work employed dance as a form of contemporary spiritual practice based in what she termed ecstasy, or what Irigaray might refer to as *joussiance* (Whitford 1991). In seeking to move away from the Enlightenment norm of Platonic cosmology, which sees the pure, invisible, eternal, godly realm as separated out from the material, visible domain of the body, Roth placed the incorporation of body, emotions, mother and the feminine right at the heart of her spiritual practice – shamelessly committing the ultimate heresy of combining god, sex and the body in unified and ecstatic relationship with each other.

God for Roth was located in the moment, present in each unique human expression, all equally important. She believed the way to this was through the physicality of the body, here and now, in whomever or whatever was in front of and around us. Brought up during the emotional and sexual repression of the 1950s, Roth sought to empower all who worked with her from what she saw as the prison of socially conditioned roles and taboos about expressing power, anger or sexuality in public. She suggested that liberation from the imposition of cultural strictures limiting what can and cannot be expressed lay in the process of freeing life energy within. The body itself was framed as the ultimate site of life affirmation or denial. Her students were encouraged to address what Twine refers to as 'the oppressor within' (Twine 2001: 33; see also Starhawk 1987). Roth did not privilege women as necessarily any more embodied than men. While she saw motherhood as valuable, it was to be held in balance with the role of father, and both sexes were encouraged to engage creatively with the world around them. Although her work was not directly addressed to environmental challenges, she was passionately committed to the notion that a healthy society needs to recognize the value of the body and emotions as sources of wisdom, balanced with the mind.

Roth's ethos had much in common with the philosophy and practice of German psychoanalyst Wilhelm Reich, a man whose books were burnt by both the Germans and the Americans (Corrington 2003; Kripal 2007). Reich and his work are also closely connected to Esalen, as he took refuge there shortly before his arrest in the 1950s. Writing on subjects such as *The Mass Psychology of Fascism*, Reich (1975) drew very clear links between authoritarian systems of leading and following, and the ways in which cultures relate to the issue of the free expression of what he termed life energy, or 'orgone'. Parts of his work influenced a wide range of cultural figures from Norman Mailer to Michel Foucault; perhaps his most enduring theoretical contribution is in the argument that culture is written into the body in the form of 'character armouring', the ways in which socialization shapes and is stored within the body's musculature and embodied physicality (Corrington 2003; Puttick 1997). Reich became such a controversial figure that he was imprisoned by the US Federal Drug Administration, where he died in jail in 1957 (Corrington 2003; see also Kripal 2007). Although Roth began her work in psychiatric wards and schools, unlike Reich she became a highly financially successful entrepreneur and a much loved and admired public figure in some parts of the counter-culture.

Roth's development into a leader for the community she spoke to and practised with illustrates a number of tensions between radicalism and effecting change. Over time, she began to practise what some scholars refer to as 'distancing' (Grint 2010; Puttick 1997) through devices including designer clothing, limousines and the construction of a conventional modernist organization to promote and enable her work. Arweck (2002) comments on the way in which new religious movements sometimes construct a spiritual elite. Roth used to refer to followers as '*the*' dancing tribe. Membership was exclusive, and fitted with Arweck's profile of the membership of new religious movements as affluent, well educated, and middle class. In ecofeminist terms this raises concerns about homogeneity being presented as heterogeneity. The community had very few black members, no First Nation Peoples, few older members and no children. As Roth's work grew in popularity and exposure, it seems to have engaged very closely with ethics of capitalist production, consumption and very conventional organizing/managing practices.

In 2006, the two UK directors of Roth's work left the organizational umbrella to work independently as the School of Movement Medicine. Susannah and Ya'Acov Darling Khan's political roots lay in the nuclear protest movement. They decided after 18 years of working with and representing Roth's teachings that personal growth was no longer enough to meet the demands of an increasingly challenged world, and therefore decided to form a new organization based on the three goals of environmental sustainability, social justice and human fulfilment. The latter aim became just one strand of a much wider agenda of economic and social change. Like Roth, they have established the body, the feminine and nature at the centre of teachings that employ dance and movement as their core spiritual practice. They are also, again like Roth, located in the marketplace of the New Age.

However, the School of Movement Medicine signals concern with global environmental issues by organizing itself in several ways. It initially allied with Fundación Pachamama in Ecuador, an organization which was responsible for leading activity relating to the struggle for indigenous land rights. The Fundación was shut down by Ecuador's government at the end of 2013, just weeks before a plan to open some 2.6 million hectares of rainforest to new oil drilling. In spite of this, the School and the community associated with it continue to fundraise for both Achuar and Sapara peoples in Ecuador. The British government's refusal to grant visas to representatives from the Achuar to visit the UK for an annual fundraising event in 2013 (an event that also doubles up as a 'religious' ceremonial space) saw the community directly involved in political processes, lobbying the British Home Secretary among others. Founders and others in the community continue to pursue an educational campaign intended to raise awareness of and finance for the Fundación. This issue is viewed by the community as a shared global threat from what the Achuar refer to as the Dream of the North, what we would describe as industrialized modernity, with the shared task of working to protect the global commons represented by the rainforests. The School and the community associated with it have raised over £250,000 in recent years, much of which has been donated to the Pachamama Alliance and Survival International, an organization working, as its name suggests, on survival issues faced by indigenous peoples, often in conflict with corporate interests.

The School is also involved in a number of other arenas concerned with promoting the need for environmental sustainability and social justice. These include the need for organizational transformations in these realms through the Be The Change Symposium, working across the political divide in Israel and Palestine, and encouraging environmentally focused business practices such as train instead of plane use, and organic food production and consumption. As a reasonably reflexive community, members are aware that complacency about achievements is not an appropriate response to a troubled world. Fundraising is described as one end of a community spectrum, which also includes a considerable amount of international travel. This is clearly seen by several interviewees as a significant paradox, a shadow of the New Age movement as a whole (Young 2015). Such 'shadows' are felt and expressed by many members of the community, sometimes described as ethical dilemmas and in other instances as hypocrisies. According to participants themselves, contradictions include commuting and car use, waste production from consumerist lifestyles, and the economic privilege required to engage with this community in the first place. It has also been observed that the founders' lifestyles are achievable only because of the profit margins provided by followers. Interviews conducted in the community also revealed concerns about insufficient political engagement, narcissism on the part of some of those in the community, and insufficient time left to engage effectively in the mitigation of climate change effects. The up-side, if there is one, is the awareness that exists about these issues, and that criticisms are generally made in the knowledge that they reflect and are embedded in much wider systemic issues that afflict most contemporary Western communities. Critique, in keeping with community practices, is on the whole offered from an observational rather than a judgemental position, as part of the struggle to assess what can then be engaged with in ongoing change processes.

## Being radical, being tempered

The ambivalence expressed in the Movement Medicine community's reflections and organizational practices is a central feature of what Meyerson and Scully (1995) describe as a deliberate strategy employed by change agents they call 'tempered radicals'. Members of this group remain 'loyal' to the causes espoused by their organizations, but in other ways are committed to more radical values than those expressed within them. Interestingly, this seems to be a dynamic that works in two directions within Movement

Medicine. As a belief system, it attracts some members who are more politically radical than membership of a profit-making endeavour implies. They participate in order to reap political and social supports to be gained from membership of an organization with commitments that are more politically radical than most mainstream organizations. In addition, many members are also employed within much more conservative organizations, so that this organization may simultaneously represent one of their more radical commitments.

This fits well with the range of ways in which being radical and tempered intersect, as described by Meyerson and Scully (1995) – for those who fail to find an easy fit in the organizations they join because certain aspects of their experience and identity render them outsiders. The life experiences attached to such a position therefore function to strengthen (or temper) them in ways that assist in addressing injustice and inequality. This can leave people unwilling to accept the status quo and committed to seeking strategic ways to engage with change in the form of tempered solutions. As Meyerson and Scully (1995) point out, these individuals may be pivotal players as change agents, loss of whom through burn-out or co-optation might impoverish important change processes in organizations. Finding effective ways to maintain their commitment to change presents particular challenges for tempered radicals as the experience of living with identity conflicts pulls them in a number of different directions, creating a permanent state of emotional ambivalence.

The advantage for the organization, and perhaps also for wider society, is that the 'outsiders within' position affords these people a particular kind of dual subjectivity. Outsider status creates a lack of total identification with the organization, values and practices that makes critique possible, lending the ability to problematize things that others take for granted. Insider status generates the opportunity and access to work for change. Because tempered radicals work within the confines of organizational structures, they also tend to gain the rewards associated with membership of those structures. However, they may find themselves open to the criticism of others who also view themselves as outsiders, as well as those more conservative elements within their own organizations.

Among the positive advantages, however, is the opportunity to engage in a series of incremental, small changes that may, in the long term, add up to significant social change, and to be less likely to provoke defensive reactions from the surrounding systems (Frost and Egri 1991). This may include a grounded assessment of what is or is not possible at different sites and different times. It may also generate life-affirming, spontaneous, authentic local action that benefits those around it in ways that can be entirely unpredictable in effects and consequences. These outcomes may resemble gentler, kinder and more compassionate approaches to change than any revolutions led by violence and aggression (Heelas 2008), the classical form of social change that perpetuates the hyper-masculine forms that ecofeminism is committed to dissolving (Puttick 1997). Tempered radicals may bring the small innovations, vitality, educative processes and much needed shifts to organizing and managing which an ecofeminist perspective suggests enable the adaptation and change needed to meet the demands of a globally challenged environment.

That is essentially our point in this chapter. We write it in a week when many scientists are expressing considerable alarm about the immanent collapse of several large glaciers in Antarctica due to human activity and the likely displacement of millions of people worldwide as a consequence. This makes Jones and Stablein's (2006) question of whether tempered radicalism actually works all too apposite. In an environment in which neoliberal economics seems, at least for now, to be triumphant, where minimal 'adaptation' seems to be the order of the day, perhaps we need to enquire more deeply into the question of how to achieve untempered change, by what sorts of means, where, and to what ends. The tempered language adopted by mainstream institutions to address issues such as continuing inequality, lack of diversity, and very partial social justice can help to reinforce and reify the notions of place encompassed in terms like margin and centre, resulting in tokenism and superficial redistributions of power and material resources. It is undoubtedly true that the business models of capitalism are always seeking to recuperate power and depoliticize radical interests, most recently to locate social justice and environmental issues second to profit motives. Bearing this in mind, it seems that if the goals of ecofeminism are to be served in the longer term, those of us interested in them must continue to employ critical frameworks in order to analyse asymmetrical power relations and attempted colonizations on an ongoing basis. The ongoing costs of environmental degradation continue to be paid by the world's more materially impoverished, who are also still blamed for population increases, which in and of themselves have less influence on global systems than Western consumption rates (Mies and Shiva 1993). Debates about the socio-cultural significance of movements that may be unified by the same basic desires for health, happiness and wellbeing, regardless of the market distortions that may become interwoven with them, will no doubt continue. In the meantime, membership of more than just one organization or community where attempts are being made to address pressing issues may enable the pursuit of deliberate, self-reflexive strategies to hold open spaces for change, consolidate gains made in the past, and advance change agendas within the increasingly totalizing expressions of global capitalism. This is the alternative we see to what Meyerson and Scully (1995) term tempered loyalty to the corporations that often provide our employment opportunities. If we also remember the lack of hierarchy that is a principle of ecofeminist cosmologies and praxis, we must conclude that all liberation struggles have value and cannot be graded from A to F. The ultimate judge, jury and executioner with regard to human efforts to generate life-affirming change within our immediate future is, after all, most likely to be life itself.

## Notes

1 Nature's reappearance within sustainability discourse, as 'environment', does not necessarily herald a fundamental paradigm shift (Sullivan 2011).
2 'Paganism is the only religion to have developed theology that not only perceives the Goddess as equal or superior to the God, but follows through by giving women equal or superior spiritual status. It is also the only religion that contains a specifically conscious feminist branch: feminist witchcraft' (Puttick 1997: 245).

## References

Arweck, E. (2002) 'New religious movements', in *Religions in the Modern World*, edited by Woodhead, L., London: Routledge, 264–287.

Banerjee, S.B. (2008) 'Necrocapitalism', *Organization Studies* 29(12): 1541–1563.

Bateson, G. (1972) *Steps to an Ecology of Mind: Collected Essays in Anthropology, Psychiatry, Evolution and Epistemology*, London: The University of Chicago Press.

Beckford, J.A. (1984) 'Holistic imagery and ethics in new religious and healing movements', *Social Compass* 31(2–3): 259–272.

Bird, F. (1980) 'The pursuit of innocence: new religious movements and moral accountability', *Sociological Analysis* 40(4): 335–346.

Bullis, C. and Glaser, H. (1992) 'Bureaucratic discourse and the goddess: towards an ecofeminist critique and rearticulation', *Journal of Organizational Change Management* 5(2): 50–60.

Carrette, J. and King, R. (2005) *Selling Spirituality: The Silent Takeover of Religion*, London: Routledge.

Christ, C. (1997) *Rebirth of the Goddess*, New York: Routledge.

Christ, C. (2003) *She Who Changes: Re-imagining the Divine in the World*, New York: Palgrave Macmillan.

Clark, J., Langone, R., Schechter, R. and Daly, R. (1981) *Destructive Cult Conversion: Theory, Research and Treatment*, Weston, MA: American Family Foundation.

Coffey, A. (1999) *The Ethnographic Self: Fieldwork and the Representation of Identity*, London: Sage.

Corrington, R.S. (2003) *Wilhelm Reich: Psychoanalyst and Radical Naturalist*, New York: Farrer, Straus and Giroux.

Curry, P. (2011) *Environmental Ethics – An Introduction*, Cambridge: Polity Press.

Darling Khan, S. and Darling Khan, Y. (2009) *Movement Medicine: How to Awaken, Dance and Live Your Dreams*, London: Hay House.

D'Eubonne, F. (1974) *Le Feminisme ou La Mort*, Paris: Pierre Horay.

Eisler, R. (1987) *The Chalice and The Blade*, San Francisco: HarperCollins.

Frost, P.J. and Egri, C.P. (1991) 'The political process of innovation', in *Research in Organizational Behavior*, Volume 13, edited by Staw, B. and Cummings, L., Greenwich, CT: JAI, 229–295.

Glazebrook, T. (2005) 'Gynocentric eco-logics', *Ethics and the Environment* 10(2): 75–99.

Glucksmann, M. (1995) 'Why "work"? Gender and the total social organization of labour', *Gender, Work & Organization* 2(2): 63–75.

Grint, K. (2010) 'The sacred in leadership: separation, sacrifice and silence', *Organization Studies* 31(1): 89–107.

Harner, M. (1980) *The Way of the Shaman*, New York: Harper & Row.

Heelas, P. (2008) *Spiritualities of Life: New Age Romanticism and Consumptive Capitalism*, Oxford: Blackwell.

Hess, D.J. (1993) *Science in the New Age: The Paranormal, its Defenders and Debunkers, and American Culture*, Madison: University of Wisconsin Press.

Homer-Dixon, T. (2006) *The Upside of Down*, Washington, DC: Island Press.

Jones, D. and Stablein, R. (2006) 'Diversity: from the margins to the centre', in *Handbook of Workplace Diversity*, edited by Konrad, A., Prasad, P. and Pringle, J., London: Sage, 146–168.

Kieft, E. (2012) 'Dancing as a tool for emotional and mental wellbeing, and personal growth: anthropological research on "Movement Medicine"', PhD thesis, University of Roehampton, UK.

Kripal, J.J. (2007) *Esalen: America and the Religion of No Religion*, Chicago: University of Chicago Press.

Lasch, C. (1979) *The Culture of Narcissism*, New York: Norton & Company.

Lau, K. (2000) *New Age Capitalism: Making Money East of Eden*, Philadelphia: University of Pennsylvania Press.

Lomborg, B. (2001) *The Sceptical Environmentalist: Measuring the Real State of the World*, Cambridge: Cambridge University Press.

Lovelock, J. (2006) *The Revenge of Gaia*, London: Allen Lane.

Merchant, C. (1980/1990) *The Death of Nature: Women, Ecology and the Scientific Revolution*, San Francisco: Harper.

Meyerson, D. and Scully, M. (1995) 'Tempered radicalism and the politics of ambivalence and change', *Organization Science* 6(5): 585–600.

Mies, M. and Shiva, V. (1993) *Ecofeminism*, Melbourne: Spinifex Press.

Naess, A. and Sessions, G. (1984) *Basic Principles of Deep Ecology*, available from http://theanarchistlibrary.org/library/arne-naess-and-george-sessions-basic-principles-of-deep-ecology.

Orbach, S. (1994) *What's Really Going on Here? Making Sense of our Emotional Lives*, London: Virago.

Plumwood, V. (1993) *Feminism and the Mastery of Nature*, London: Routledge.

Porritt, J. (2005) *Capitalism as if the World Matters*, London: Earthscan.

Puttick, E. (1997) *Women in New Religions: In Search of Community, Sexuality and Spiritual Power*, New York: St Martin's Press.

Radford Ruether, R. (1992) *Gaia and God: An EcoFeminist Theology of Earth Healing*, San Francisco: HarperCollins.

Radford Ruether, R. (2005) *Integrating Ecofeminism, Globalization and World Religions*, Lanham, MD: Rowman & Littlefield.

Reich, W. (1975 [1946]) *The Mass Psychology of Fascism*, Harmondsworth: Penguin.

Roszak, T. (1978) *Person/Planet: The Creative Disintegration of Industrial Society*, Lincoln: iUniverse, Inc.

Roszak, T., Gomes, M.E. and Kanner, A.D. (1995) *Ecopsychology – Restoring the Earth, Healing the Mind*, Berkeley: University of California Press.

Roth, G. (1990) *Maps to Ecstasy – Teachings of an Urban Shaman*, London: Aquarian Press.

Roth, G. (1999) *Sweat Your Prayers: Movement as Spiritual Practice*, New York: Penguin Putnam.

Roth, G. (2004) *Connections: The Five Threads of Intuitive Wisdom*, New York: Penguin.

Schur, E. (1976) *The Awareness Trap: Self-Absorption Instead of Social Change*, New York: Quadrangle Books.

Sennett, R. (1977) *The Fall of Public Man*, New York: Knopf.

Shrivastava, P. (1994) 'CASTRATED Environment: GREENING Organizational Studies', *Organization Studies* 15(5): 705–726.

Sinclair, A. (2010) 'Placing self: how might we place ourselves in leadership studies differently?', *Leadership* 6(4): 447–460.

Spretnak, C. (1999) *The Resurgence of the Real – Body, Nature and Place in a HyperModern World*, New York: Routledge.

Starhawk (1982) *Dreaming the Dark: Magic, Sex and Politics*, Boston, MA: Beacon Press.

Starhawk (1987) *Truth or Dare: Encounters with Power, Authority and Mystery*, New York: HarperCollins.

Stevens, P. (2012) 'Towards an EcoSociology', *Sociology* 46(4): 579–595.

Sullivan, S. (2011) *Banking Nature? The Financialisation of Environmental Conservation*, Open Anthropology Cooperative Press, available at http://www.openanthcoop.net.

Twine, R.T. (2001) 'Ma(r)king essence: ecofeminism and embodiment', *Ethics and Environment* 6(2): 31–58.

Weber, M. (1930 [1904–1905]) *The Protestant Ethic and the Spirit of Capitalism*, London: George Allen & Unwin Ltd.

Whitford, M. (ed.) (1991) *The Irigaray Reader*, Oxford: Blackwell.

Wilson, B.R. (1976) *The Contemporary Transformations of Religion*, Berkeley: University of California Press.

Wuthnow, R. (1978) *Experimentation in American Religion*, Berkeley: University of California Press.

Young, A. (2015) 'Leader as dreamer: alternatives to modernity', PhD thesis, University of Exeter.

Young, A. (forthcoming) 'Towards a deconstruction of leadership and cosmology: the re-embodiment of the sacred', in *Exploring Re-embodiments: Law, Philosophy and Ecology*, edited by Sullivan, S. and Thomas-Pellicer, R., London: Glasshouse Books/Routledge.

# Index

Tables are shown by a reference in **bold**.